Bordering social reproduction

Manchester University Press

WOMEN ON THE MOVE

Women on the Move is a transdisciplinary book series that focuses on unveiling the presence and multiplicity of experiences of women in migration processes. The series bridges the gap between historical and contemporary approaches, its objective being to publish books on women's migration from a wide variety of perspectives, time frames and geographical outlooks, with a combination of quantitative and qualitative approaches. The books published in the series seek to deconstruct the sexist stereotypes that have marked the history of migration by revealing both women migrants' agency and resources, as well as their vulnerabilities and the challenges faced in past and present experiences of migration. The interplay between gender and migration at the core of the series invites authors to develop multifactorial perspectives of women's migration and to disclose how gender shapes migration and how migration shapes gender.

To buy or to find out more about the books currently available in this series, please go to:
https://manchesteruniversitypress.co.uk/series/women-on-the-move/

Series editors

Marie Ruiz, Université de Paris and Université de Picardie Jules Verne, France
Sónia Ferreira, Universidade Nova de Lisboa, Portugal
Cecilia Menjívar, University of California, Los Angeles, USA

Editorial board

Emma Bond, University of St Andrews, UK
Gabor Egry, Institute of Political History, Hungary
Heike Drotbohm, Johannes Gutenberg University Mainz, Germany
Carol Farbotko, Commonwealth Scientific and Industrial Research Organisation, Australia
Eric Fong, Chinese University of Hong Kong
Stephanie Hemelryk Donald, Monash University Malaysia
Elaine Moriarty, Trinity College Dublin, Ireland
Irudaya Rajan, Centre for Development Studies, India
Uzma Rashid, United Nations mandated University for Peace, Costa Rica
Victoria Souliman, University of New England, Australia
Inga K. Thiemann, University of Exeter, UK

Bordering social reproduction

Migrant mothers and children making lives in the shadows

Rachel Rosen and Eve Dickson

MANCHESTER UNIVERSITY PRESS

Copyright © Rachel Rosen and Eve Dickson 2025

The rights of Rachel Rosen and Eve Dickson to be identified as the authors of this work have been asserted in accordance with the Copyright, Designs and Patents Act 1988.

An electronic version of this book has been made freely available under a Creative Commons (CC BY-NC-ND) licence, thanks to the support of the ESRC (grant number ES/X000265/1), which permits non-commercial use, distribution and reproduction provided the author(s) and Manchester University Press are fully cited and no modifications or adaptations are made. Details of the licence can be viewed at https://creativecommons.org/licenses/by-nc-nd/4.0/

Published by Manchester University Press
Oxford Road, Manchester, M13 9PL

www.manchesteruniversitypress.co.uk

British Library Cataloguing-in-Publication Data
A catalogue record for this book is available from the British Library

ISBN 978 1 5261 8927 1 hardback

First published 2025

The publisher has no responsibility for the persistence or accuracy of URLs for any external or third-party internet websites referred to in this book, and does not guarantee that any content on such websites is, or will remain, accurate or appropriate.

EU authorised representative for GPSR:
Easy Access System Europe, Mustamäe tee 50, 10621
Tallinn, Estonia
gpsr.requests@easproject.com

Typeset
by Cheshire Typesetting Ltd, Cuddington, Cheshire

Dedication

For the children and mothers who have shared their lives with us.

Contents

Acknowledgements	*page* viii
Introduction: Bordering social reproduction	1
1 Enforcing destitution and debt	24
2 Weathering through social reproduction	43
3 Existential erasure and its discontents	61
4 Childhood in the shadows	78
5 Secrets and silences	98
6 Doing time	115
7 (En)countering 'race'	131
Conclusion: Contesting welfare bordering	150
References	158
Index	172

Acknowledgements

It is difficult to know where to begin acknowledging the many people that have inspired us and stretched our thinking as we have worked on this book. It has been a long (longer than imagined!) labour of love that has extended through a global pandemic; in an international context of intensifying ethno-nationalism; and across grassroots organising that has grown, faltered, and been renewed in multiple forms.

As much as we are the named authors of this book, we know that it would never have been possible without our friends and comrades from NELMA, Project 17, Akwaaba, the Anti-Raids network, Displaced Collective, Grassroots Women, Haringey Migrant Support Centre, IWGB, Kalayaan Centre, and more. Our efforts to reflect upon and analyse the material and psychic realities which we write about in this book will never be ours alone. They emerge from informal conversations, shared projects of common cause and the contested, impossible, yet profoundly necessary efforts towards solidarities we have been grateful to be a part of.

We are deeply grateful to the British Academy/Leverhulme small grant fund for providing the seed monies that enabled us to engage with the lives of mothers with NRPF and their children through ethnographic fieldwork [grant number SRG19\190192 s]. Funding from the Economic and Social Research Council to expand this pilot research [grant number ES/X000265/1], and a fellowship from the Independent Social Research Foundation for Rachel, have made it possible for us to dwell carefully and analytically with this material and the words of our interlocutors, and helped us to carve space otherwise unavailable in the neoliberal academy for the writing of this book.

We appreciate the sage advice and active encouragement of our publisher, Shannon Kneis, and the incisive comments provided by two anonymous reviewers. An earlier version of Chapter 1 was published in *Critical Social Policy*.

Our heartfelt thanks go to everyone at Project 17, Haringey Migrant Support Centre, and Together with Migrant Children for introducing us to our interlocutors in this book. We recognise this is no small task in the context of the overburdened system of civil society support necessitated by the welfare bordering we write about in these pages. We thank you for making the time and energy, and for gently but persistently holding us to account, against the tradition of extractivist research.

Most of all, we are grateful to our interlocutors, the mothers and children whose voices and experiences animate the pages of this book and who opened up their lives to us despite the border violences they are forced to endure. To you, we say: we are inspired by your refusals to be rendered surplus and your endeavours to make meaningful lives. We hope that this book in some way meets you in these efforts and that we have done justice to your insights. It is our hope that the ideas developed in these pages can contribute to struggles against the pernicious, punitive and extractive processes of racial capitalism – refusing their divisions and nurturing the knowledge that things can be different, and collectively we can make it so.

It goes without saying that all errors, omissions and offences are ours alone. Much as we would prefer that mistakes would not happen, we do not want such concerns to serve as an excuse to stay quiet in the face of welfare bordering. We look forward to deepening our understanding through further dialogue and learning from questions and challenges where we have faltered in our aims.

Introduction:
Bordering social reproduction

This is a book about borders. It does not speak primarily about those edifices of concrete, metal and barbed wire which separate, filter, and often violently exclude, although it is impossible to consider the borders we discuss without the presence of these historically produced megastructures. We write here of the invisible, yet consequential, borders that define which bodies, or – more aptly – which people, receive support and which do not, even when all other options for sustenance have failed. This book is about those who are punished and neglected simply because they crossed one of the hard physical borders of the nation without state permission, or because they do not leave when the state demands. These are people whom the British state attempts to reduce to what Giorgio Agamben (1998) calls 'bare life' or those who are, because of systemic racism, 'vulnerable to premature death' as Ruth Wilson Gilmore (2007) puts it.

We write in these pages about *welfare bordering*: the United Kingdom's (UK) imposition of intangible borders that nonetheless deny people the means to life through a draconian policy masked by the bureaucratic language of 'no recourse to public funds' (NRPF). Whether facing homelessness, ill health or deep impoverishment, NRPF pushes people into the shadows of the UK's welfare state, forcing reliance on hope, hustle and whatever support might be available from friends, family, strangers or – in some instances – local authorities. This faint and fragile version of an already austere nation state might be characterised as shadow welfare provision, placing families with NRPF both in the shadows of the welfare state and only able to avail of a shadowy version of the former. Life in the shadows, then, raises the spectre of existential erasure and degradation of life, making efforts to achieve visibility a demand for life at the same time as placing into peril the means and methods of surviving threats of detention, deportation and welfare bordering for those living in precarious migrancy. Life in the shadows is to always risk exposure to the state and to intimate others, yet such lives are often problematically obscured from view – allowing Britain's myth of itself as a welcoming and supportive community of value to persist and its violent practices of welfare bordering to go unquestioned.

Yet this is not only a book about borders. This is a book motivated by the insistence of our interlocutors that they are more than disposable surplus bodies and 'ungrievable lives' (Butler, 2016). With our interlocutors, mothers from Britain's former colonies and their children who are subject to NRPF in the UK, we ask: what happens when people on the move who are made to pay for their 'undesirability' through a policy that seeks to deny them the means of life nonetheless endeavour to make and sustain meaningful lives? Our answers to this question aim to keep visible the processes that produce and sustain welfare bordering, which likewise seek to naturalise their existence and operations. At the same time, our ambition is to acknowledge the complex and life-affirming ways in which people endeavour to weather the violence which lies at the heart of racial capitalism and the UK's neoliberal welfare state. In so doing, in the pages of this book, we seek to walk alongside our interlocutors to offer fine-grained insights about their life-making, or social reproductive, practices under conditions of duress – practices which ultimately point to the fragilities of repressive border regimes and the possibilities of alternatives.

Welfare bordering through NRPF

In the UK, migrants 'subject to immigration control' are not allowed to access most welfare benefits, social housing or support tied to benefits, such as extended childcare services. This is stipulated in the 'no recourse to public funds' (NRPF) immigration condition in the Immigration and Asylum Act 1999. Rather than viewing NRPF as a relatively new phenomenon, however, we view it as part of a century-long story of exclusion, one that continues to expand and morph as new groups come under its auspices (points we develop in Chapter 1). The NRPF condition is currently imposed on undocumented migrants and most migrants with time-limited permission to stay in the country. Around 1.376 million people with time-limited 'leave to remain' are subject to NRPF in the UK (Fernandez-Reino 2020), while a further approximately 674,000 undocumented people have NRPF by default (Jolly et al. 2020). The NRPF condition is a long-term one, often spanning decades. For example, undocumented families can often expect to have NRPF by default for close to ten years, followed by at least another ten years once they manage to get on the state's longest route to settlement.

The scant existing research on NRPF highlights that it negatively affects people who are already economically and socially marginalised (O'Neill et al. 2019), such as undocumented single mothers from Britain's former colonies and their children. NRPF has been consistently shown to trap migrants in conditions of destitution (Jolly, 2018), debt (Dickson et al., 2023b), and homelessness. For mothers with NRPF who are excluded from the formal labour market by virtue of their migration status or because they cannot access childcare, having no access to social support means being heavily reliant on informal networks (Benchekroun, 2024). Some become 'subject to coercive control' when this support is unavailable or fractured, for instance by domestic violence (Dudley, 2017), as well as subject to exploitation and abuse in employment and housing (Price and Spencer 2015; Smith et al. 2021).

For families with NRPF who endure such extreme hardship, the only potential state support available comes from cash-strapped local authorities under Section 17 of the Children Act 1989, which in practice is minimal and difficult to access (Dexter et al. 2016). Alternatively, some families who have regularised their status can apply for 'change of conditions' to remove NRPF from their visa due to conditions of destitution. These applications are also onerous and complicated. A recent survey found that 90 per cent of those who apply without third sector or legal support are turned down (Woolley, 2019: 47), and for the 55 per cent who are ultimately successful, a new application must typically be made every two and a half years alongside compulsory visa renewals, regardless of the family's economic situation. Previous research on NRPF has tended to focus on short-lived moments of crisis when families seek support from the local government or third sector organisations, and therefore come out of the shadows. But if NRPF is such a long-term condition, or even one without seeming end, how do families navigate it over time and what are its long-term effects? This question animates our discussion throughout the book.

Research and advocacy have tended to treat NRPF as a discrete policy area, often one that is considered so complex that it receives little attention in campaigning or wider discussions about immigration policy in the UK (Rosen and Dickson, 2024). While a policy in itself, such that it is not unusual for local authorities to have 'NRPF teams' and discrete workers for processing Section 17 applications from families subjected to the condition, NRPF can be best understood as sitting at the interface of welfare and migration regimes in the UK. We use the notion of 'regimes' to move away from a singular story about national policy or local implementation, instead highlighting the multi-scalar articulation and variety of programmes; policies; institutions – including state, market and household; and symbolic processes involved. Migration and welfare regimes may be analytically separable but are thoroughly entwined in practice (Williams, 2014). As such, if welfare in advanced capitalist countries is, broadly speaking, 'understood to pool and redistribute wealth raised through taxation for the benefit of the members of the political community' (Bhambra, 2022: 8), including their care, protection and well-being, one question that arises is who is a member of this political community?

Indeed, for van Oorschot (2000: 34), this is the *fundamental* welfare question: 'Who should get what, and why?' The answer to such a question is fraught, but its archetypical figure is that of the citizen, who – in exchange for rights and entitlements – agrees to live within the country's laws, institutions, expectations and so forth. Beneath this simple assumption, however, lies a series of complexities, not least competing legal, social and geographical ideas about the constitution of citizenship or 'political community'. Are people under 18 years old citizens in their own right or only 'future citizens' subsumed under some version of *paterfamilias* or corporate parenthood by the state until achieving legal adulthood (Larkins, 2013)? Are the people that resource a welfare regime part of the political community to which it applies, even if they live in far-flung parts of the world connected only by empire or neocolonialism (Bhambra, 2022)? Do those without immigration and citizenship 'papers' have no relation to the state at all (Tonkiss and Bloom, 2015)? What degree of importance is granted to immigration status vis-à-vis residency in constituting welfare citizenship when the two appear to be in conflict?

As these questions imply, welfare regimes set limits on who is seen to be entitled to social support. They can do this in multiple ways, such as through means testing for support in liberal welfare states like the UK (Esping-Andersen, 1990) or through ideas about belonging – in other words, consideration of whether someone is 'one of us' (van Oorschot, 2000). It is here that the UK's migration regime steps in. NRPF is a policy answer to the question 'Who should get what, and why?', placing an increasing number of newly arrived and long-term residents in the category of outsider to the political community and therefore shunting them into the shadows of the UK's welfare regime. But the 'us' is not just the result of the legal ascription of citizenship status or the NRPF condition. According to Anderson (2013: 2), the 'us' is also a moral production, or what we are inclined to call a socio-political production. She explains, 'Modern states portray themselves not as arbitrary collections of people hung together by a common legal status but as a community of value, composed of people who share common ideals and (exemplary) patterns of behaviour.' Crucially, this imagined community of value, which is closely linked with the nation, exists by setting out the terms of its exclusions (Valluvan, 2017) such as 'Non-Citizens' – understood as foreigners and (im)migrants. This is perhaps best demonstrated by the rising clamour of voices suggesting that a key welfare policy problem in the UK is scarcity of resources which, the nativist argument runs, should be protected for 'our own' (for critiques see Rosen et al., 2021; Anderson, 2013).

It is partially for this reason that critical race and migration scholars contest a common story told about welfare in the UK. In this story, Britain's welfare state is a tale of working-class success, with the achievement of one of the most comprehensive and universal welfare systems in the world (Mitton, 2009) only to have its golden age destroyed by the advent of neoliberalism. Originally modelled on the 1942 *Beveridge Report*, the British welfare regime was viewed by its social democratic proponents as a way to mediate capitalism's inequalities through state interventions to ensure decent wages and to provide workers with adequate health, education and sustenance (Esping-Andersen, 1990), albeit that critical commentators point out this was little more than 'social compromise between capital and labour' rather than a 'socialist alternative' (Harvey, 2007: 15).

This tale continues with the entrance of neoliberalism as capitalists' answer to their declining share of profits by the 1970s and indeed questions about the political viability of capitalism itself. In the decades since, the UK's welfare regime has been marked by rapid marketisation, privatisation and contracting out as part of neoliberals' toolkit of profiteering (Brennan et al., 2012). Alongside these seismic shifts, the UK's neoliberalising welfare regime individualises risk and responsibility, requiring individuals to be increasingly self-sufficient (Kilkey, 2017), in effect dampening social solidarity. Neoliberal changes have also enabled capital to 'unmoor' from place (Katz, 2002), and evade contributing to welfare systems through the widespread use of offshore tax havens. In this context, retrenched welfare services and support have become increasingly targeted, only available to those limited few who meet a series of restrictive conditionalities (Lambie-Mumford and Green, 2017). As Guentner et al. (2016: 396) point out: 'The rationale of public welfare has shifted from the founding principle, "from cradle to grave" (Attlee government 1945–1951) to the concept "from welfare to work" under Blair.' In combination with over a decade of austerity measures and central government retrenchment following the 2008 financial crisis and ensuing 'global slump' (McNally, 2010), this has meant that the UK has shifted to a limited liberal welfare regime (Esping-Andersen, 1990) where support is increasingly focused on the most destitute, with the rest securing (better) services via the market, making welfare provision increasingly guarded, stigmatised, paternalistic, and punitive in the neoliberal era (Wacquant, 2009).

To some degree this story is true, mapping as it does changes in the way that welfare is understood and organised in the UK, as well as its intensifying use as a site of profiteering for capital, but it implies – incorrectly – that, prior to the rise of neoliberalism, Britain's welfare state met its universalist aspirations in practice. This assertion is not historically accurate, nor does it provide sufficient understanding of the current proliferation of bordering, including of welfare itself. For although Britain's welfare provision has traditionally been framed as a national project of redistribution, it has been funded by international systems of extraction and taxation from times of empire to the present (Bhambra, 2022). The imperial irony here is that those from (neo)colonies who financed the infrastructure of the British welfare state were and are often excluded from its provisions and services even when physically present in the UK. The state has sought to accomplish this through a combination of nationality and immigration policies (El-Enany, 2020), such as those set on deterring long-term settlement by forcing racially marginalised commonwealth subjects into the vagaries of the private housing market (Hayes, 2002). Our primary point here is that the exclusion of non-citizens from welfare did not just begin with neoliberalisation or the UK government's proclamation of a 'hostile environment' for migrants in 2012 (Mills and Klein, 2021), as the story often goes.

Just as it is important to recognise both changes and continuities in the UK's welfare regime, it is crucial to consider the ways in which this intersects with its migration regime. As Kundnani (2023) argues, the story of the rise of neoliberalism is as much about its response to decolonialisation efforts in the Global South and anti-racist struggles around the world as it was to rising workers' movements in the North. In pressing for independence, formally colonised countries moved towards nationalising control over natural resources, transforming foreign-owned private assets into public ownership and raising the spectre of reparations for the impacts of colonialism and chattel slavery. This meant that 'neoliberals were confronting ... the breakdown of racial and colonial boundaries that had previously set limits to demands for social justice' (Kundnani, 2023: 165). It is no surprise then that, alongside marketisation, the 'gyrations and chaotic experiments' of capitalists and their state bedfellows which ushered in neoliberalism (Harvey, 2007: 15) produced an ever-enlarging infrastructure of policing, incarceration and bordering technologies, essentially redrawing and buttressing a 'global colour line' (De Genova, 2018: 1766) (and see further discussion in Chapter 7).

Indeed, commentators agree that recent decades have borne witness to a 'multiplication of borders' (Mezzadra and Neilson, 2013), moving them 'from the margins into the centre of political and social life' (Yuval-Davis et al., 2019: 1). Boundaries around Europe have been deterritorialised and externalised via increasingly sophisticated technologies and security measures. Most importantly for our purposes, in current years there has also been a proliferation of internal borders, in what Van Der Leun (2006) describes as the shift from 'gatekeeping at the border' to 'gatekeeping access to services'. NRPF is an obvious example of such gatekeeping of services, denying people access to services provided via 'public funds'. In the UK, this process has also co-opted teachers, health care professionals, social workers and landlords into the role of border guard, making decisions about who is 'deserving' of the multiple forms of social support which make up 'public funds', thus implicating everyday citizens in shoring up the internal boundaries around welfare and services necessary for daily life.

In delineating multiplication, Mezzadra and Neilson (2013: 7) argue that borders are not simply walls, barriers or blockages, but are 'equally devices of inclusion that select and filter people and different forms of circulation in ways no less violent than those deployed in exclusionary measures'. This way of apprehending the 'partial inclusions' of migrants, at once within geopolitical borders whilst still being heavily regulated, restricted, subordinated and rendered as 'second class', even when granted legal citizenship and the right to reside, is a crucial point we develop in this book. For the purposes of Mezzadra and Neilson (2013) and others, this partial inclusion is about the stratification of labouring bodies, reminiscent of De Genova's (2002) notion of 'deportability', where the capitalist state and its corporate partners use even the distant threat of forced return in an effort to render migrant labour cheap and pliable.

The notion of deportability, and its ugly bedfellow immigration detention, certainly applies to those who are undocumented and have NRPF by default, as they are stranded in the liminal space of 'non-existence', both physically present and yet legal non-entities (Gonzales et al., 2019). To date, however, the important body of scholarship on deportability has focused on detention and forced return and their implications for labour power exploitability. But these state migration control strategies are complicated legally, morally and politically by the presence of children. International commitments to the UN Convention on the Rights of the Child (1989), also embedded in national laws, make it difficult for the UK to deport locally born or long-resident children and their carers – primarily mothers. Indeed, the right to private and family life, an important legal mechanism for undocumented families in the UK to resist expulsion (Desmond, 2018), represents a particular frustration to neoliberal migration regimes seeking to 'control migration' (see Chapter 1).

What happens, then, to those whom nation states regard as undesirable, but who are deemed non-deportable or non-detainable legally, morally or politically? This question takes us to the heart of the arguments we make in this book. Thinking with our interlocutors, we show how the imposition of NRPF as a state strategy of migration control and deterrence, an attempt to make the UK less appealing for people on the move, operates by enforcing destitution and debt on 'undesirables'. We conceptualise this as a form of welfare bordering which, we argue, operates alongside detention and deportation as tripartite border technologies.

Early on, we thought about NRPF as a form of what Ruth Wilson Gilmore (2007) calls 'organized state abandonment', akin to O'Neill and Roberts's (2019) description of NRPF as 'state sanctioned necropower', where racially marginalised migrant families are left to fend for themselves with minimal resources and without access to a social safety net if needed. We have come to see that abandonment on its own does not sufficiently account for NRPF's use as a punitive form of neoliberal welfare statecraft (Wacquant, 2009). An alternative way of conceptualising NRPF has been as a form of 'welfare chauvinism', picking up on the concept's widespread usage in political sociology and beyond (Careja and Harris, 2022). In defining NRPF in such terms, Guentner et al. (2016: 393) explain welfare chauvinism as 'the ideological construction of a specified out-group as both threatening and morally inferior so that action to punish, exclude or incapacitate its members is necessary on both moral and existential grounds', thereby providing both 'form' and 'rationale' for inclusions of 'good citizens' and exclusions of 'non-citizens'. However, naming this process as chauvinism runs the risk of reducing it to individuals' discriminatory thoughts or bad feelings.

Although moral judgements are certainly central to imaginaries of the community of value, our preference is to understand NRPF as an exemplar par excellence of a process of *welfare bordering*. This formulation draws our attention directly to the intersections of welfare and migration regimes and points towards the systemic and institutional exclusions, or 'partial inclusions', from social support at and within the boundaries of the nation state. Building on literature on bordering, it prompts consideration of how people are filtered into different forms of social support, or no public support at all, via structural as well as everyday bordering practices, without reducing this to individual maleficence. To take but one example, social workers do not deny support to homeless families with NRPF, leaving them on the street or in uninhabitable temporary accommodation, because these frontline workers are monsters. Infrastructures of welfare bordering are far more entrenched and institutionalised in the UK than a single individual's beliefs and attitudes, such that they persist regardless of whether denials of support are articulated in the racialised terms of nativism or whether individual workers express frustration and sadness for the restrictions placed on what they can offer. This is not to say that their actions are not part of the process of welfare bordering, simply that welfare bordering is not reducible to their attitudes. Furthermore, while the concept of welfare bordering assumes that some sort of redistribution process is in place in a political community, it does not assume the form of social support provided or the rationales for its withholding – giving the concept purchase beyond the UK. In short, attending to welfare bordering invites us to consider with precision the (inconsistent) ways in which punishment, subjugation, detention, deportation and denial of support operate in relation to each other and with what effects. Indeed, just as neoliberalism was certainly not the only possible response to anti-colonial, anti-racist and workers' struggles, there is no necessity to welfare provision as a site of marketisation nor must it be a site where the nation is marked and made (see Chapter 7). Things could have been, and can be, different.

That said, as we show throughout the book, welfare bordering as it has developed in the guise of NRPF serves to deny migrant mothers and their children the means of life, in a context where deportation and detention are largely not possible. However, departing from accounts which focus primarily on lack or depletion through the long-term impoverishment enforced by NRPF, families' efforts to make and sustain meaningful lives in the shadows of Britain's neoliberal welfare state serve as an important reminder of the limitations, contestations and indeed fragilities of welfare as a site of bordering. To help us make sense of the idea of 'making and sustaining lives', we turn to the literature on social reproduction.

Life-making practices, or social reproduction

A starting point for much analysis of social reproduction is the question: if labour makes the commodity, who makes the labourer? (Taha and Salem, 2019). This is a crucial question for linking the practices involved in making and sustaining life to capitalism, showing that it is a political question as to where lines are drawn between paid and unpaid work; private and public spheres; workers and non-workers; and, indeed, to the production of these categories at all. The question also jolts us into a recognition that workers do not appear every morning (or night) replenished and regenerated for another day of (hard, dirty, difficult) labour, ready not only to produce the commodity but surplus value for capital. For, as Marx (1976) made clear in his stunning, if by now familiar, elaboration of the source of profit in capitalism: this is none other than the worker's actualised labour power. In posing the question about the labourer in this way, we are reminded that everyday, intimate family practices or 'life' to quote a favourite mantra of the UK policy world ('work–life' balance) are not separate realms – with the everyday, family or 'life' representing a bastion apart from capitalism. Instead, the question draws our attention to every loaf of bread ever baked, every curry simmered or coffee brewed. It reminds us not to dismiss each floor swept and mopped, toilet scrubbed and dish washed. It puts centrally in our mind the mountain of diapers changed, wounds bandaged, tears soothed and stories told. Social reproduction does not let us forget, indeed it demands that we bring into sharp relief, all those daily and long-term acts of repair, replenishment and replacement that enable workers to report to work. It reminds us that this labour is necessary for capital but hidden from its wage calculus and therefore one of the dirty little secrets of capital's own regeneration and accumulation practices. And, as critical scholars of 'race' and colonialism remind us, some people are simply rejected from wage labour entirely as capital relies on 'more dispersed methods of scraping value from the business of human life' (Bhattacharyya, 2024: 36). These are the edge populations required to rationalise carceral, migration and social services; the captive consumers and debt servicers of a monetised economy; and the labouring subjects engaged in the effort of sustaining the viability of natural and social life in the face of revanchist social policy (Bhattacharyya, 2024; Newberry and Rosen, 2020; Federici, 2014).

To some degree welfare 'successes' won in the mid-twentieth century in Britain represented a silent reckoning with the question of how the worker appears ready to work every morning – a refusal to accept that the costs of social reproduction should be born stoically, sacrificially and often dangerously by the labourer and his family alone. If the use of the masculine possessive reads awkwardly in the twenty-first century, that is good, but know that we have used it here purposively. Decades of research and activism have made clear that the labour of producing the worker is highly gendered, shouldered disproportionately by women in both unpaid and low-/underpaid capacities, naturalised as labours of love and unskilled feminised work (Vogel, 2000; Bhattacharya, 2017; Federici, 2012). Increasingly, it has also become clear that the relegation of reproductive labour to 'the family' is neither a necessary part of capitalism, nor does it describe the myriad of ways advanced capitalist countries like Britain are handling their 'crisis of social reproduction'. With ageing populations, retrenchment of social support and rising impoverishment, the question of who is producing the worker, and how, is more pressing than ever for capital and its state backers. One way this reproduction has been accomplished is through the use of internal or international migrant labour in what has come to be referred to as a 'global care chain' (Parrenas, 2000). Here, border regimes select and filter, providing partial inclusion to workers in order to secure reproductive labour often at a cheaper cost and in more precarious circumstances than local workers (Kofman, 2012), whilst producing social reproduction gaps in the countries where their labour was reproduced in the first place.

In this sense, we can see that social reproduction and welfare (in its broadest sense) are bound up with each other, in terms of who provides reproductive labour, where and under what conditions. Is the labour of making lives supported in some way by the state (e.g. through welfare support and services), capital (e.g. through taxation) or left to people to negotiate on their own? Who pays for reproduction, and how, when the British state seeks to shrink its welfare budget and capital untethers from place? A key point here is that the labour of regenerating and replenishing lives is not simply in the interests of capital, but it is also a necessity for human existence. For this reason, Marx (1976: 718) stipulates: 'The capitalist may safely leave this to the worker's drive for self-preservation and propagation.' Social reproduction doubles as both source of life and site of exploitation.

Such labour occurs on a highly uneven terrain, as the discussion of migrant care workers suggests. Not only is reproductive labour in each link of the chain increasingly devalued – morally and economically – but this exemplifies the point above about liberal welfare regimes. Those who can afford to purchase welfare support for their reproduction do so, often relying on what is effectively subsidised by the use of migrant labour – including mothers with NPRF as we discuss further in Chapter 3 (and see Erel, 2018). Those who cannot may rely on welfare support for their reproduction, but how do families address their social reproduction needs when they are impoverished *and* support is denied through welfare bordering? This question brings us to the heart of the second core argument of our book.

Building on theorisations of social reproduction as stratified in its achievement, and therefore its effects (Colen, 1995; Parrenas, 2012), we pay close ethnographic attention to how families navigate life's labour in the precarious circumstances shaped by welfare bordering. Rai and colleagues (2013: 86) are instructive here, suggesting that in contexts of extreme inequality, for those who are only ever partially included, reproductive labour can effectively 'deplete' or 'exhaust', rather than regenerate, in the effort of survival. They point to the 'critical gap between the outflows – domestic, affective and reproductive – and the inflows that sustain their health and well-being', including welfare services and supports. Reproductive labour can be extractive and harmful when depletion is greater than sustenance. Likewise, Yasmin Gunaratnam (2020) speaks about the 'slow wearing down of black bodies' in the labour of provisioning, highlighting the racialised stratification whereby Black and Brown people are far more likely to experience depletion, rather than sustenance, through reproductive labour.

The notion of depletion serves as an important warning, but our worry is that its raw calculus neither reflects the ways in which our interlocutors sought to represent the complexities of their lives, nor the insights of social reproduction theory as to its dual character: producing labour for capital and lives that are never fully exhausted by it. In response to these concerns, in Chapter 2, we introduce the novel conceptual apparatus of 'weathering' for the study of contingent and contested effects of welfare bordering on the reproduction of life. This allows us to break with reductive readings which have dominated critical scholarship about NRPF, showing that lives always exceed the stories that policies construct and impose, while never losing sight of the impact of enforced debt and destitution on the conditions of life and livelihood. Throughout the book, we demonstrate the ways migrant families refuse the existential erasure and punitive conditions of enforced destitution, while simultaneously living its violence. The analytic of weathering we develop draws attention to processes of wearing, withstanding, fortification and toughening, and allows for engagement with the dynamic and multi-faceted ways in which mothers and children in precarious migrancy position and represent themselves both within and beyond the hardship produced by NRPF.

Indeed, children and childhood are central to discussions of social reproduction, typically in the guise of childbirth, child rearing and child socialisation. Having children is at once viewed as pivotal to hopes for the future (Narotzky and Besnier, 2014), futures which are often otherwise deferred by precarious migrancy (Jacobsen and Karlsen, 2021), and as reproductive labour's greatest burden (Rosen, 2023). Framed in this latter way, children can appear as a route into hardship and deprivation. Yet, both approaches typically neglect children's own experiences and perspectives, replicating a figuration of the child as essentially dependent on independent adults, the vulnerable subject par excellence in contradistinction to the self-sufficient adult, and the voiceless Other. For this reason, it is hardly surprising that critiques of NRPF, and political efforts to address its violences, are often framed around narratives of the 'in-need child', policy terminology embedded in the Children's Act 1989 in its specification of Section 17 support.

We pause here for a moment to home in on the ways in which children and childhood appear, differently, in this book. We set out from the burgeoning body of literature which makes the case that childhood, like motherhood and family, is not a universal with essentialised characteristics, but is better understood as a socially constituted position, relation, bureaucratic category, embodied inscription, interpellation and/or performance which changes over time and place. This is not just an empirical nod to the 'multiplicity' of childhoods (Balagopalan, 2019) or motherhoods. Nor is it simply a descriptive statement about the diversity of families and heterogeneity of family life where sedentarism, cohabitation, love, care and biological kinship are only some of the many variations that are possible or considered desirable (Baldassar and Merla, 2014). To leave our understanding at the level of the descriptive empirical – telling no more than a neutral story of diversity – flattens the inequities and injustices which shape the conditions and lived experience of migrant family life.

More so then, for us, insights about the deeply politicised social constitution of childhood, along with motherhood and family, compel reflection on the ways in which they are produced and the work they do as people go about the everyday business of making lives within the UK's racialised borders and neoliberalising welfare regime. In this regard, a series of concurrent trends in Euro-America derive their discursive force from portrayals of 'the family' as a site of crisis (Cooper, 2017), where familial bonds purportedly need strengthening and their 'values' revived to address 'social decay' – as in the 'Troubled Families' policy trend of the UK in the 2010s (Crossley, 2016). On the one hand this has led to the increased responsibilisation of families, characteristic of neoliberal individualism. This is little more than a rationalisation for the refamilisation of social reproduction (Newberry and Rosen, 2020) where parents are cast as '*a* (or *the*) determining force in how their children turn out' (Rosen and Faircloth, 2020: 5). On the other, this has led to increasing state intervention, often in neoconservative and right-wing populist terms. Surveillance, regulation and intervention into families is on the rise in the name of producing 'proper' subjects (Gillies et al., 2017) as well as the British nation as an archetype of white Englishness (Erel, 2018).

Such scrutiny and policing of intimate lives is particularly pronounced for destitute migrant mothers and children as they may be constituted as bodies out of place (Reynolds and Orellana, 2009), undesirable in such racialised and classed conceptions of the nation. But it also reflects destitute families' material conditions of existence which mean that their lives are often lived in public – in playgrounds, schools, religious institutions, public transit and so forth – and therefore they are open to more intensive scrutiny and governance (Lisiak, 2017). One consequence is that migrant mothers are often blamed for their children's living conditions and everyday struggles, as well as held individually responsible for their social and educational outcomes. This is despite the often extreme limits bordering their access to resources and state support (Heidbrink and Statz, 2017; Erel, 2018; Erel et al., 2017; Benchekroun et al., 2024) and compounded by heteronormative and Eurocentric constructions of the family where, for example, physical co-presence is conflated with 'good' care, stigmatising families who live apart due to migration regardless of whether such separation is experienced as disruptive or problematic in practice (Baldassar and Merla, 2014).

In other cases, practices which are seen as necessary or valuable by migrant families may be pathologised or penalised, particularly where they contradict hegemonic understandings. For example, dominant ideas about children as essentially dependent and developing at predictable milestones rub up awkwardly against children's language brokering for adults in institutional settings, caring for siblings, working to pay off family debts or send remittances – practices which are often highly valued within migrant families (McGovern and Devine, 2015; Crafter and Iqbal, 2021; Leon and Rosen, 2023). Despite offering evidence of children's complex capabilities and the interdependence of life, children living in precarious migrancy are often deemed unchildlike when engaged in these practices, not the 'at risk child' but instead 'the risk' (Heidbrink, 2014). One point to draw out here is that these social categories – childhood, motherhood, the family – are exceptionally malleable, and therefore easily reconstituted, but at the same time remarkably overdetermined, often in ways that exclude or preclude edge populations from the respect and protection the categories might otherwise offer (for an example of the ways in which undocumented children are the impossible subject of campaigns which draw their force from assumptions of children's exceptionalism, see Rosen and Dickson, 2024).

Despite the often-subjugating ways in which childhood, motherhood and the family are put to work by the racialised state, these positions and institutions nonetheless hold ethical meaning and value, including for those whom they exclude or oppress. Motherhood may bring a sense of importance, regarded as key to nurturing relations of care and solidarity and engaging in 'culture work' across transnational lives (Erel et al., 2017). Childhood may be viewed as a precious time, offering hope into the future (Rosen and Suissa, 2020). Family life may be experienced as a haven or a site for resisting racism and exclusion (hooks, 2014; Erel et al., 2017). We write these points with some trepidation, however, concerned to recognise everyday yearnings while seeking to avoid fetishising or romanticising institutions which are themselves shot through with inequities and power differentials. For instance, children's experiences are often subsumed into their parents' as though they are one and the same. Mixed statuses within families (which may include citizens and non-citizens) produces differential access to support and services, and therefore, as with hegemonic positionings of childhood, breeds difficult dependencies. As Gargi Bhattacharyya (2024: 50) cautions: 'Somehow we have to stretch our ability to think ourselves in a way that allows us to see our most precious practices as arising in dialogue with our torment.' Throughout the book then, we are at pains to engage with those institutions, positions and imaginaries which animate the lives and values of our interlocutors while recognising and troubling hegemonic and reified constructions of childhood, motherhood and the family.

In so doing, and by engaging children, as well as their mothers, as research interlocutors, we consider what they have to show us, what keen insights about the impacts of precarious migrancy they have to offer, in ways which both parallel and are distinctive to those of their mothers. We argue that welfare bordering makes the reproductive labour of children as well as mothers an essential, yet fragile, family project of common cause, which tends to be obscured when advocacy and support are framed within exceptionalist narratives about childhood or if a calculus of depletion does not sufficiently consider affect and emotions, the animatory force of hopes and dreams, and generational social positions alongside class, 'race' and gender. Our interlocutors remind us over and over that, despite the violence of welfare bordering and the denial of life that NRPF represents, their collective effort of making and sustaining life can be filled with reciprocity and love. We choose to think of this as a world-making labour which on its own cannot end racialised border violences or ensure that human needs are met, but which still produces spaces where such subjugation cannot fully tread and where sparks of opposition to injustice may even be fomented.

Research methods and ethics

The stories we share in this book are the outcomes of various in-depth encounters we have had with mothers and children subjected to no recourse to public funds (NRPF) on our joint research projects. *Social reproduction in the shadows (Shadows)* ran from 2019 to 2021 and specifically focused on how single-mother families with NRPF engaged in processes of provision and care in the context of the UK's 'hostile environment' for immigration. Our analytic process, however, has far exceeded this period, and indeed continues in our current expansion of this first study. In our initial project, we focused on single-mother families because, as discussed above, research has shown that this group has been most negatively impacted by NRPF – something we also knew from our own non-academic work on NRPF and which was borne out by the third sector organisations who supported us with recruitment. These organisations worked overwhelmingly with single-mother families. This had analytic repercussions for our project, which we pick up on throughout the book. It's important to note, however, that relationship status was often fluid for mothers we met, with periods of single parenthood sometimes punctuated by, for instance, intermittent reunions with fathers or other romantic relationships.

When we began *Shadows*, our intention was to engage in 'day in the life' ethnography, spending time with family members during their everyday activities but for more focused periods of time and place than typically associated with ethnographic research. Early in the process, the Covid-19 pandemic hit globally, putting our carefully laid plans to rest. We revised our approach to ensure that we could maintain social distancing for the well-being of our participants and ourselves. We are well aware of the difference between the deep immersion associated with face-to-face ethnography and the restrictions of scheduled and screen restricted encounters of online research, which our participants often undertook using the small screens of mobile phones. We did, however, draw on insights from in-person ethnography, designing interactions and activities with the aim of generating finely grained and richly textured data from the flow of everyday life.

In total, we spent time with ten families, including ten single-mothers and sixteen children, as part of *Shadows*. This included ethnographic observation with three families prior to the pandemic and, with the others, ethnographic-inspired activities during the pandemic. Our online methods included real-time video tours of living spaces and 'day in your life' WhatsApp conversations, using photos, audio, video and text to share activities over the day. We combined this with narrative interviews with mothers, simply posing the request 'Could you tell us your story of living with NRPF', and then following our interlocutors' lead. Most of the mothers spoke for extended periods of time with little need for prompts. Interviews with children focused on a pre-completed activity. Participants were invited to choose either to take pictures of their lives based on several prompts, such as things that make you feel good or are hard, or to complete a journal filled with both blank pages and activities, such as 'Three wishes' or charting daily movements. We have largely included verbatim portions of our interlocutors' stories, without correcting for grammar or duplication. Discursive styles – such as repetition – serve as important features of their narratives, serving to emphasise specific points or work through reoccurring questions and themes we pick up throughout this book.

The interactions and conversations we had with participants about their lives often touched upon difficult and distressing topics. Given this, we took the lead of our interlocuters in interviews and conversations, allowing them to set the topics and limits. We felt the need to be particularly careful not to replicate negative experiences of interviews (e.g. invasive social services assessments) and therefore generally avoided direct questions. For instance, if another person entered the room during an interview or visit, we did not ask who they were, but allowed participants to decide whether to explain the situation to us. Sometimes this left us with many questions, but we nonetheless felt it was important. We also reminded participants throughout that they could withdraw, stop, pause or change the research encounter. Before speaking directly to children, we explained to mothers the methods we would use and how we would approach the conversations, which were adapted according to the language used to talk about such issues within the family. As in the case of our interactions with mothers, we followed the lead of children in these conversations rather than imposing our own agenda. The only more direct question we asked, with parental consent, was at the end of interviews, at which point we asked whether children had heard of the term 'no recourse to public funds' and what they thought it might mean. In recognition of the material conditions in which our participants were living and to thank them for their participation in the research, we offered refreshments and gift vouchers. Anonymity and confidentiality were particularly important, given participants' insecure immigration statuses. Names and other potentially identifying details have therefore been changed throughout this book.

Our ethnographic fieldwork is accompanied by textual analysis of government statements, policy documents and media coverage to help paint a picture of the public debates and contextual framing of our interlocutors' lives. In Chapter 1, however, we take a more comprehensive look at material from the period of January 2011 to August 2012, a period spanning the introduction and confirmation of new family migration rules, and in Chapter 7 we home in on Equalities legislation. Our analytic approach to this material was informed by critical discourse analysis (Fairclough, 2003) and involved close attention to frequency, valence and framing of coverage and specific terminology, as well as silences, in relation to an analysis of the broader material and discursive contexts in which these emerged.

We feel it is important to note a few things about the nature of our ethnographic fieldwork and its limitations. First, this book does not represent an exhaustive account of the lives of our interlocuters, nor indeed of living with NRPF. In the scheme of their lives, our contact with the families in this book was fleeting and limited by the research process. We consider our contributions as reflecting situated and partial knowledge – there are many things we may not have been told, may not have understood and may never know. What it was possible or impossible for families to share with us will have been shaped by who we are and who we present as – including our 'positionality' as women racialised as white, without experience of undocumented migration, with British citizenship and high levels of formal education. These factors may have been experienced as constraining, marking our difference and potential gulfs in our capacity to understand – something, perhaps, Rita draws our attention to in Chapter 3, when she repeatedly asks Eve if she understands what she is being told. Yet, like De Noronha (2020: 33), we are 'cautious about what can be inferred from either racial proximity or difference'. As he continues, 'There is always more going on, something in excess of racial categories, and positionality should be about more than listing categories of identity.' We have also both witnessed our 'difference' as something that might, at times, potentially facilitate conversations that it may otherwise feel impossible to have. For example, one time when Eve accompanied Lucy, a Caribbean mother with NRPF to a local authority, as they sat in a McDonalds eating chips while they waited for social services to decide whether to house Lucy and her daughter, Lucy told Eve what she called 'the story of her life' – a harrowing tale she said she'd never been able to tell anyone before. It was as though this incredibly painful story Lucy told, with all its deep regrets and shame, could be told to Eve precisely because she was different – so far removed from her everyday and the social world in which she often felt, like some of our participants, persecuted by those who appeared more similar to her in some respects (e.g. in terms of 'race', class and nationality), because of her exploitability as an undocumented woman. And while we remain alive to the gaps in our fieldwork, the unuttered sentences, the things we saw but could not understand or the things we did not see at all, and their part in the story we offer here, we were also deeply moved by our interlocuters' willingness to share their stories with us and to let us into their lives.

Secondly, even though we are co-authors of this book, our roles in the research on which it is based have been different. Due to the nature of academic grant funding and its various constraints, Eve carried out the fieldwork with the families included throughout this book, while Rachel designed the methods we used. The project was co-conceived – drawing primarily on Rachel's previous work on social reproduction and Eve's work on NRPF – and we co-analysed the data. We feel this book is deeply collaborative, the result of endless conversations, thinking together and, indeed, often struggling to disentangle ourselves from the thought of the other. We have written this book together and it reflects our joint labour – something that can often risk being obscured by the fraught terrain of author order. At the same time, this is a book – despite the uniform 'we' with which we write – in which we are speaking to one another, and in which our different interests, approaches and styles are put into dialogue. There are times, therefore, when each one of us emerges more clearly, as for instance Rachel does in Chapter 4, developing lines of thought from her ongoing work on children's positioning and participation in social reproduction (e.g. Rosen, 2023; Rosen and Newberry, 2018). Or, when we hear Eve more strongly in Chapter 3, as she foregrounds questions of psychic life, reflecting her long-held interests and ideas (Dickson, 2023). This conversation between us has been incredibly productive and is precisely what has led us to the main intellectual contributions of this book.

Finally, the impetus for and ideas discussed in this book come not only out of our research, but also our ongoing community activism and political commitments, including to publicly engaged scholarship for social justice. For example, we have been heavily influenced by our involvement in North East London Migrant Action (NELMA), an organisation which campaigned to defend the rights of all migrants and ran an accompanying scheme for people with no recourse to public funds (NRPF), and Grassroots

Women, a feminist and anti-imperialist women's organisation in Canada which engaged in collective struggle for universal and liberatory childcare and against the racist exploitation of migrant domestic workers (Rosen et al., 2017). All this to say, our desires to challenge welfare bordering, such as the NRPF condition, do not begin or end with this book, and we hope to continue to contribute to struggles for free movement, both in and outside of our academic work.

Our interlocutors

For all their shared experiences, the mothers and children who populate the pages of this book are a heterogeneous and diverse group. Some, as in the case of Samantha and Tanya, migrated to the UK from Nigeria and Jamaica as children to join their parents, only to later discover that they had no legal status in the country. Others, like Rita and Ijeoma, arrived in the UK later in their lives, attempting to flee experiences of abuse in Nigeria and to make new lives. While they migrated at different times and for different reasons, the mothers we met had all been living in the UK for long periods of time, often for more than ten or fifteen years. Their class backgrounds were varied – for example, one mother described living a middle-class life in Nigeria, cared for by a nanny and other household staff as a child, while others described conditions of extreme poverty in their childhoods. Similarly, migration routes reflected a plurality of entry routes and circumstances leading to settlement in the UK. Some, like Abiola or Martha, had come on visitor visas for short trips to see friends and family but had ended up staying as their situations changed – for example, when Martha's son had an accident and required specialist healthcare in the UK to recover. The children we met had spent most, indeed often all, of their lives in the UK, and in some cases, they had never left the country. Many had British citizenship or should have had, but, as in Sam's situation, were struggling to prove it in their father's absences. In some families, there were other children we never met because they did not, and were not allowed to, live in the UK – barred from joining their mothers and siblings by the state's migration rules. Their presence was mostly spectral for us, often coming into the frame only when they were symbolically represented – for instance, when Shanice tells us in Chapter 4 that the suitcases that fill the room she shares with her mother are full of items her mother plans to send to her siblings in Ghana.

What our interlocuters had in common, amongst other things, were the borders they had to navigate in their everyday lives. These ranged from the drawn-out processes of endeavouring to regularise migration status – a continual cycle for those with legal status as well as those without, as we see in Destiny's case in Chapter 6 – to the micro-borders of the everyday, where public services, informal work and interpersonal relationships became part of the wider bordered terrain. Some families in this book were undocumented and seeking regularised status based on Article 8 rights to family and private life under the European Convention of Human Rights (ECHR). Their applications often rested on provisions in the immigration rules for legal status to be granted if a child has lived continuously in the UK for at least seven years and it 'would not be reasonable to expect them to leave the UK', or if a child has British citizenship – whether by birth or naturalisation. Other families we discuss in subsequent chapters had already made successful applications on these grounds and had temporary thirty-month visas with an NRPF condition. They were on a family migration route known as the 'ten-year route to settlement', which requires four separate applications for temporary status to be made, before applicants can apply for permanent residence – something we discuss in more detail in Chapter 1. The only exception was one mother who was undocumented and applying for regularisation on a slightly different basis. Tanya was making what is often called a 'half-life application' when we met her, because she was between 18 and 24 years old and had lived in the UK continuously for more than half her life. Like the other applications mentioned above, if successful, this application would have placed Tanya on the ten-year route to settlement. All our research participants were subject to NRPF – whether directly, because of a lack of legal status or as a visa conditionality, or indirectly, as in the case of children with British citizenship, who cannot claim welfare benefits or other 'public funds' (as defined by the immigration rules) in their own right.

While we see these legal categories as important to register and understand, given that they profoundly shaped the lives of the families we met, we do not wish to reduce our interlocuters to such bureaucratic statuses. We are also mindful not to reduce people's relationships with the state, or indeed their rights vis-à-vis the state, to questions of citizenship or 'noncitizenship' (Tonkiss and Bloom, 2015). Instead, we recognise that the ascription of precarious, mixed or non-citizenship statuses within and across families creates the possibility of particular forms of domination over their lives. In the chapters that follow, we attempt to engage with these complexities meaningfully, showing how such statuses constrained family members at the level of the everyday, as well as the ways in which they challenged, withstood and navigated the borders with which they had to contend. We are deeply grateful for all that they have taught us and for their continued efforts to make life in the shadows.

Outline of the book

In Chapter 1, 'Enforcing destitution and debt', we explore processes of internal bordering, tracing the ways that NRPF and enforced destitution and debt have come to be understood, imposed and normalised in the UK. Homing in on the 2012 expansion of NRPF to families who had previously been eligible for residency and support through human rights legislation, we draw on policy and public debates to make the case that NRPF is a post-hoc, punitive measure *enforcing* destitution and debt on racially marginalised postcolonial subjects. We conclude with a discussion of more recent shifts in discourse around NRPF, as well as the continued expansion of the policy, to consider the question of 'where next' for NRPF and its increasing contestation.

Moving beyond policy and responsive campaigning, which only tell us part of the story, the next three chapters focus on the lives of those subject to NRPF. Here we introduce the concept of 'weathering' as an analytic tool for comprehending the complex interplay between bordering that makes lives impossible and the lives of people who refuse to accept such impossibilities. Chapter 2, 'Weathering through social reproduction', sets out from a problematisation of the scant literature on NRPF, with its overemphasis on wearing, lack and survival for naked human existence. Rather than viewing migrant mothers and children as victims who are passively 'done to', an argument implied in some of the NRPF literature, we explore the complex planning, calculating, strategising, navigating and dreaming that animates daily life as well as the time, energy and labour required to sustain it. Taking our cue from the way our interlocutors seek to present their own lives, weathering enables a focus on the simultaneity of wearing, riding out and withstanding.

While Chapter 2 puts the concept of weathering to work in relation to material practices of sustaining everyday life, Chapter 3, 'Existential erasure and its discontents', does so in relation to the psychic lives of mothers. Following our interlocutors' narratives of feeling radically alone in their impoverishment, jettisoned by the state and unable to seek support from those around them due to the extremity of their hardship, we conceptualise the experience of enforced destitution as a form of psychic precarity, even erasure. For many, reclaiming value lies down the path of motherhood, whether the productive potential of having a child who can confer regularised immigration status on the family or as a relational mode generative of meaning, value and futures – however far deferred. Yet, as we argue, the psychic fluctuations of value, where existential erasure looms large, produce a radical responsibilisation of the individual or family unit and create fertile ground for hyper-exploitation, subjugation and usury of migrant mothers as workers, friends and partners.

If motherhood is viewed as a source of value, where does that leave childhood? In Chapter 4, 'Childhood in the shadows', we turn our attention specifically to questions of how children in families with NRPF are positioned and position themselves. In policy, welfare contexts and in families, children are often simultaneously the object of intervention, a potential route to access support, a route to settlement and the silenced subject of advocacy campaigns. Engaging children as interlocuters, we highlight the complex ways in which they laboured under NRPF, contributing to maintaining the household, engaging in caring and reparative emotional work and navigating bureaucracies – often finely attuned to their families' situation. Family survival was narrated many of our young interlocutors as a collective, albeit fragile, project of common cause.

The next two chapters in the book focus on the spatial-temporal shaping of life with NRPF and life-making practices occurring under this duress. In Chapter 5, 'Secrets and silences', we take up the question of space, specifically considering the way that housing and domestic life are conditioned by NRPF. Documenting families' experiences of homelessness, cramped shared accommodation, dependence on the 'hospitality' of friends and strangers and exploitative private rentals, we argue that the enforced destitution of welfare bordering compels fraught intimacy and a sense of dangerous proximity. We trace the ways that mothers and children use secrets and silences as 'practices under duress', both a necessity and, at the same time, multi-layered, contradictory and always already impossible. Secrets and silences, we argue, operate as efforts to weather acute proximity with dignity and to make lives liveable in unbearable circumstances.

Weathering is fundamentally a temporal analytic, and Chapter 6, 'Doing time', builds on the spatial focus of the previous chapter to explore the use of time delayed as both a tactic of state power over space-time and migrant endurance under duress. Between enforced destitution, punitive debt and the challenges of completing official routes to settlement while subject to NRPF, it is evident that the UK's 'hostile' migration regime operates in the long durée. Yet, in conversation with our interlocutors, we argue that time, like space, and in their interface, may be harnessed as a border technology but this is never a smooth and seemly process. We trace the ways that migrant families not only come to terms with time as a bordering technology, but in weathering with fortitude, persistence and planning, put time to work in aid of making a legal case for status and in claims to belonging. We argue, however, that this refusal of NRPF's existential erasure through 'doing time' to regularise or remove the NRPF condition provides no simple panaceas.

In Chapter 7, '(En)countering "race"', we take a step back from the close portraits of our interlocutors as they navigate life's labour in the context of the UK's welfare borders. We attend to silences in policy, advocacy and previous scholarship to understand how NRPF can be presented as 'raceless', with its racialised effects justified despite the right to equality being an ostensibly a legal obligation. We demonstrate that in policies, institutions and everyday interactions, NRPF can be understood as imbricated in the racial logics and fabric of British society, operating through migration status and nationality as well as racially coded but seemingly 'race neutral' characteristics and competencies. Developing understandings of how and why NRPF can be understood as a tool of state racism is, we argue, important politically as well as intellectually, an effort we begin in this final chapter and which we hope will be continued, by both us and others, beyond the life of this book.

Conclusion

Through historicised policy analysis and rich ethnographic insights, this book makes two core arguments. First, we claim that welfare bordering is part of tripartite racialised border technologies within deportation regimes, alongside detention and deportation. We focus here specifically on the imposition of NRPF in the UK, which we conceptualise as a key mechanism of welfare bordering – a form of punitive exclusion from the means of life and central to the (re)production of the racialised nation state. Second, we advance the concept of weathering as a way to move beyond analytics of heroic resilience or bare life in efforts to make meaningful lives, making the case for inclusion of the social status of childhood, subjectivities and space-time in analyses of stratified social reproduction. These insights are analytic, but they have real-world impact not least because they point to the necessity of finding new ways to challenge welfare bordering – a point we pick up again in more detail in the conclusion.

1

Enforcing destitution and debt

There was a rare furore around the NRPF condition in 2020, when, at the height of the Covid-19 pandemic, the then Prime Minister Boris Johnson revealed his own surprise at the policy's existence (Mills, 2020). While Johnson's political gaffe was largely interpreted as an example of his own incompetence, his initial reaction and later defence of the policy suggest that the oft-claimed 'naturalness' of NRPF is more contrived – even by the standards of Conservative politicians – than is generally assumed. Welfare bordering is typically presented as a necessary and natural facet of national migration regimes. These policies, we're told, 'make sense', demarcating as they do boundaries of (un)deservingness that accord with nativist national imaginaries. Their basic premise, therefore, often goes unquestioned. Even those who advocate against them rarely call for their abolition. We rarely hear slogans such as 'everything for everyone'. Instead, advocates make more 'reasonable' asks – a specific group should be exempted on exceptional grounds, or a particular provision (e.g. free school meals) should be made available for all. Our imaginaries of change, as we've discussed elsewhere (Rosen and Dickson, 2024), are thus often also captured by the very logics of welfare bordering that we attempt to contest – the idea, for example, that Britain's welfare system is not for all. All this to say, the so-called 'sense' of policies like NRPF are deeply ingrained in our social world and our horizon for change. How welfare bordering is justified and framed, then, is something we cannot afford to neglect. With this in mind, we might think of this chapter as attempting to take the policy, or at least some of its 'sense', somewhat apart.

We start with an in-depth discussion of the NRPF rule before homing in on the most recent direct extension of NRPF – the 2012 changes to the family migration rules. Through close attention to how this policy extension was framed and constructed, we interrogate the justification of NRPF. Focusing on the criminalisation of migrant families and the engineering of citizenship on highly restrictive notions of the neoliberal British nation, we show how long-resident migrant families regularising through Article 8 of the ECHR were constructed as a 'social problem' that prescribed particular policy solutions. We make the case that NRPF was – and continues to be – intentionally subjugating and punitive, most aptly understood as a policy of enforced destitution and debt imposed on racially marginalised postcolonial subjects. Lastly, we turn to more recent shifts in discourse around NRPF, as well as the continued expansion of the policy, to consider the question of 'where next' for NRPF and its increasing contestation.

The basic rule: 'no recourse to public funds'

While its antecedents can be traced back much further, as we go on to discuss, the 'no recourse to public funds' condition was first introduced in the immigration rules that accompanied the Immigration Act 1971 and was initially used to control entry at the border by requiring those entering to prove financial self-sufficiency to show they would not be in need of public funds (Sainsbury, 2012). With the Immigration and Asylum Act 1999, NRPF was imposed as a condition of leave, restricting welfare support for those 'subject to immigration control' and making individuals liable for enforcement action if they claimed 'public funds'. Those 'subject to immigration control' include undocumented migrants and most migrants with time-limited leave to remain, such as students, people with work visas and those on family visas. Rather than denoting a bar on all publicly funded services, the NRPF condition prohibits access to a specified list of 'public funds', which are determined by the immigration rules. Under current legislation, NRPF restricts access to local authority housing assistance and most welfare benefits, as well as other forms of support tied to benefits, such as extended childcare services and, until recently, free school meals (Rosen and Dickson, 2024). For the purposes of the immigration rules, education, health and social care do not constitute 'public funds'.

Research suggests that single-parent families, mainly headed by mothers, are most negatively impacted by NRPF (Anitha, 2010; Price and Spencer, 2015), particularly those from former British colonies who are already economically marginalised (O'Neill et al., 2019; Price and Spencer, 2015). Price and Spencer (2015) found that Nigerian and Jamaican nationals made up 51 per cent of parents with NRPF who sought local authority support, with a significant number of others coming from Ghana and Pakistan. Indeed, the mothers who we introduce in the subsequent chapters of this book are from Nigeria, Ghana and Jamaica. In theory, destitute families with NRPF should be able to access local authority support under Section 17 of the Children Act 1989. Though not originally intended for the purpose, local authorities can provide accommodation and financial support to some families with NRPF under this legislation. Data from the NRPF Network (2022) shows that at least 1,650 families (comprising 2,903 dependants) were supported by seventy-two local authorities across the UK as of 31 March 2022. Of these, 61 per cent (1,000 families, 1,711 dependants) were supported by London local authorities. However, the overall number of destitute families with NRPF is likely to be much higher. As well as legal restrictions in the Nationality, Immigration and Asylum Act 2002 excluding some families from Section 17 support, frontline workers' conceptions of 'deservingness' are a key determinant of who is able to access support (Jolly, 2018). High numbers of families who seek local authority support are wrongly turned away and those who are supported are often provided with exceptionally low levels (Dexter et al., 2016). These are issues that emerge over the course of the next six chapters – from Mobo's concerns about his mother's mistreatment by social services in Chapter 4 to the spatial constraints imposed upon families by their Section 17 accommodation in Chapter 5. For cash-strapped local authorities, lack of funding to cover the costs of supporting families with NRPF – which rose by 22 per cent in 2022–23 to £77.6 million (NRPF Network, 2024) – is a key issue. With families' needs being exacerbated by punitive immigration restrictions, Section 17 support is often seen by local government bodies as a form of 'cost-shunting' (London Councils, n.d.) – which we understand in this book as part of a shadow welfare system.

Although relatively hidden in migration scholarship, NRPF represents a key plank of Britain's migration regime and its most pervasive manifestation of 'welfare bordering'. It effectively consolidates a century of immigration controls on welfare support and its reach is rapidly expanding. As such, it is an important case for considering bordering processes that work across migration and welfare regimes. As we discussed in the introduction to this book, we understand NRPF as a form of 'welfare bordering' – wherein migration policy and its enactment set limits on social support. Existing literature tends to link the widespread use of NRPF to either the Immigration and Asylum Act 1999, which contains the current iteration of the rule, or the emergence of the UK's self-proclaimed 'hostile' immigration environment in 2012. This risks both presentism and methodological nationalism by obscuring NRPF's longer history, as well as the colonial roots of European welfare states (El-Enany, 2020) and the role of local, national and supra-national bodies in welfare bordering (Yuval-Davis et al., 2019). Rather than a new phenomenon, NRPF should be understood in the context of a century-long history of exclusion. The UK's first modern immigration legislation (Aliens Act 1905) sought to control entry into the UK as a way of limiting access to welfare support, in that case to impoverished eastern European Jews, and subsequent laws set on deterring long-term settlement. Indeed, recognition as a member of the 'political community' and therefore deserving of welfare, argues Shilliam (2018), has been racialised in Britain from 'abolition to Brexit' to serve 'elite' interests, a historical process embedding whiteness as a constitutive feature of working-class respectability, with 'the "slave" – and thereby the condition of blackness' – representing the quintessentially undeserving.

While previous research has focused on the detrimental impacts of NRPF on migrants (Jolly, 2018; Anitha, 2010), there has been limited attention to theorising the NRPF policy's providence and shifting application. Focusing on the 2012 extension of the condition, as we do in this chapter, offers us a way of understanding how NRPF has been justified and framed, as well as which migrants have been targeted by its ever-widening application. The 2012 changes to the family migration rules that we discuss here, moreover, directly affect all of the families whom we focus on in this book, shaping the possibilities and impossibilities of their migration trajectories in the UK. As such, this chapter helps to contextualise the ethnographic material we introduce in the chapters that follow.

The 2012 changes to the UK's family migration rules

Rather than addressing the evident problems created by the NRPF policy, in 2012 the British state extended NRPF to migrant families who were exercising Article 8 rights under the European Convention on Human Rights. While not technically part of the infamous 'hostile environment' policies set in motion by the former home secretary Theresa May – who in 2012, announced that her 'aim is to create, here in Britian, a really hostile environment for illegal immigrants' (Kirkup and Winnett, 2012) – this extension of NRPF was part and parcel of an intentionally punitive policy approach characterised by the very same logic. 'What we don't want,' May continued, 'is a situation where people think that they can come here and overstay because they're able to access everything they need.' May's justification for the 'hostile environment' speaks to the implicit aims of this expansion of NRPF in 2012, which sought to make life unliveable for those who had once overstayed. While continuous with decades of immigration controls in the UK, this particular extension was contemporaneous with an intensification of border controls targeting, above all, those deemed to be 'illegal' migrants.

The 2012 extension, as we shall see in the subsequent chapters, had significant implications for our participants, all of whom were seeking or had been granted 'limited leave to remain' on the basis of these 'rights to private and family life', which had previously accorded migrant families the right to both stay and access social support alongside other UK residents. In this chapter, we consider why the NRPF policy was applied to families exercising Article 8 rights, and how to best characterise the extension, through analysis of government statements, policy documents and media coverage. In so doing, we make the case that NRPF was a punitive and exclusionary post-hoc measure where racially marginalised mothers from former British colonies, and their children, were made to 'pay' for their 'undesirability' through a draconian policy that denied them the means of life. We contend that destitution and debt were, and continue to be, *enforced* through NRPF.

The 2012 extension of NRPF was part of a raft of changes to the family migration rules, made by the then Conservative-Liberal Democrat government as part of its attempt to reduce net migration from the hundreds of thousands to the tens of thousands. Prior to these changes, where removal was deemed to breach an individual's right to family and private life, discretionary leave to remain was granted outside of the normal immigration rules. This status permitted residence for three years, during which families had access to public funds. Once individuals accrued six years of discretionary leave, they could apply for permanent residence. The 2012 changes, which purportedly brought Article 8 within the immigration rules, imposed a narrow interpretation of the right to family and private life on decision-makers and the courts. These changes ended the process of granting discretionary leave to remain to those whose Article 8 rights had been recognised and set out new routes to settlement for them and others, which were more stringent and punitive. The most relevant grounds for making an application under the rules for undocumented families already resident in the UK were seven years of residence by a child or being the parent/carer of a British citizen child. It is worth noting that these were the grounds on which the families we turn to in subsequent chapters were seeking or had been granted 'leave to remain' – visas which allowed them to legally live and work in the UK. In some cases, the children in this book were British citizens upon birth because their fathers were British or settled, but in others, children registered as British citizens after ten years of continuous residence in the country – often at great cost and after extensive periods of waiting, as we see in the case of Abiola and Akin in Chapter 6. Other children and young people who appear elsewhere in this book came to the UK at a young age, or were born in the UK, but were not yet old enough to register as British citizens, often qualifying instead under the 'seven-year rule' outlined above. We note this not to make distinctions between the 'deservingness' of children along the lines of nationality or citizenship – something we raise concerns about towards the end of this chapter – but to point towards some of the ways in which migration regimes produce multi-status families (De Noronha, 2020), splintering family members from one another through differentiated legal categories and statuses. These multi-status family structures reveal the ways in which the nativist logic underpinning NRPF – that 'our' resources should be protected for 'us' – is racialised even on its own terms. British citizens with migrant parents, including some of the children in this book, are excluded from this ethno-nationalist imaginary, unable to access the resources of the welfare state purportedly intended for its nationals.

When the 2012 changes were made, 'probationary' periods were also extended for all, with shorter routes to settlement reserved for those who met 'eligibility' requirements. These requirements included stipulations that applicants must not have 'overstayed' by more than twenty-eight days and that they must be financially self-sufficient, which were, and remain, particularly difficult for families applying for legal status from the position of being undocumented. Those who did not meet the eligibility requirements, but who could not be removed due to Article 8, were subject to the most arduous and costly route to settlement: the ten-year route. Migrants placed on this route were, and continue to be, required to make four separate applications for temporary status ('limited leave to remain') over ten years, which is usually subject to NRPF, before they can apply for permanent residence – something we see in practice in Destiny's case in Chapter 7, where we explore the temporal dimensions of NRPF. The majority of those on the ten-year route are from Africa and Asia, with over half of applicants between 2016 and 2020 from Nigeria, Pakistan, India, Ghana and Bangladesh (McKinney and Sumption, 2021).

Constructing the 'problem' and the 'solution'

As critical policy scholars point out, 'social problems' do not pre-exist policy, but policy is part of what creates them (Taylor, 2006; Schön, 1993). This is not to say that there is no material basis for policy interventions, but that things which come to be seen as 'problems', and the ways that these 'problems' are named and framed, create possible responses. Along with 'policy silences' (Freedman, 2010), this makes other responses unsayable, even unimaginable.

Compared to other changes to the family migration rules in 2012, the extension of NRPF and the creation of the ten-year route to settlement received limited public attention, less scrutiny and, by extension, less resistance than other changes. At the same time, families with Article 8 rights were subsumed within the broader rhetoric justifying the family migration changes. Our discussion, therefore, moves between general framing of the 2012 family migration changes and specific reference to families previously granted discretionary leave to remain. We point here to ways that migrant families were rendered as criminals and citizenship was engineered based on highly restrictive and neoliberal notions of the British nation.

Leading up to the 2012 changes, migration to the UK was built up as a problem for Britain by both media and state, with then Immigration Minister, Damian Green, commenting: 'For too long the immigration system was allowed to get *out of control*. This Government will tackle abuse of the system and get net migration back down to the tens of thousands in the lifetime of this parliament.' (Dawar, 2011; emphasis ours). The overwhelming sense was that there was a 'numbers problem' which urgently needed addressing so that immigration could be brought back 'under control'. This is language that, more than a decade later, we see continue to shape policymaking around immigration in the UK. While the targets have shifted – as the contemporary preoccupation with Channel crossings shows (Davies et al., 2021) – these discourses remain pervasive, producing policy 'problems' and their 'solutions', as we see exemplified in the former UK government's 'stop the boats' campaign (Sunak, 2023).

In the case of the 2012 family migration rules, media coverage and government statements focused on high-profile cases which combined to paint a picture of a broken, incoherent and out of control immigration system. 'We all know the stories' stated Theresa May (2011), then Home Secretary, during her party conference speech. 'The violent drug dealer who cannot be sent home because his daughter – for whom he pays no maintenance – lives here. The robber who cannot be removed because he has a girlfriend. The illegal immigrant who cannot be deported because – and I am not making this up – he had a pet cat …' Sensationalised headlines in the right-wing press decried 'sham marriages' and a system 'sabotaged' (Slack, 2011) by human rights law, with 'alarming cases including foreign killers allowed to stay in the country despite committing horrendous crimes' (Doyle, 2011).

Alongside making it more difficult to enter the UK legally, Theresa May turned to family migration routes to 'mak[e] it harder for long term migrants to settle in the UK and chang[e] rules about bringing family members into the country' (Dawar, 2011). The Home Office launched a public consultation on family migration on 13 July 2011, which was mentioned over fifty times in UK media coverage before the changes were announced in parliament on 13 June 2012, amplifying a sense that there was a problem with family migration but that a solution was on its way. During the period, government spokespeople began a discursive shift away from simply reducing net migration to that of a system designed to 'work for Britain' (Green, 2012). At its heart, this implied that immigration needed to be *controlled by the state*. In what follows, we highlight more specifically how this logic was mobilised in relation to the 2012 extension of NRPF.

Criminalising migrant families

Writing in the *Brentwood Gazette*, Conservative Councillor Ball (2011) asserted:

> Those who want to contribute and make a life here with their family are welcome, but too often in the past the family route has been abused as a means to bypass our immigration laws. That includes too many times where we have seen Article 8 used to place the rights of criminals and illegal migrants above the rights of the British public.

Throughout the period, phrases concatenating 'criminals' and 'illegals', like Ball's, were used consistently, serving to discursively link, even equate, irregular immigration status with criminality and thereby justify migrants' expulsion or refusal. (The power of these labels and the subjectivities they produce is something Ijeoma alerts us to in Chapter 3.) On launching the family migration consultation, Damian Green pledged to redress 'the [favouring of] rights of criminals and illegal migrants above the rights of the British public' (Woodhouse, 2011) and the consultation document stated: 'Those who remain in the UK unlawfully, either overstaying their leave or entering without leave, are also breaking the law' (Home Office, 2011).

While the families affected by the 2012 extension of NRPF were in most cases previously undocumented, the state's frustration with their presence in the UK related precisely to the fact that they had acquired *the legal right to stay* in the country through Article 8. The criminalisation of these families was not only achieved through discursive elision but through widespread framing of Article 8 rights being used to 'abuse the system'. As in Tony Ball's statement above, family migration was singled out as a serious route for abuse: 'A MAJOR review of the human right to a "family life" will be launched this week amid mounting evidence that it is undermining Britain's immigration system' (Doyle, 2011). In its consultation document, the Home Office (2011) implied that people were 'gaming' the system: 'Settlement in the UK is a privilege. It should not be achieved simply by evading our detection for a number of years.'

In these accounts, one branch of policy (immigration rules) was understood as 'the law', while another (human rights) was portrayed as a means to evade the law. Here 'human rights' – as symbolised by the European Convention on Human Rights (ECHR) – was also emblematic of the perceived hegemony of the European Union in pre-Brexit Britain, essentially constructed as a threat to national sovereignty in the long lead-up to the country's withdrawal from the EU. This framing rendered human rights, and the migrants who mobilised them, a social, even criminal, problem necessitating a 'crackdown on abuse of the family route' (Home Office, 2011).

Framing these families as 'criminals' implied a victim, in this case the British public, with headlines screaming about the 'Human Right to Sponge off UK' (Slack, 2011). Also depicted as victims were 'rule following' migrants, who were rendered 'deserving' because of their compliance. In its consultation document, the Home Office (2011) wrote:

> We do not think it is right that a person who remains in the UK unlawfully should be able to gain advantage by only informing us of their private or family life when they face removal from the UK. We will seek to ensure that in future those who apply through the proper channels are in a better position than those who do not. Those who want to rely on the law should comply with the law.

The sense that non-compliance resulted in undeserved rewards, over and above those granted to people who met the immigration rules, was echoed in the Home Office's (2012b) *Statement of Intent: Family Migration*: 'A grant of Discretionary Leave provides automatic access to public funds and places the person in a better position than those who meet the rules.' The end result was that the Home Office (2012b) proclaimed: 'We shall end the situation where those claiming the right to enter or remain in the UK on the basis of ECHR Article 8 – the right to respect for private and family life – do so essentially without regard to the Immigration Rules.' Such efforts to undermine the ECHR continue today, with right-wing politicians representing the convention as an impediment to Britain's jurisdiction over its borders. The former government's attempt to offshore the processing of people seeking asylum in Rwanda is a case in point, as anti-EU discourse was mobilised to gain support for a much more extensive overhaul of the British state. Our point is *not* to (re)instantiate a distinction around 'deservingness' by emphasising the *legal* immigration status families gained through Article 8, in order to make a case that they should be considered amongst the 'deserving' of settlement rights. Our point is that *'illegality' is a political not an existential status*, one that is produced through changing legalised routes to mobility and settlement (Crawley and Sklepari, 2017; De Genova, 2002). Most fundamentally, Britain used its 1981 Nationality Act to limit or deny racially marginalised, Commonwealth citizens – upon whom its wealth was built – access to legal routes to residence and citizenship (El-Enany, 2020). In the specific case we focus on, families who had previously had a means for achieving legal status (discretionary leave to remain) and survival, either through work and/or access to services and support, became discursively criminalised. As we discuss further below, long routes to settlement combined with recurring high application costs and no access to social provision are impossible for many families, thereby producing 'illegality'. This sits in sharp contrast to the depiction of 'illegality' as an ontological state-of-being in the state's framing of criminal, system abusers.

Engineering the racialised neoliberal British nation

In keeping with its emphasis on making immigration 'work for Britain', much government rhetoric focused on ideas of 'selection'. 'Reducing net migration and ensuring community cohesion is not just about reducing the numbers coming to the UK; it is also about being more selective about those who stay permanently,' argued Damian Green (2011). Such sentiments ostensibly accept liberal multicultural presumptions that settlement, belonging and even citizenship are open rather than determined by birth right. However, here we argue that the logic of selectivity, *always* on the state's terms, represents a classed, raced and gendered engineering of the British nation (a point we develop further in Chapter 7).

The state's framing of selectivity was based on representations of migrants as coming from two distinct groups. One group was depicted as undesirable and problematic. This group was painted as 'a burden on the taxpayer' repeatedly by government ministers, or what was derogatorily referred to as engaging in 'benefit tourism' (Slack, 2011), 'unable and on occasion unwilling to integrate into British life' (Green, 2011), uncompliant and abusing the system. In contrast, another group of migrants was depicted as desirable for Britain, those 'who will benefit Britain, not just those who will benefit from Britain' (Green, 2012). Core to desirability were ideas about legal compliance with immigration law, over and above human rights law, something financially and politically out of reach of many family migrants. In contradistinction to the 'undesirables' were ideas about economic contributions and status, epitomised by the slogan of 'attracting the brightest and best global talent to Britain'. Amongst those deemed desirable were 'foreign investors and entrepreneurs', 'the best teachers, researchers and students' and 'talented doctors and nurses' (Cameron, 2011).

The rendering of particular groups of migrants as 'economic burdens' and others as 'hardworking, wealth creators who can help us to win in the global race' (Cameron, 2013) can be understood as part and parcel of the logic of the UK's neoliberalising welfare-migration regime. This logic is evident in the reduction of human mobility and its governance to economic rationalities, exemplified by the invocation of cost-benefit calculations. Seemingly reasoned and evidenced, such analyses were always on the state's terms or in the interest of a mythic British nation: 'Reducing the volume of people eligible to claim these benefits/credits, through reducing the volume of family migrants coming to the UK and increas[ing] the time before which they can settle, equates to a saving to the UK Government' (Home Office, 2012a). This rhetoric, however, created a false depiction of control over labour migration, attempting to obscure demand for cheapened migrant labour power and the filters which continued to produce it, most notably through the deportability of the undocumented population (De Genova, 2002) and short-term worker visas. What we add to this discussion is a reflection on what happens to those who have not been selected for entry or settlement as 'pure labour power' (Oliveri, 2012) by the neoliberal UK state through processes of filtration and control, and yet still find themselves amongst the partially included within its geopolitical borders.

In reducing immigration to neoliberal rationalities, other ways of framing responses to migration were silenced: for instance, human rights to land, life, livelihood and mobility or reparations for colonial appropriations. In this framing, the solution to the 'social problem' of 'undesirables' was seen to be greater state control over immigration, and indeed the makeup of the nation. This was to be achieved through cherry-picking those migrants considered desirable and 'breaking the link between temporary migration and permanent settlement' (Green, 2011) for those who were not considered desirable for settlement.

It is worth noting that whether referred to explicitly or not, both these groups of migrants were set over and against the British public and British ways of life. 'Excessive immigration also brings pressures, real pressures, on our communities up and down the country,' Cameron (2011) stated. 'Our communities' might be read as a reference to people who were already in the UK, as distinct from those outside seeking to immigrate. Such a naïve reading, however, belies the more complex and historically laden assumptions about just who the 'British public' is, and what constitutes 'British ways of life', including who has a right to the resources, support and spaces within the UK's national borders. As Yuval-Davis et al. (2019: 16) argue, an 'autochthonic politics of belonging' has become increasingly hegemonic in Britain, serving as 'social and political triggers to "reborder" the state and to keep its resources exclusively for those who "really belong". Based on little more than the assertion that '"I was here before you"' (Yuval-Davis et al., 2018), this claim to belonging is vague at best, but more likely violently restrictive, not only for those who seek to enter the UK but also those who are already here.

The families we focus on in this book exemplify this point. They were already living in communities across the UK, attending schools, working, participating in social and religious life and so forth. Yet in this 'policy silence', these families are constructed as outsiders always external to 'our communities'. This is a highly racialised process, points out El-Enany (2020: 5), rooted in the contemporary extension of Britain's colonial empire through immigration law: 'Immigration law is also the prop used to teach white British citizens that what Britain plundered from its colonies is theirs and theirs alone. "Others" are here as guests.' As noted above, the majority of families affected by the 2012 changes are from former British colonies, deeply affected by the colonial present of the migration regime.

The positioning of these families as 'undesirable', yet un-removeable due to Article 8 rights, is also deeply classed and gendered. Notably, the majority of the families facing destitution because of NRPF are headed by a single mother (Woolley, 2019) with highly gendered responsibility for young children, as we see throughout this book. Denied access to childcare and other forms of social support, combined with gendered inequalities in incomes, mean that such financial requirements are particularly prohibitive (see also Shutes, 2017). In combination with the financial requirements and elision of 'brightest and best' with entrepreneurs and investors, family migration is effectively a privilege of the well-off (Sirriyeh, 2015) and the 2012 extension of NRPF is deeply classed, raced and gendered.

Enforced destitution and punitive debt as immigration control

If the UK state's framing of the 2012 extension of NRPF was as a 'rational' policy solution to so-called lack of immigration control and towards a mythic British nation, its effects, we argue here, were purposely punitive towards unremovable migrants whose presence the state was forced to accept. Indeed, the language of 'punishment' for those who failed to comply with the rules was explicitly used by Theresa May (2011) in her speech for the Conservative Party conference:

> The meaning of Article Eight should no longer be perverted. So I will write it into our immigration rules that when foreign nationals are convicted of a criminal offence or breach our immigration laws: when they should be removed, they will be removed. [...] I will never be ashamed to say that we should do everything we can to reward those who do the right thing, and I will never hesitate to say we should punish those who do the wrong thing.

The introduction of the ten-year family route, and the default position that leave granted on the route be subject to NRPF, was one of the ways in which this sentiment was enacted. Migrant families who were unable to meet the Home Office's eligibility requirements but who could not be removed due to Article 8 received the punishment of a longer, ten-year route to settlement – as we see in the cases of Serwah and Destiny in the following chapters. Although the ten-year route was precisely for those who were not deemed financially self-sufficient, NRPF was nonetheless automatically imposed. While in principle the policy provided discretion to grant recourse to public funds in 'exceptional circumstances', in practice families were forced into destitution (Woolley, 2019). In 2014, following a legal challenge, the Home Office was forced to introduce a process whereby people with certain forms of leave to remain subject to NRPF could apply for 'a change of conditions' to allow them to access welfare support.[1] This process defined 'need' for access to public funds narrowly, requiring applicants to prove 'destitution' or imminent risk of destitution, 'reasons relating to the welfare of a relevant child which outweigh the considerations for imposing or maintaining the condition' or other exceptional circumstances. While the latter two requirements suggest a relatively wide scope for discretion, they are rarely the basis on which applications are granted. Further, applications are often slow and onerously bureaucratic, thereby not offering an adequate safeguard against destitution. Since applicants have to prove that they are destitute to be eligible, many fear that making the request could jeopardise their leave to remain, particularly if there are financial stipulations attached to their visas. Home Office data shows that an average of 3,628 'change of conditions' applications per year were made between 2018 to 2022 – with an exception in 2020, which saw a spike in applications due to the pandemic (Cuibus and Fernandez-Reino, 2023). In the last six years, around a third of these have been refused. In keeping with other evidence of which groups with NRPF are more likely to experience destitution, high numbers of applications are made by those from Nigeria (who made up a quarter of applications in 2017–22), Pakistan, Ghana, India and Bangladesh (Cuibus and Fernandez-Reino, 2023).

But to return to the 2012 changes, the connection between destitution and NRPF, already well established, was well known to the Home Office at the time, who had long been informed of it by local authorities supporting destitute migrant families under Section 17 of the Children Act 1989. In 2009, responding to the recommendation made by local government bodies that local authorities be reimbursed for the costs they incurred supporting people with NRPF, Lin Homer, then Chief Executive of the UK Border Agency, stated:

> the priority must be to tackle the problem at source by addressing the presence or status in this country of these individuals concerned rather than perpetuating and risking exacerbating the problem by making specific additional financial provision for local support services for this category. (LGA Asylum and Refugee Task Group, 2009)

Here Homer invokes the idea that welfare support operates as a 'magnet' incentivising migration from non-citizens deemed undesirable by the state, claiming that if local authorities were adequately funded to provide support to those with NRPF, it would exacerbate 'the problem' (the presence of undocumented migrants). The denial of the means of life for migrant families was thus represented as shoring up both internal and external borders. Working in tandem with austerity measures, refusal to reimburse local authorities for the costs of providing a 'parallel welfare system' (Price and Spencer, 2015) to migrants with NRPF can be understood as an implicit policy of *enforcing destitution* as a mechanism of immigration control. In response, under-funded councils attempted to deter migrants with NRPF from seeking support through 'gatekeeping' tactics such as threatening to remove children from parents (Dennler, 2018), and, where forced by advocates to provide support, offered only minimal levels. The extension of NRPF in 2012 compounded these issues, which the Home Office had been explicitly warned of by the NRPF Network in response to its family migration consultation.

Discussions of 'enforced destitution' as a tool of immigration policy have tended to focus on asylum-seekers, but these insights are also relevant to other groups of migrants. Enforced destitution serves as an attempt to starve out unwanted migrants who are within the nation state (Chakrabarti, 2005); as a more explicit form of coercion, where access to support is tied to 'voluntary return' (Kirkwood et al., 2016); and as part of the state's efforts to deter future migration (Mayblin, 2020). Speaking to the Education Committee (2012), Damian Green stated on the one hand that, '[d]estitution is very explicitly not used as a tool', and on the other, that it was essential for the government to counter the idea, '[g]et to Britain illegally and the streets are paved with gold'. Green continued by arguing that deportation was the most effective method for preventing migration. The (unofficial) policy of enforcing destitution through NRPF can thus be seen to work alongside the deportation regime in 'sending a message' on immigration.

The 2012 extension of NRPF perpetuated the already existing exclusion of those who were only ever 'partially included' even as they moved into a legitimated legal status within the migration regime. Where before the transition from irregular to regular status had provided access to support and services, and therefore ostensibly the alleviation of destitution – a common plight of the undocumented (Gonzales et al., 2019) – the new family migration rules meant that impoverishment would continue regardless of legal status. The changes in 2012 can thus be understood as 'ongoing expressions of empire' (El-Enany, 2020: 2) that, through the denial of access to Britain's colonial spoils, produce and enforce destitution on predominantly Black, Asian and working-class families from countries formerly colonised by the British Empire.

The impossibility of the ten-year route

The extension of the NRPF condition works alongside other punitive requirements of the ten-year route, such as high renewal fees, which combine to subordinate and impoverish families relying on Article 8 to stay in the UK. The fact that the overall cost of the ten-year route is significantly higher than the other, shorter routes suggests that these families are being made to 'pay' for their undesirability. Through a drawn-out process of extraction, those on the ten-year route are expected to pay the application fee (currently £1,048 per person) four times, alongside a fifth fee for permanent residence (Indefinite Leave to Remain). In addition, the immigration health surcharge must be paid upfront for the full thirty-month duration of the visa – currently £1,560 for each individual application. Although it is possible to apply for a fee waiver, rejection rates are high. Between 2013 and 2018, 72–90 per cent of applications were rejected (Mohdin, 2019). There is no fee waiver for the final application for Indefinite Leave to Remain, which is currently £2,885 per person. The sheer cost of the route, therefore, renders many families destitute. In turn, with loans as *the* means to obtain and maintain legal status and survival, destitution is enforced through long-term debt and debt servicing – as we see in Destiny's case in Chapter 6 – which serves to regulate and impoverish families well beyond the life of the ten-year route (Dickson et al., 2023b).

This effect is intensified by other requirements for maintaining leave, which ensure 'legality' and permanent residence are kept out of reach for many. For example, the rules specify that, if a person on the ten-year route 'overstays by more than 28 days, they will have broken their continuous leave and have to restart the route if they continue to qualify for it' (Home Office, 2012b). This means that something as minor as forgetting to include passport photographs with an application could result in illegalisation and restarting the route entirely. The rule is particularly punitive for families refused fee waivers, who are given just ten working days to submit an application and pay the fee. The requirement, which effectively means that those on the ten-year route are just one step away from losing their legal status, both produces 'illegality' and further enforces destitution and debt by making it highly likely that families will 'fall off' the route and be forced to start again.

There is also a serious question about whether permanent residence will ever actually be achieved by many families on the route. In some cases, years of destitution and debt may ultimately end in deportation. According to the Home Office (2012b):

> to continue on or complete the route, the migrant parent or carer will have to satisfy the UK Border Agency at the next application stage that, where

the child has turned 18, there continues to be a reason why it would breach Article 8 for the migrant parent/carer to be removed from the UK.

If parents of children who were born in the UK have waited for their children to turn 10 – whereupon they become eligible to register for British citizenship – before applying for legal status, they may face considerable difficulties over the course of the ten-year-route in continuing to prove that their removal would constitute a breach of Article 8 once their children turn 18. This may also be an issue for those who applied at an earlier stage in their children's lives if they 'fall off' the route and have to restart. As the policy is in its infancy, it remains to be seen whether parents/carers will be given deportation orders when their children turn 18. In other cases, permanent residence may be unobtainable because of the extortionate cost of the final application, or because of difficulties passing the 'knowledge of language and life in the UK' test. Families will thus be trapped in a cycle of perpetual bouts of 'limited leave to remain' without access to public funds, confined to paying high fees only to be (forever) temporary.

Together, these factors make it highly likely that many people on the ten-year route will be subject to the perennial threat of destitution, debt and illegalisation. The formal inclusion of these families within the immigration rules can therefore be understood as a 'process of exclusion through inclusion' (Mezzadra and Neilson, 2013: 148). Bringing Article 8 within the immigration rules ensured on the one hand that the right to private and family life would be narrowly interpreted, meaning that fewer families would be able to achieve regularised status, and on the other, that greater regulation, restriction and control could be exerted over those to whom the state had to (unwillingly) grant legal status. This subjugation involved racially marginalised, working-class migrant families being internally included, while at the same time excluded from the welfare state, impoverished and subjected to punitive debt.

Our analysis of the 2012 extension of NRPF and the ten-year route with which it works in tandem have shown how these punitive post-hoc measures functioned to subjugate 'undesirable' migrant families whose presence threw into question the efficacy of the state's controlled migration regime. Forced to juridically accept these families who had neither 'complied' with the immigration rules, nor were able to meet its neoliberal requirements, exclusion was and is reasserted through state produced and enforced destitution and punitive debt. Constructing these families as non-self-sufficient at the same time as effectively reducing their ability to support themselves, regardless of whether they 'contribute' to the nation (Erel, 2018), created the situation where removal or exclusions from social support were presented as always in the best interests of the nation. Further, the 2012 changes which served to make life unbearable for migrant families from former British colonies also worked to violently extract profit through immigration fees and long-term debt-servicing.

Where next for NRPF?

Just over ten years on from this policy change, we are witnessing new directions for the NRPF restriction. On the one hand, NRPF has been expanded to new groups of migrants. Since Brexit, European Economic Area (EEA) citizens and their family members are also subject to NRPF if they arrived on or after 1 January 2021. Others who arrived earlier but did not make an application under the EU Settlement Scheme are also likely to be caught by the NRPF rule, though the Home Office is accepting late applications where the applicant can prove there were 'reasonable grounds' for missing its official deadline (Home Office, n.d.). While the Nationality and Borders Act 2022 threatened to further extend the reach of NRPF, with fears that the condition would be used to punish people seeking asylum who arrived in the UK via so-called 'illegal' routes, plans for differentiated statuses for refugees were dropped less than a year after they were introduced (Yeo, 2023). But the spectre of NRPF's increasing application nonetheless remains, and we are yet to see how the latest legislative attack on migrants' rights (the controversial Illegal Migration Act 2023) will be implemented.

On the other hand, however, for all its relative invisibility, we have undoubtedly seen a significant shift in attention towards NRPF in recent years, as discussions have increased in research, policy, advocacy and even in the wider public domain. There were more references to NRPF in parliament during the Covid-19 pandemic than ever before, as the global epidemic exacerbated precarity for marginalised groups and prompted public debate in Britain about migrants' access to the welfare safety net. Where before it had been unusual and arduous to get MPs to take notice of the negative impacts of NRPF, at the height of the pandemic there were no less than four parliamentary debates focused on the topic in a single nine-month period. At the same time, applications for the NRPF condition to be lifted soared – rising from 843 in the first quarter of 2020 to 5,665 in the second quarter (Cuibus and Fernandez-Reino, 2023). As before, these applications could only be made by those on family and human rights routes to settlement, and applicants were required to demonstrate destitution or an imminent risk of destitution. Those on the shorter five-year route who were granted access to public funds were initially automatically moved to the more punitive ten-year route discussed above.[2] The vast majority of those subject to NRPF, however, were not eligible to apply. Stories of hardship in the media proliferated, as international students became reliant on foodbanks, migrant workers lost employment, and migrant women were put at even greater risk of domestic abuse, which rose across the UK (Bulman, 2020; Kaur, 2020). Their exclusion from the welfare safety net was exposed. As ideas about who was deserving of welfare support began to shift under the pressure of the health crisis (however temporarily), support coalesced around a temporary suspension of NRPF. This call was widely supported by MPs across political parties, local government bodies, local authorities, high-profile charities, the Children's Commissioner and even celebrities such as the British actor Dame Emma Thompson (Simmonds et al., 2020; Children's Commissioner, 2020; Marsh, 2020; *Shropshire Star*, 2020). While the urgency of the conditions being experienced by migrants with NRPF in these times clearly moved many to challenge what had heretofore seemed a vital organ of Britain's migration regime, the discourse was also haunted by the public health risks represented by destitute migrants, whose sufferings were seen to pose a threat to the rest of the population (Vincent, 2020). What's more, issues with NRPF and their potential solutions were discursively framed around the 'exceptional times', as though the problem lay with Covid-19 itself. This obscured the long-standing harms caused by the policy, which of course did not disappear when the pandemic eased.

Yet, the policy certainly remains under more scrutiny than before. Calls for a suspension have been replaced with more meagre asks, such as shorter routes to settlement, the extension of Child Benefit to British children in families with NRPF, and changes to childcare provision (Work and Pensions Committee, 2022). Meanwhile, NRPF has even found its way into the cultural domain, featuring in the popular Netflix series *Topboy*. To reduce this shifting policy terrain to Covid-19 alone would seem to elide other factors, such as the resistance to the 'hostile environment', which though perhaps fainter do seem to be part of the picture. A broad range of organisations and groups – from the big to the small – now campaign around NRPF, and some parliamentary interest continues. Legal challenges carry on quietly in the background, often winning concessions, policy tweaks and sometimes more substantial policy changes, such as the recent expansion of free school meals to children in families with NRPF. Advocacy across these domains, however, continues to be marked by ideas of deservingness, notably in the figure of the child and particularly the 'British' child. As we have written about elsewhere (Rosen and Dickson, 2024), these representations sometimes derive their power both from disempowering, hegemonic imaginaries of childhood and long-standing colonial, nativist, and sedentarist ideas about non-citizens as 'undeserving' drains on Britain's welfare system – the very logic that underlines welfare bordering. What is contested, then, is not so much the premise and violence of NRPF, but often only its application to specific groups who have mistakenly ended up in the camp of the undeserving. There is, then, a need for a shift, not just in immigration policy, but also in campaigning against welfare bordering. What sort of alternative futures can we imagine if we jettison a framework of deservingness and exceptionalism altogether? This is a question we return to and pose again in the conclusion to this book, as we consider new ways of challenging welfare bordering in light of our ethnographic encounters with families affected by NRPF.

Despite its long history and increasing public profile, relatively little is known about the impact of NRPF and how families make their lives in these impossible conditions. Policy and responsive campaigning only tell us part of the story. In the upcoming pages of the book, we turn to these questions through in-depth engagement with families endeavouring to make and sustain meaningful lives in the shadows of Britain's bordered and austere welfare state.

Notes

1 Those eligible to make these applications include migrants on family visas; the ten-year route to settlement (Family and Private life); leave to remain based on other human rights grounds under the ECHR; and people with a British National (Overseas) visas. In October 2023, following a legal challenge, the Home Office broadened eligibility to migrants on other kinds of visas. However, these applicants need to demonstrate that there is a human rights barrier to them returning to their country of origin alongside the other criteria.
2 This was successfully challenged in the courts in March 2023 – see Deighton Pierce Glynn (2023).

2

Weathering through social reproduction

'I can't even wash the baby's clothes and dishes continuously because of the water,' Serwah explained. Motioning to a kitchen chair, she continued: 'I have to sit down here, wait until the water is coming out, to quickly get the water out of the sink and to put it in the toilet. Otherwise, all the house will be flooded.' The sink that would not drain played an ongoing refrain in the lives of Serwah and her children: Miriam (aged 13), Luke (9) and Joshua (1). During another visit Serwah commented: 'Because the sink is blocked a long time, everything that I wash, fry, and cook, I have to get the water and put it from the sink into the toilet.' A bucket sitting within easy reach of the toilet attested to the intensive process involved in something as seemingly simple as washing a bowl or a cup. 'You can't wash a lot. So, every week I only wash once … Every time I wash, I have to wait. And me and Miriam will get the water at both ends. Some we will get the water from the sink and put it in the toilet. That one is very stressful for me. That one is.' Serwah's use of repetition, in this case of the words 'that one', was a rhetorical strategy she commonly deployed. For us, this seemed to function as an emphatic echo to ensure her listener was aware that she was making an important point. But it also suggests that the blocked sink was only one of many problems related to her living conditions, albeit one that weighed heavily on her.

When we met them, the family of four were living in a small, two-bedroom flat owned by a private landlord in South London. In Serwah's room, which she shared with her youngest son Joshua, a small double bed was covered by a burgundy blanket, loosely pulled over the bed. It would have dominated the small windowless room, except for the pile of bags and suitcases in one corner. Without any furniture to contain them, these overflowed with clothes and other personal items. 'It's quite a mess because we don't really have that much space,' explained Miriam one day. Although the pile overwhelmed the small room, it did not contain much by the standards of many London households. The family had lived here for three years, and in London for over ten, but the bags gave the impression of rapid mobility – a material representation of their precarious life. Items had been grabbed when needed and replaced when not, and all could be easily zipped up into the suitcase and stuffed back into the bags, quickly ready for another move. The suitcases reminded us of the many stories we have heard of destitute families showing up at local authorities with suitcases in tow and nowhere left to go – an experience Serwah and her children had also endured.

The next room, which Luke and Miriam shared, had a similar feel. Here though, clothes tumbled out of two sets of plastic drawers. Despite Serwah's efforts to create a sense of permanence and comfort in the older children's space, it was a source of frustration not to have a wardrobe for her children or herself, she explained. A metal frame bunkbed lined one side of the room, but the beds were 'not good', Serwah commented, and she would replace them if she could afford to. A side table with a lamp sat next to the bunk bed. Miriam mentioned that the main light in the room burnt out over a year ago, but the landlord had not fixed it. At some point, the small lamp also broke, and the children used the torches on their mobile phones to see when it was dark.

In the small bathroom, large holes were visible in the plaster next to the toilet and Miriam explained that the heater had broken but that the landlord had not replaced it. Later, it became clear this was not only a problem in the bathroom, but that the heat in the whole flat was intermittent. 'The heating is on and off,' Serwah explained. 'For two months now it's not off. That's what I'm praying for. If it's off, I don't know what would happen. I'm praying that it's still going to be there like that.' Cold and damp London winters are notorious, and it is not uncommon to hear of mould growing on the walls of badly maintained flats leading to sickness and even death (Brown and Booth, 2022).

In the main room, a burgundy two-seater and matching armchairs lined the border of a matching burgundy red carpet. Clothes hung over the backs of the furniture. Serwah explained that when she went to bed, she had to take clothes off the laundry line in her room and lay them on the furniture to dry, sometimes returning them to her room in the morning. The small eating table where Serwah waited to catch the water before it overflowed from the sink doubled as the space where Miriam and Luke did their schoolwork and had their meals while Serwah fed Joshua on the couch. It was clear though that members of the family often missed out on meals. Serwah mentioned preparing breakfast and dinner but said nothing about lunch, and the family often ate dinner by 4.30pm, possibly because they had not had anything to eat since breakfast. Miriam noted that her mother often would not eat so the children could: 'Cos normally we don't have enough food for our ... to eat. So, if there's a little bit, she'll give it to me and Luke.

Joshua has his own separate baby food. So, she'll give it to me and Luke, and then she just has tea or something.' At other points, the children's narratives indicated that they also missed meals. When Luke commented, 'We don't really have, like, breakfast breakfast ... Like, normally, I have cereal. But, but, I don't eat it anymore,' Miriam nodded in agreement.

Over ten years of living with 'no recourse to public funds' (NRPF) had taken their toll on the family. At that time, reliant solely on Serwah's wages from twice-weekly night shifts in a small residential facility assisting people with dementia with basic living and care needs, the family found themselves deep in debt. The only friend Serwah ever mentioned took care of the children when she worked but had recently said she could not do more than two nights a week. Serwah's friend lived in similarly precarious circumstances. Unable to afford paid childcare, Serwah's work options were heavily restricted. Not having the 'right to rent' for years due to being undocumented, and months of rent arrears due to their destitution, had left the family with limited legal options to hold the private landlord to account for ensuring adequate heating, water and other necessary utilities. Despite recently regularising her immigration status with a thirty-month grant of Limited Leave to Remain, Serwah, who is originally from Ghana, and her children continued to be barred from receiving any benefits due to the NRPF condition.

Serwah had been trying to obtain a 'change of conditions' on her visa which would remove NRPF and allow her access to mainstream welfare support. It should be self-evident that a lack of food, being in rent arrears due to inability to pay and the incapacity to move elsewhere despite the abysmal state of the heating, lighting and drainage in the flat were indications that the family was destitute, or at risk of destitution – a key criterion for receiving a 'change of conditions'. Yet Serwah's application was still under review during the time we met with her, and she described the unbearable 'wait' given the 'slowness' of the process. 'They always say I have to wait because they have not decided if I'm qualified for the benefits.' She spoke with incredulity about being told she could not get support because she was not homeless: 'That's what they told me. They said I'm not homeless ... I can't even pay the rent ... The money I receive with two days and nights is not enough to pay the rent. I need help for the rent. They say I'm not homeless and the landlord didn't throw me out, so they can't do nothing.' While Serwah expressed shock that a sort of negative exceptionalism could place her family in such extreme and dire conditions, the family's experiences are unfortunately not unique at all. Like Serwah, other mothers and advocates have reported difficulty successfully obtaining a 'change of conditions' or support from local authorities under Section 17 of the Children's Act. Extensive gatekeeping practices often lead to extended periods of assessment despite urgent situations of street homelessness, uninhabitable accommodation, domestic violence and more. Some families are simply incorrectly turned away from support.

What do families do in such a situation – where they are denied the means of life for such extended periods through the policies and practices of welfare bordering? What are the material, social and psychic consequences of living life under such conditions of duress? How do mothers with NRPF and their children think about, and seek to represent, their own lives and life-making practices? In this chapter, and the ones that follow, we respond to these questions, attending to the (im)possibilities of life's labour under welfare bordering. We look sidewise at what advocates refer to as a complex and complicated policy terrain, which lies at the conflux of various immigration statuses and aspects of Britain's welfare provision and the technical calculus of policy abstractions such as destitution, need and reliability which may allow for a brief reprieve in the NRPF condition. In contrast, we pay close attention to what families' practices and narratives tell us about the concrete experiences of living with NRPF over time, about the compulsions, exclusions and violences this form of welfare bordering produces and which, we argue, form part of the state's tripartite border technologies. At the same time, we endeavour to listen closely to families' struggles for meaning, sustenance and indeed lives that exceed those proscribed by NRPF. We refer to this as weathering through social reproduction, an analytic frame which we begin to develop in this chapter and deepen over the course of the book.

Hardship and lack

If we return to Serwah's narrative above, it is not surprising that the little that has been published about NRPF by advocates, activists and researchers focuses on the hardship it causes (e.g. Jolly et al., 2022; Pinter et al., 2020; Woolley, 2019). This literature tells a story of misery and lack, be this of resources, food, somewhere to live, ontological security or access to other basic rights of citizenship – much as we hear in Serwah's account. Indeed, in many ways, Serwah's story, like others with NRPF, is reminiscent of Agamben's (1998) formulation of 'bare life', and the camp as a state of exception where the law does not apply, as it has been taken up in much of the migration literature. Scholars have made use of this concept to highlight the ways migrants are stripped of all humanity by repressive border regimes, and to demonstrate how this permits their exclusion from any social and political rights, reducing them to simple biological existence (Ghorashi et al., 2018; Whitley, 2017; Dines et al., 2014). Although we might say that NRPF even denies biological existence or, more precisely, the right to biological existence, given the state of destitution it produces, making even physical life intolerable and unsustainable, with families like Serwah's living in the heart of one of the world's richest cities going without food, heat and adequate sewage systems. Given the extreme difficulties of making lives with NRPF, particularly for those who are already marginalised, efforts to highlight its violences are crucial interventions in public discourse and more so, we would suggest, in the face of the resounding public silence on the matter. As we pointed out in Chapter 1, even the former Prime Minister Boris Johnson appeared to be unaware of his government's policies denying social support to most migrants.

Such formulations of the hardship and lack produced by NRPF resonate with theorisations of social reproduction as being 'depleting' rather than regenerating which we wrote about in the introductory chapter (Rai et al., 2013; Dowling, 2016) as families engage in the effort of survival in liminal and marginalised positions with no possibility of social support. We can see that, for Serwah and her children, the time and energy required to achieve something as basic as emptying a sink exerts a substantial toll, highlighted by Serwah's repeated invocations of the stress caused by the state of disrepair of the flat in which she and her family were forced to live. It was not just the non-draining sink that weighed heavily, however, or the intensity of labour required for acts of daily life which may be unnecessary or minimal in many London homes. But the energy of Serwah, Miriam and Luke was absorbed by the effort of making lives in the context of inadequate and unchallengeable housing conditions. Life with NRPF produces an intensity and extensity of everyday labour, with each task made more difficult by the conditions in which the family is forced to live. The substantial demand on their time as well as their physical and emotional resources is non-recuperable in many ways, stolen away from other life-making endeavours – be they restorative acts of care, nourishment, leisure, schooling or paid work.

In this sense, conceptualisations which draw our attention to depletion offer important ways of considering the draining nature of reproductive labour and, in Serwah's words, the 'suffering' caused by the enforced destitution of welfare bordering and stratified social reproduction. Similarly, approaches highlighting hardship and lack through dehumanisation and the reduction of migrants to 'bare life' importantly turn the spotlight on the violent effects of an immigration policy that is intentionally punitive and not simply a broken system with unintended effects. We understand the appeal, even the importance, of such approaches, particularly when they are mobilised by advocacy or activist groups. An emphasis on hardship may be understood to move or motivate the public by provoking sympathy or a sense of moral outrage that such extreme levels of destitution may be occurring only next door.

Indeed, scholarly and advocacy literature often points to the moments of most extreme destitution and crisis when families have exhausted all other potential sources of support and wind up seeking it from voluntary organisations and the local state. At some points, Serwah had found herself in such dire and extreme situations. 'I remember when their dad left us when Miriam was 7. The landlord came to collect,' Serwah explained. 'I went to the council. They didn't help. They didn't help us,' she echoed herself, stressing the depth of the family's crises and her incredulity at the lack of support. 'We went there in the morning until night. They didn't do anything for us ... I told them everything, and they said they will get back to me. I sat down till night. They didn't come back,' Serwah continued, highlighting the long period of waiting that many families face when trying to obtain support from the local state when forced to live in the shadows of Britain's national welfare system. 'I went to the desk and the man says, I forgot his name, he said, "You must come back." He said, "She's finished. Go home. She's gone." I said, "Why? I want to talk to somebody." He said, "Everybody has gone. Nobody is in the office." So, I said, "No, somebody is there." He said I should go ... So, I didn't go back again,' she concluded.

Serwah's experiences of gatekeeping, dismissal and calamity are unfortunately not at all unusual, with similar stories populating materials produced by advocates and activists (Morgan, 2024). For those intent on galvanising public opinion in the face of xenophobic narratives of migration or what is perceived as apathy in challenging state policies which cause harm, it may seem that the most horrifying or excessive cases will be the ones with the greatest impact. Yet many of the families with NRPF whom we have talked to and spent time with – including Serwah's – do not tell a story of crisis as punctuating an otherwise benign and copacetic life in the UK. Instead, they tell a story of the long durée, a riding out and wearing that may be marked by moments of extreme crisis, yet are rarely marked by a return to calm. They also do not see themselves (solely) in terms of distress and hardship. As we go on to discuss, lack is not the (only) story they want to tell about their lives. The mothers with NRPF and their children who spoke with us cannot and do not want to be reduced to 'naked human existence' (Dines et al., 2014: 431), and a raw calculus of depletion does not seem to adequately account for the complexity of their lives.

The bareness of 'bare life'

'They give me good advice. They help me through things,' Miriam commented one day about Serwah, Luke and Joshua. 'We have a close bond with each other.' The family often did research activities together, handing the phone back and forth and cuddling, teasing and joking with one another. When Serwah would speak, Miriam stayed close by or hung her arms around Serwah's neck. During the calls, we caught glimpses of Joshua being carried by Miriam, climbing on Serwah or sitting on Luke's lap. He always seemed to be held and snuggled by someone in the family while he laughed at the activity or waved at people on and off frame. They appeared close and protective of each other, and we had the sense that what mattered most to the family were the four people who lived in the space. We might think of the care, love and concern we observed between them in terms of 'homeplace'. bell hooks (2014: 42) uses this in reference to Black family life in the US as sites of regeneration, away from the onslaught of systemic racism and enforced destitution 'where all black people could strive to be subjects, not objects, where we could be affirmed in our minds and hearts despite poverty, hardship, and deprivation, where we could restore to ourselves the dignity denied us on the outside in the public world'. In contrast to conceptualisations of reproductive labour as depleting or even a site of expropriation, including in families, hooks draws our attention to the renewing aspects of the labour of everyday existence undertaken even momentarily away from the control and violence of the racialised nation state and – relatedly – this labour's ongoing possibilities for evading commodification (Davis et al., 2020).

However, practices of care, affirmation and repair are not, hooks asserts, simply natural phenomenon. To reduce them in such a way, she contends, is little more than a spuriously gendered reading of the labour of life that is most often accomplished by women. Nor is such labour easy or even always possible, she continues, as is evident in Serwah, Miriam and Luke's narratives, given the denial of resources through welfare bordering, the fracturing of families through the production of multiple immigration statuses, and the intensity of labour required in conditions of enforced destitution. hooks proposes, therefore, that we must attend to the efforts and the will required to maintain homeplace as it is 'always subject to violation and destruction', not least because of its centrality in efforts to 'build a meaningful community of resistance' (hooks, 2014: 47). Love, as it is nurtured in the labour of everyday life such as that we witness in Serwah's family, is central to such fortitude and potential resistance to welfare bordering.

For despite the many stresses and struggles she had endured, and shared with us, Serwah's narrative of her life was replete with tales of strength, fortitude and dreams for her children. 'I told Miriam the way I suffered to raise her. She understands, and I hope she makes me proud.' Strength, in Serwah's narrative, seems to come through enduring the impossible over immense stretches of time and passing on lessons to her children so they would not have to experience the same hardships. 'Every time I tell Miriam,

I hope you are going to listen, so you know, and you won't suffer.' Serwah often spoke about the children's father, explaining the difficulties he caused them through deception, cheating and absence of support. 'I always tell Miriam. I know she's not a big girl, but I always use my life to advise her because some men can make you go down. All your dreams went off.' Some of the proffered advice was addressed explicitly to the children and at other times the 'lessons' she enumerated could easily be overheard in the small living space: 'Don't follow and live my life. Finish school get a good job and get a big place … before you talk about marriage. I say, "Don't forget to buy me a car and a house."' Her emphasis on intergenerational reciprocity over time as 'the morality of a shared life' seemed to invoke meaning and seek value, and they resonated with ideas about 'good' parenthood and childhood in Ghana, where she was from (Twum-Danso Imoh, 2022: 13). The children were never directly invited to comment or respond to Serwah's commentary, despite often being present or nearby as she testified about her experiences. Yet her sacrifices and struggles also pervaded their narratives. Miriam, when commenting about the cost of school meals for children in the context of Serwah saying she could not afford to pay for lunches, did not mention the impact on herself or the other children, but that of adults, and Serwah specifically: 'Yes, I think most parents who are suffering and can't afford much should get free school meals because that would help, because they have to pay rent. First, they have to get the food and then that's just too much. So, I feel like they should give some parents who are suffering, give their children free school meals.'

Advice giving and receiving, as an act of practicing hope for the long term, appeared as an intergenerational project in the family. A dialogic family narrative was born out of the small space of the flat and the physical closeness of the family (but see Chapter 5 for the complexities of such intimacies). Miriam articulated a shared narrative on behalf of the children of wanting to make Serwah 'proud', something she explained as a response to Serwah's efforts, 'because she's struggled a lot for us, so when she gets old, we, all three of us, wanna make her proud'. This tale of mutual duty and dependence speaks to dominant Ghanaian ideas about intergenerational relations (Twum-Danso Imoh, 2022), albeit that these – like any cultural notions – are dynamic, transformed through transnational mobility and everyday life.

Luke and Miriam also spoke several times about their dreams of having a house or good car. These may seem to simply be articulations of neoliberal desires of material accumulation which proliferate in the heart of global capitalism. But as they revisited these ideas over several conversations, it became clear that their dreams (also) centred around improving the basic conditions of life for their mother. Miriam commented at one point: 'Me and Luke have promised her, like, when we grow up, we're gonna save money to buy her house. And then a car next. So that's our promise to her.' Angela Y. Davis reminds us that in the context of systemic racism possibilities for flourishing were and are always a shared endeavour for Black communities: 'Individual achievements were also collective steps forward, refutations of the ideology of racial inferiority.' (Davis et al. 2020). We can hear something akin to this point in Miriam's words here, in the sense that achievements of a decent place to live, or a more expedient way to travel with a large family, are never simply the result of any single individual's actions nor something to be celebrated alone, but a shared project of the family. The circumstances of life-making in the context of welfare bordering make this a fragile family project to be sure and families themselves are fraught and complex sites, not independent from the social inequities that pervade the wider societies they are a part of. The family, we caution, is an institution like others, and we should be careful not to romanticise it. For example, as we go on to discuss in Chapter 4, Miriam and Luke's own struggles and fears, and experiences of destitution, emerge fleetingly and do not seem to form part of the collective family narrative or even seem to be speakable in the presence of others.

To put this in a different way: there is no doubt that living in enforced destitution because of NRPF had caused significant hardship, or 'suffering' as Serwah and her children emphasised. Likewise, the impact of being undocumented, the effects of rentierism and the emotional, physical and social violence condoned within patriarchal relations had all taken their toll. But the lives of the family members and their narratives spoke of something much more. Care and concern pervaded their interactions, with hope ever present – although often in the form of a distant future which may never be achievable. Whatever immiseration the state causes through NRPF, this was not a family being passively 'done to' as is implied by representations of NRPF as a form of 'statutory neglect' from the state, akin to what 'would be considered as neglectful if caused by a parent or carer' (Jolly, 2018: 2). This characterisation seems to miss the complexity of the lives being lived under NRPF, risking evoking a spectre of families with NRPF as the 'vulnerable child'. Likewise, the small window Serwah, Miriam, Luke and Joshua offered us into their lives lays to rest any sense of lives stripped of meaning such as that suggested by the metaphor of 'bare life' or indeed their non-citizenship simply being a condition of negation (Tonkiss and Bloom, 2015). Instead, we caught glimpses of a family engrossed in the labour of sustenance, care and meaning making *together*, in and against the world, and despite a state that sought to render them vulnerable and destitute.

Our concern, then, is that, while drawing our attention to the deep violences of welfare bordering, an overemphasis on wearing, depletion and bare life can erase the dynamic and multi-faceted ways in which our interlocutors understood themselves and their actions in the world. When families' stories are flattened to a singular dimension of hardship, this not only obscures their efforts to make lives, but it obfuscates their struggles to make their lives meaningful. In other words, what may be intended by critical scholars and advocates as an act of concern and impulse for change may wind up being experienced as one of suppression and subjectification. At the same time, an overemphasis on regeneration falls into a similar trap, discounting the intensive and extensive nature of reproductive labour for the marginalised. Accordingly, we view our project here as an effort to move beyond a vacillating and dichotomous view of 'life's work' (Mitchell et al., 2003) which either reduces it to a cold calculus of augmentation minus depletion or treats it as necessarily replenishing, loving, mutual and even generative of resistance to injustice. The question for us becomes how to apprehend and valorise our interlocutors' efforts to make and sustain meaningful lives without losing sight of a draconian policy that seeks to deny them the means of life and a border regime designed to make it impossible. To respond to this problematic, or untenable bifurcation, we turn back to the narratives and practices of those mothers with NRPF and their children who we spent time with.

Weathering enforced destitution

Taking our cue from the way our interlocutors sought to present their own lives, our effort in this book is to develop a corrective to depictions of families with NRPF as *only* lacking or depleted, or the family as a site that is always, or even necessarily, marked by care and resistance to systemic racism, as is bound up in the concept of homeplace. Instead, we propose 'weathering' as an analytic which allows us to keep the complexities of life in play. Like a wind-trained tree, permanently and ever more deeply bowed, weathering speaks to the wearing down that happens through outside forces such as bordered welfare regimes. But it simultaneously speaks to a riding out, a withstanding, a toughening and a solidity, unlike depletion, lack or bare life. Weathering draws attention to processes of wearing, withstanding, fortification and toughening, and allows for engagement with the creative, dynamic and multi-faceted ways in which mothers and children in precarious migrancy position and seek to present their own lives within and beyond the hardship produced by NRPF. Seen in this way, weathering in the shadows of Britain's neoliberal welfare state is not simply a reworking of the available, but weathering implies the creation of something new. The erosion of bark as it is exposed to the elements does not just imply its disintegration, but smoother textures and new patterns are made in the process. Likewise, weathering welfare bordering speaks to the hopes that many families nurture in the shadows, the creative practices they must and do develop to sustain themselves, and the ways in which they strive to assign and maintain the value of their lives. To be sure, these are intensive and difficult labours given the injustices of welfare bordering, but that does not and should not write them off as inconsequential.

'One thing I decided is to, if there's three or four things that are dirty, I will, I will use the bucket, I will use the bath. Soak it in, and in the afternoon, there's nobody at home to use the bath. Then, I wash it, to reduce the cost. Because whilst I'm not working and the government is supporting, the money is not enough for me to take some to the laundrette,' explained Jessica. She came to the UK from Ghana and was undocumented when we met her. Jessica lived with her 16-year-old daughter Shanice in London, with other children still living in Ghana. The shared bathroom where she did her laundry was in a hostel where the two had been placed by the local authority after receiving Section 17 support. The bathroom had a typical high-sided tub found in many British homes and the bucket where she soaked the clothes was shorter than the tub walls. Jessica had to bend over completely just to reach the clothes and scrub each item by hand. She balanced the soapy items on the narrow ledge of the shared tub until she was ready to rinse them. Staying bent over the low bucket, she would wring out the clothes before bundling them back into the bucket to take to their single private room in the multiple occupancy building.

'In my mind, I said, let me plan it this way and do it that way so that we can have, we can save the money until the end of the month. That's another ... To the end of the month, that we can be okay,' Jessica continued, explaining her careful quantifying of laundry weight and a calendrics of washing to determine what to wash by hand in the shared bathtub and when to forfeit precious funds on bus fare to get to a laundrette and pay to use the washing machine. As with Serwah and Miriam's carefully choreographed emptying of the sink that will not drain, Jessica's daily life was animated by complex practices involving planning, calculating and strategising – all aspects of what we are referring to as weathering practices. Without working plumbing and utilities, white goods such as washing machines, or sufficiently heated homes to enable laundry to dry in a reasonable amount of time, accomplishing everyday acts of replenishment takes immense time, energy and a careful weighing up of highly restricted options.

Reproductive labour is not just stratified by the availability or lack of physical infrastructures such as these, however, but about resourcing, which is largely monetised in a marketised economy. For those who manage to find periods of paid labour, wages are carefully allocated. For Serwah, priority was given to food and a mobile phone, essential for coordinating work shifts, staying in contact with advocates and for Miriam and Luke to do their schoolwork – a particularly pressing issue during pandemic lockdowns. Some mothers told us they bought low-cost items in bulk when income from piece work allowed, never to be thrown out just in case the items became necessary, whilst others directed any possible extras to saving for applications to regularise their immigration status. Given the highly limited funds families with NRPF have available, it is often not possible to purchase everything that is needed. Many of the mothers we spoke to told us about accessing donations of food, clothes and home goods from charities. This means that mothers with NRPF and their very young children are often occupied by daily treks across London. Their movements are tied to the opening days and locations of food banks which are not restricted to those with regularised immigration status or to charities without eligibility requirements, well-researched sites of support which can be lost in a moment if families are moved to far-flung locations as a condition of receiving support from local authorities.

Reproductive labour is a far more time- and resource-intensive endeavour for the impoverished and excluded than for the (more) comfortable citizen-worker or citizen-parent. This means that how, and even if, the labour of reproduction is accomplished is never guaranteed. Following bell hooks, a key point here is there is no natural necessity to these families' efforts, and no singular path that families take. Instead, we think about their life's work as a series of carefully laid plans and judicious balancing acts taken in an effort to ensure that lives are sustained and spaces of hope are nurtured. Weathering, as a verb, and an active one at that, impels us to look and listen closely to the ways that mothers and children with NRPF *navigate* the restraints of welfare bordering. Heeding their complex acts of planning, doing and telling enables greater empirical insights and more holistic ontological understandings. But we also see the analytic of weathering as an invitation to engage in a form of ethical and political answerability to the way we understand our interlocutors invited us to hear and understand their experiences and reflections.

'So, we're just running to help each other, you know,' Serwah commented about her friend, the 'one person' that she 'has'. She explained that when the children's father left them unexpectedly, she ended up moving in with her friend: 'I don't have anywhere to go. [But] it's small. The kitchen, everything, is tiny together. So, me and my children we slept in the lounge. It was very small. So, I put something on the floor for my children. There are two, and me. I slept on the sofa. And my friend and her son sleep in the bedroom. It was very difficult. Very difficult.' As this suggests, not all resourcing of social reproduction is financial, and many families – including Serwah's – seek support from informal networks of friends, acquaintances or extended family, in some ways bringing us back to Davis's assertion that the making of daily lives is necessarily a collective endeavour for those marginalised by the racial state. Yet people in these social networks, these communities, like Serwah's friend, are often in equally precarious positions, frequently destitute themselves, with irregular immigration status, or similarly struggling to balance childcare and paid sources of income. As a result, asking for help requires a very nuanced analysis of the distinct types of support that might be available from each individual, careful consideration of how and to what extent this support might be reciprocated, and with what effects. For example, during the period that Serwah and her children lived in their friend's living room, the two families shared childcare responsibilities. 'I wake up early at 6 o'clock and go to work, and she will take Miriam and Luke to school and take her son as well. And I come back at four. She will start work at five and finish at nine in the evening,' Serwah explained. 'I was taking care of my friend's children with Miriam. It was very difficult. That was very difficult.' Serwah's repeated use of the word 'difficult' to describe this co-living arrangement across our multiple conversations with her reinforced the extent of these struggles, but it also served to highlight her ingenuity and endurance in the face of such challenging conditions. It also underscored her concern to reciprocate her friend's hospitality in whatever way she could.

'You need to go in for asking people for help,' Jessica commented. 'But who exactly is the one you're going for help? That is the question.' Her words highlight how fraught it is to ask for support, hinting at the impossible demands it can place on a relationship. As a result, many of our interlocutors spoke about making every effort to avoid pressurising family and friends by placing unmeetable demands on them. It was not uncommon for children to speak about silencing their own needs, whether at home or school. We heard, for example, Miriam and Luke's quiet comments about not wanting to eat breakfast anymore. For Miriam, this was largely about trying to avoid making demands except in exceptional circumstances, an effort to limit the amount that Serwah sacrificed for the children. For mothers, asking for help was not something to be undertaken lightly because it always ran the risk of opening oneself up to situations of hyper-exploitation, expectations of repayment through sexual favours or punitive and paternalistic demands for gratitude. Although reluctant to speak about her own situation directly, Jessica explained that having NRPF meant that 'people take advantage to make fun of you because they know you are not having status in this country'. In some cases, she went on, reluctant to offer details, this was about 'mis-using you'. At other times, it was about knowing that if there is trouble you 'just keep quiet', unable to 'call the police' because of being undocumented. Homeplace, or the collective resistance fostered in the labour of making lives away from the intense subjection of the racial state, which Black feminist scholars offer us, is highly contingent for those who live in precarious migrancy. It is filled with complex determinations about if and how far the labour of life can be shared and navigated with others in the context of welfare bordering. It requires emotional fortification, deep preparation for withstanding the ways asking for support transforms relationships, for good or bad, including producing unbearable obligations. In Jessica's question, 'who is the one you are going to', we hear something of the way that even the act of deciding whether to ask for help is a conundrum that can occupy and wear.

There is no doubt then that a single fissure in carefully constructed, but exceedingly fragile, strategies for life-making can mean the difference between having food on the table that evening or not. These daily struggles are not just the result of being at the whim of unscrupulous landlords or being unable to make complaints due to their immigration status. Nor is it simply that families do not have sufficient funds from the small amount of support they may receive from local authorities or from low-paid work, as in Serwah's case, to cover the ever-rising costs of living. The point is that welfare bordering through NRPF serves as a critical facet in the stratification of reproductive labour, fundamentally constraining the possibilities for life-making practices and 'disorganising' family life in ways which may disrupt its potential as a site of regeneration and resistance (Davis, 1971). However, unlike the abrupt ruptures caused by detention and deportation, enforced destitution produced by NRPF is a border technology that operates through its grinding and persistent presence.

Weathering, as a temporal analytic, prompts us to attend to those impacts on life-making practices which may not be immediately noticeable or those which do not produce a fixed outcome at a particular point in time, instead calling us to think about processes of immiseration, regeneration and remaking over extended periods. Indeed, time features centrally in the use of destitution as a border technology: in the afterlives of colonialism as they pervade borderings under racial capitalism and the use of time delayed as both a tactic of state power and migrant endurance – ideas we continue to develop in more detail throughout the book. Equally, the temporal focus provoked by an analytic of weathering allows for attention to the long-term impacts of NRPF, its grinding impacts on everyday life including and beyond moments of extreme distress which feature in the literature to date and, at the same time, the deferral of desires for uncertain futures, particularly as they figure in ideas about childhood. Many of our interlocutors' accounts of their life-making practices are motivated by imaginaries that something good will happen in the future, whether when children are of an age where regularisation becomes possible or in children's distant futures. As Serwah and her children spoke about their lives, putting in time to weather the violence of NRPF was imbued with their love for each other and a dream that, one day, things would be different. 'My advice, if she will listen, is going to help her a lot,' Serwah repeated about Miriam in another conversation. 'I hope she will listen. I tell her a lot of … She knows. She says, "Actually my mother always tells me: Don't follow and live my life. Finish school get a good job and get a big place." I say, "Don't forget to buy me a car and a house." I told her, the way I suffered to raise her. She understands, and I hope she makes me proud.'

Indeed, the narratives of mothers with NRPF and their children who we have met are replete with messages of fortitude in the face of extreme exclusions, everyday wisdom honed and mobilised in the context of impossible choices, and sparks of hope that serve as refusals (Simpson, 2017) of the impossibilities of a 'bare life' forced upon them by the relentless state violence of the UK's border regime. These ascriptions reappear in analyses of NRPF which spotlight only lack and depletion – even if these are done in the effort to interrupt or seek restitution for enforced destitution. Across our ethnographic fieldwork, we heard many examples of refusing such erasures and families' ongoing efforts to make meaningful lives. 'Not wallowing' is how Samantha, another mother, put it, instead focusing on the creation and telling of family stories as a way of lovingly and collectively withstanding welfare bordering technologies. During one conversation, she and her son Sam jointly reconstructed the narrative of a book she had made for Sam, in the process telling what was by that point an obviously well-trodden story of this important gift and its meaning for the family. Samantha read out the dedication: 'This is a fairy tale for a special boy like you. We hope you have fantastic adventures surrounded by those who love you most.' This use of stories to build a collective sense of hope, its affirmation of the value of the interconnected lives of the family members, again brings to mind hooks' notion of homeplace and Serwah's use of 'lessons' from her own life, and aimed at ensuring her children avoid the mistakes she felt she had made in order to bring about more positive futures that were not available in the here and now.

There is certainly a sense of the cruel optimism that Lauren Berlant (2011) writes about in these dreams and the social reproductive practices they sustain, given the extremes the British state is willing to go to exclude and penalise those unwanted others with irregular or time-limited status who can neither be deported or detained in current legislation. And to be clear, there are no guarantees in the UK's hostile environment that citizenship – as legal status, as feeling or social rights (Isin and Nielsen, 2008) – will come to pass. Nor does citizenship, in any of these guises, offer guarantees for life in the context of the UK's neoliberal welfare state. However, rather than falling into a paternalistic trap of dismissing dreams as a type of false consciousness, we seek ways to engage with our interlocutors' hopes, imagination and meaning making, as well as their relations of care. Dismissing these too easily, and only focusing on infrastructures, resources and policies, cannot adequately account for the production of life itself.

We are reminded here of Bev Skeggs's (2013: 24) potent warning to keep alive the interplay of value and values. 'We may be disenchanted, alienated and experience anomie and [be] subject to the imperatives of neoliberalism, market populism and capitalist realism,' she comments, 'but these are not the only social relations that shape us', nor are they the only relations that define us. In other words, if we reduce all practices and relationships to a logic of commodification, where those who are consigned to the edge of circuits of capitalist value *are* 'surplus' or lacking, or that unwaged labour *is* valueless, we are simply allowing our analyses to be captured by capital. While life-making practices produce the labour power central to capital's accumulation of surplus – be this through waged work, unfree labour or as edge populations absorbed in a monetised economy – they simultaneously do something more. For the reproduction and realisation of labour power can be, and often is, also imbued with values – those qualitative ways in which people not only interpret life but orient themselves to things that matter or come to matter to them. As Andrew Sayer (2011: 2) puts it: 'We are beings whose relation to the world is one of concern.'

Thus when we talk about the life-making practices of mothers with NRPF and their children, arguing that the dreams and values that animate them are more than cruel optimism, our aim is to mobilise the concept of weathering to attend not only to material practices like strategising, planning, withstanding and fortifying, and the violence of welfare bordering that shapes the conditions of possibility for reproductive labour. But we strive to attend to 'values' that matter, motivate and serve as a source of evaluation of the present (Levitas, 2010). When we speak of weathering through social reproduction, we speak to those refusals of bare life which reverberated in our interlocutors' accounts. We turn instead to their efforts to make *meaningful* lives, seeking to understand what this tells us about 'suffering', as Serwah puts it, as well as what could, even should, be different. We see something of these values when Joshua gurgled happily as Luke tickled his belly while Serwah cooked nearby. We hear something of these values when Miriam explained how she wants to 'do Serwah proud'. We learn something about the value of the lives being made in the shadows when Serwah insisted that the world is not as it should be when her family was left on the street simply because she was not born in Britain. In what follows, we hear more about value and values, welfare bordering and refusals through weathering, from the mothers and children who shared small parts of their lives with us.

Conclusion

In this chapter, we have considered how families with NRPF endeavour to make and sustain meaningful lives. We have introduced 'weathering', as both verb and metaphor, for the study of the effects of welfare bordering on the reproduction of life itself. This allows us to break with reductive readings of welfare bordering which have dominated in critical scholarship, showing that lives always exceed the stories that policies construct and impose, while never losing sight of the impact of enforced debt and destitution on the conditions of life and livelihood. For it is not enough to say that, as Marx put it, 'the capitalist may safely leave [the reproduction of labour power] to the worker's drive for self-preservation and propagation' (Marx 1976: 718). This naturalisation of 'drive' obscures the heterogeneous, contingent and relational practices in which 'drives' are constituted, and the ways that divisions and stratifications of reproductive labour are produced and contested.

The analytic of weathering we have introduced here, and go on to develop further in this book, draws attention to processes of wearing, withstanding, fortification and toughening, and allows for engagement with the dynamic and multi-faceted ways in which mothers and children in precarious migrancy represent and position themselves both within and beyond the hardship produced by NRPF. The story we are telling here is not one of heroic resilience, but neither is it a story of bare life. Instead, the mothers and children we have met invite us to attend to the interplay between enforced destitution and struggles to make meaningful lives. Sustaining this duality is both intellectually enriching and politically imperative for efforts to challenge the pernicious effects of NRPF.

In some ways, our use of weathering parallels that developed by Hamilton et al. (2021) to attend to the differential every day and embodied experiences of navigating *the weather* over time, a proposal we became acquainted with late in the process of writing this book. Their 'meteorological' use of weathering is an important reminder that the 'total climate' that must be weathered is not just social but environmental, an admitted gap in our own formulation of the concept and area for further interrogation. For them, however, the question becomes how might we 'weather better' together, while our usage operates in a less normative, and rather more descriptive and analytic, register. In many ways, this reflects our efforts to better understand the complexities of people's life-making practices while subject to NRPF which have often been obscured in research, policy and advocacy. But it also relates to our aim in the book, and beyond, to confront the brutal and adverse contexts that our interlocutors are forced to weather. We view our efforts here as a very small part of an explicitly political project, not intent on finding ways to 'weather better' the violences of welfare bordering, instead aiming to challenge the pernicious effects of NRPF and contest the very political economy shaping its conditions of existence in the first place, ideas which we go on to develop in more depth in the following chapters.

3

Existential erasure and its discontents

What might it mean for the subject to bear the violence of the conditions we've described thus far at the level of the psyche? This chapter seeks to explore two overlapping questions: what does the experience of enforced destitution do to psychic life? And, secondly, how are these conditions survived psychically? Keeping alive the interplay between being 'worn down' and 'withstanding' encapsulated by our concept of 'weathering', here we attempt to think through what happens at the intersection of bordering technologies that 'slowly kill' (Tazzioli, 2020) those they target, and the desires to survive, remain and resist that emanate from the subjects who experience and endure this violence. Following Tazzioli (2020), we find 'both the paradigm of the bare life and the image of the autonomous subject that acts according to free will ... inadequate for understanding the modes of subjection and constriction exercised upon migrants'. In this sense, weathering helps to give form to the complex and multiplicitous processes of subjectivation at play here, allowing us to hold on to the contradictory ways in which subjects are pulverised, transformed and deteriorated by the border regime, and, at the same time, how they withstand these forces – how they are hardened, shaped and made by them.

While an increasing body of literature has importantly begun to engage with questions of affect and emotion in relation to borders (Lewis, 2005; Mills and Klein, 2021; Clarke and Garner, 2005; Gilroy, 2005; Casas-Cortes et al., 2015; Tyler, 2013), the interior lives of those at the sharp end of migration regimes have tended to receive less attention, particularly in the case of undocumented migration. Yet, as we go on to show, border technologies also operate psychically (see also Dickson, 2023). Equally, when we consider the strategies employed by those who are targeted by borders, we must pay heed to the countertactics that operate in the psychic register, including the love, care and homeplacing we discussed in Chapter 2. As Imogen Tyler (2021: 18) has written in relation to stigma, 'people's experiences of being stigmatised are a critical source of "sociological imagination" ... and a vital resource in collective struggles against the capture of human lives in the exploitative, dehumanising machineries of capitalism'. With this in mind, this chapter draws on ethnographic field notes and narrative interviews with mothers to consider the psychic dimensions of their lives with NRPF, ideas we pick up in relation to children in future chapters, albeit to a lesser extent.

Radical responsibilisation

The transcripts from our interviews with mothers were particularly marked by references to 'nobody' and 'no one'. These invocations, denoting an absent presence that was deeply felt, seemed to gesture towards something important about the fabric of everyday life as a mother with NRPF. It was as though the life-making practices that we discussed in the previous chapter often occurred against a profoundly unpopulated backdrop, characterised less by what it contained than what it lacked. And what it lacked were these other bodies, the other people *who were not there* – symbolised by the repeated use of 'nobody' and 'no one'. This deserted landscape was a striking image that emerged from the process of reading our participants' accounts alongside one another. Though perhaps it was not so much an image at all, but something much harder to grasp – an affective texture that could be felt across our material, irreducible to a particular individual or instance, and, precisely for that reason, difficult to represent.

In our attempt to grapple with this ubiquitous yet elusive feeling, we tried to think about what these utterances were telling us. What was being communicated, for instance, when Serwah, whom we focused on in the last chapter, spoke of having no one to turn to if her two eldest children were ill at the same time: 'It's only me. Nobody is around to call. Nobody'? Or when Samantha talked about not being able to approach close friends for support out of fear of becoming burdensome: 'I had no one to fall back on, I had no one to rely on ... Don't get me wrong, Jennifer's amazing and I could always call her, but I felt like I didn't want to saddle her. She had her own things going on.'

These uses of 'nobody' and 'no one' seemed not to be about the absence of particular people who *should* have been there, nor did they appear to be affected by the actual presence of others we saw or heard about, such as the loving relationships between family members we saw in the last chapter. They did, however, imply something about a need for others to be there, or at least an original expectation that there would be others – perhaps in a way that spoke particularly to our participants' situations as single mothers with caring responsibilities for children. These statements felt curiously untethered to objects. They called forth spectres of absent fathers, unhelpful mothers and sisters, the state and its street-level bureaucrats, but these figures existed only as shadows – never explicitly called upon or to. Instead, our participants' repeated use of negative pronouns seemed to speak to a more general metaphysical condition – a feeling of lack that, at times, appeared to permeate everything. This feeling, as we understood it, was a total and absolute sense of being radically alone as a single mother in the conditions of impoverishment. The psychic correlate of the material hardship our interlocuters were forced to endure was its own kind of destitution – a subjective life in which there was, in a deep and unrelenting sense, sometimes no one else. The force and depth of this feeling was borne out by its utter persistence. It was an affective state that was not dissipated or alleviated by the company of children, friends or neighbours, however intimate these relationships sometimes were or however much, for example, family life fostered a sense of 'homeplace'. At times, these pronouncements that there was 'nobody' or 'no one' were even preceded or followed by mentions of support from others. And yet, it was clear that such instances did not alter the quality or quantity of this affect. 'Homeplace' and radical responsibilisation, it seemed, could exist simultaneously.

Ruth Wilson Gilmore's (2007) concept of 'organized abandonment' – denoting the calculated neglect of racially marginalised people by states and capital – offers a helpful starting point for thinking through the NRPF policy in this respect. One way of understanding the state withdrawal of vital support and services from migrant populations deemed 'surplus' by racial capitalism is as a form of 'organised abandonment'– a kind of managed neglect. Another way of saying this is that these families have been purposefully forgotten by the British state – excluded from mainstream welfare support and left to 'make it on their own', despite their pre-existing socioeconomic marginalisation. They have been 'abandoned' to destitution, with the only potential state support available being the substandard accommodation and minimal funding coming from local authorities under the Children Act 1989.

The affective experience of radical aloneness that our participants felt so acutely was inextricable from this structural neglect. The mothers we spoke to often described being unable to seek support from those around them due to the extremity of their hardship. Those in our interlocuters' social networks were also often in similar situations to their own, thereby limiting the kinds of support they were able to offer to others (see also Benchekroun, 2024). But ultimately, it was the sheer level of destitution enforced by NRPF which rendered informal support from others impossible or highly fraught, with relationships breaking down, often painfully, under its strain. As Samantha told us, 'And a couple of friends that I felt like I could do that to, that I could do that with, I've done it with them, and it's always come back to bite me in the backside, so I've just soldiered on.' On another occasion, Samantha mentioned trying to keep costs down when she was working under-the-table by asking an undocumented friend to help her with childcare and paying the woman what she could afford. The arrangement had ended in a traumatic way for both Samantha and her son Sam when she discovered nail marks all over his body. Being unable to rely on others for support forced her and many of the other women we spent time with to endure relationships and situations that were harmful and painful for them and their children. Stories of exploitation and abuse were rife, though, as we see elsewhere in this book, these ran alongside other relationships of love, care and friendship. The double-bind in which mothers were caught – being on the one hand entirely abandoned by the state and thus forced to rely on informal networks for support, and nonetheless, as a direct result of this abandonment, having needs always in extreme excess of the material support such networks could offer – was compounded by single parenthood, which multiplied needs and intensified difficulties.

Tanya, a young woman who had come to the UK from Jamaica as a child, highlighted the exploitative dimensions of seeking and providing help to friends as a person with NRPF when she told us about her experience of staying with a friend:

> I take her kids to school, I clean the house every single day, seven days a week, never get a break to myself when I was pregnant with my daughter. Then when my daughter came, she never once say to me, like, oh here is £30, here and go and buy something for yourself.

Because she was staying with the 'friend' rent-free, Tanya was expected to do all the social reproductive labour for both of them, even when she was exhausted or heavily pregnant. Tanya told us that the woman often used 'abusive words', such as telling her that she should not have come to Britain and that she should be 'locked down' because she didn't have her papers. Tanya felt hurt and taken advantage of, but she had nowhere else to go and feared being told to leave. 'I would take the abuse, like take it, take it, take it, take it'. The repetition she uses here is important, emphasising the incessant nature of the exploitation and abuse she endured. The words become almost like blows as she says them.

With the experiences of Serwah, Samantha and Tanya in mind, we want to suggest that being jettisoned by the state in this way produces an affective state of radical aloneness, which, in turn, is experienced as a hyper-responsibilisation of the mother or family unit. Thinking back to Serwah, Miriam, Luke and Joshua, whom we introduced in Chapter 2, there was a heightened sense in our interactions with them of it being them (the family unit) against the world, because there was no one else who would help.

'You don't have any help, nothing. You have the children', says Serwah – gesturing towards the extreme way in which families are responsibilised under NRPF. This is not to say, however, that the families we met were not giving or receiving emotional and material support to/from others in their networks – in moments, we caught glimpses of mutual aid, care and significant friendships (as we hear in Samantha's invocation of her close friend Jennifer above) – but that the mothers we spoke to described a profound existential sense of aloneness that cut through everything, crystallised in the evocative absent-presence of 'nobody' and 'no one' in their narratives.

While organised abandonment, and the ensuing feelings of radical aloneness it often produced, created fertile ground for hyper-exploitation, the experiences of exploitation also doubled back upon the subject – serving to further entrench the sense of complete isolation. For some, the fact of being undocumented foreclosed friendship entirely. There was a sense that everyone, everywhere was ready to take advantage of them – a point we return to later in this chapter. Certainly, the stories of misuse we heard over and over again worked to instil an affective atmosphere of constant threat for us as we listened, though of course we were not in the position of the threatened subject, nor did we feel threatened ourselves. Instead, we came to associate this sense of heightened vigilance engendered by our participants' repeated experiences of exploitation with the psychic reality of being undocumented, perhaps via a process akin to the psychoanalytic notion of 'counter-transference'. This term essentially captures the psychoanalyst's affective response to the 'flow ("transfer") of unconscious dynamics' (Hollway, 2016) between themselves and the patient.

Psychic erasure

Within this affective state of feeling radically alone, the threat of existential erasure – itself a product of the 'organised abandonment' we described above – loomed large. Our sense from the conversations we had with mothers was that they were often caught up in a process of constantly defending against a total loss of self. In Samantha's words:

> It destroys you mentally. And if you're frightened to look after children, who are depending on you to be a pillar of strength and depending on you to guide them, look after them, and everything, you can't afford to lose yourself. And that's what no recourse to public funds does to people. You lose yourself. You lose your sense of identity.

Samantha's poignant description of the subjective harm of welfare bordering here moves between a narrative of psychic eradication ('you lose yourself ... your sense of identity') and a counter-narrative – almost a demand made upon the self – of survival against the odds ('you can't afford to lose yourself'). Others described 'giving up completely', feeling 'worthless', 'trapped' and like their heads were 'exploding', and many of the mothers in our research had experienced strong feelings of suicide. One mother linked 'life without papers' to 'going mad', explaining that the traumatic experiences endured as a result of being undocumented 'stay in your head' and 'don't go away', highlighting how the border is lived psychically, often long beyond the actual duration of specific legal categories (Dickson, 2023). These emotional experiences sometimes emerged in conversations in a more abstract way – evincing something of the overall psychic texture of life under duress – and at other times were more localised around specific events, relationships or roles, such as feeling unable to 'be a mother' due to the material constraints they had to endure and their resulting inability to provide for their children.

In the case of Ijeoma, it was in her relationship with her social worker that these feelings came to the fore. We met Ijeoma online during the pandemic. She was living in one room with her two young sons in hostel accommodation. She was undocumented and waiting for her immigration application to be decided by the Home Office. Her eldest son, Enofe, was almost 7-years-old. She had been supported by social services for almost six years – six years of living on minimal financial support, six years of living in the hostel, six years of waiting. During a narrative interview, she began telling us about her interactions with her social worker:

> [the stress] is out of this world. They are going to make you feel as if you are nobody. They make me feel as if I'm nobody. They make me feel as if I'm worthless ... I'm an illegal immigrant. So, there is nothing ... If you're illegal immigrant and you have kid, nobody cares. The only person that I know that care, maybe, the doctor in the hospital. Apart from that, no one cares. No one cares if you are sleeping on the street with a kid. No one cares.

Ijeoma's repetition of 'nobody' is pertinent, elucidating our more general discussion above. Here it underlines both the negation of subjecthood that she experiences in relation to her social worker ('as if I'm nobody'), and the pervasive sense of radical aloneness we touched upon earlier ('nobody cares'). In the case of the former, Ijeoma's qualifying 'as if' serves as an important trace of a split between who or what she feels she is and the processes of subjectivation she is entangled in. These distancing 'as ifs' mark a limit of subjection – Ijeoma appears disturbed and haunted by these images of herself as worthless and lacking in personhood, but her use of language indicates a gap between these representations and what she feels to be her 'self'. This distance, however, seems to collapse at the point that she announces, with sad resignation, 'I'm an illegal immigrant' – whereupon she zeroes in on her 'non-personhood' in the eyes of the nation state. Some kind of contraction has taken place, with 'illegal immigrant' coming to fix the subject discursively in place. This sense of feeling fixed within or to this category of 'illegality' came to dominate Ijeoma's narrative. Speaking of what she felt to be a kind of enforced immobility produced at the nexus between the migration regime and the shadowy welfare system of social services that came to govern her everyday, Ijeoma described a 'stuckness':

> Stay stuck. Stay stuck in the place … in my own mind. We give you house, and we are feeding you … you, just sit there. They want nobody to dream of becom[ing] somebody … Okay, maybe, tomorrow, you can become social worker. Maybe, tomorrow, you can become a nurse. No. Just stay where you are. When someone stays so long in the place, it affects the way you're thinking. It affects your thinking. It affects the way you talk. … No way out. Sometimes, I feel that I'm in the room where everywhere is locked. When I look right, it's locked. The door is locked in the front. Everywhere. … I'm so stuck. So stuck.

Here illegality becomes a 'place' – a prison – but one that is also located within the psyche ('my own mind'). This prolonged geographical confinement – to be forced to inhabit the psychic site of illegality for so long – Ijeoma suggests, has devastating consequences for thought, affect and speech. Indeed, we might say, Ijeoma's commentary seems to enact the very processes she tries to articulate. The narrative shifts between a voice that is more distinctly Ijeoma's own and the internalised voice of the punitive other (in this instance, the social worker), who comes to stand for the nation state. As soon as each tentative dream of becoming 'someone' (someone of 'value', we might add) emerges, it is shot down. The horizon of becoming is foreclosed by the imperative to 'stay stuck', to stay 'nobody'. The subject must be fixed in place – psychically, materially, discursively. This 'fixing' is tantamount to an evacuation or destitution of the subject, with the legal and discursive category of 'illegal immigrant' effectively replacing the subject proper.

It is important to note that what we have been discussing here is both what is being 'done to' the subject *and* what the mothers we spoke to felt about themselves as subjects. These are parallel processes, which at times align and coincide, but in other moments clash and collide (Dickson, 2023). Or, to go back to Ijeoma's 'as if', there is a potential disjunction, or perhaps even a radical conflict, between the 'no subject' of illegality (the 'nobody') and the subject asked to occupy the category. This subject is ultimately being impelled to annihilate itself. The disjunction or conflict, therefore, becomes a matter of life and death. Reading the hollowed out subject that we hear in the narratives of Samantha, Ijeoma and Rita (in the next section) alongside the parallel speech that contradicts, interrupts and disrupts the erasure of subjecthood, we encounter a fundamentally split subject, one that exceeds any notion of 'bare life' (Agamben, 1998). In thinking about the vicissitudes of this fractured subjective experience – the constant oscillation between breaking down and bearing out that we saw in the mothers we met – it is helpful to return for a moment to our notion of weathering. At the same time as capturing something of this slow process of psychic erasure, weathering also denotes a potential hardening, or in the words of one of our interlocuters, a kind of 'fortification'. As we continue this chapter, moving on to consider questions of psychic value, we want to hold on to this double meaning of the term.

The racialised postcolonial hierarchy of 'value'

For the mothers we spoke to, the question of psychic life or death was deeply entangled with notions of 'value'. The intersubjective field in particular was laden with a racialised postcolonial hierarchy of 'value' in which the hierarchies of migration status pervaded sexual relationships, with undocumented women often being treated as 'valueless' by undocumented men because they were not seen to offer a route to a higher migration status. This racialised sexual hierarchy is reminiscent of Frantz Fanon's (2008) writing on the production and function of sexual desire in the metropole and the colony. As in colonial Martinique, we can see something of the ways in which desire becomes imbued with, and indeed is brought into being through, the racialised forms of classification at the heart of Empire (or, in this instance, the British postcolonial state), with sexual relationships offering the potential promise of moving up, or transcending, the social order. In the words of Ann Laura Stoler (1995: 190), 'sexual desire in colonial and postcolonial contexts has been a crucial transfer point of power, tangled with racial exclusions in complicated ways'. This violent hierarchy, as we go on to show, underpinned the affective experience of radical aloneness, as well as pushing the subject to the very limits of a liveable psychic existence. It is worth noting that the questions of psychic value that we focus on here may be especially pertinent to feminist studies of social reproduction, which have given rise to debates around the value (in the Marxian sense) of reproductive labour. Here we attempt to attend to the interplay between this Marxian notion of value and questions of value in the ethical, moral and subjective domains, which as Skeggs (2014: 1) argues, are 'always dialogic, dependent and co-constituting'.

We were confronted by these issues of value most powerfully in our conversations with Rita – a middle-aged Nigerian woman who had been undocumented in Britain for over a decade. Rita was living with two of her children, Joseph (aged 7) and John (aged 3), in a pristine but small one-bedroom flat in East London. She was in the middle of a battle with the Nigerian High Commission to get a passport issued for her immigration application. It was the first time in her adult life that she had not been trapped in an abusive relationship. Rita explained to us that she had three children with three different fathers – all of whom had been abusive towards her.[1] Her migration to the UK had not interrupted but perpetuated the abuse. When we met, Rita spoke forcefully about these abusive relationships with men. The narrative she gave of her life was structured by gendered violence – a raw story told in episodes of physical, emotional and financial abuse. This narrative structure was circular and disorienting, with the horrific violence Rita had experienced exceeding and escaping any sense of chronology or linearity. As we listened, and later read her transcript silently and aloud, we lost sight of where we were, what was happening or who the perpetrators were. We had been enveloped by a narrative blur – one that operated at a rapid and bewildering pace – anchored only by the visceral brutality of the violence depicted. The violence, moreover, was dramatically performed by Rita to Eve. Rita took on the personas of her perpetrators as the story unfolded, acquiring other voices, gestures and vocabularies as she did. Rather than reproducing the scenes of violence that we heard, and therefore risking 'reinforc[ing] the spectacular character of black suffering' (Hartman, 1997), we choose to focus here on the narrative devices Rita employed, which we feel tell us something about the form of this violence and its lived reality.

As we tried to follow the 'big' and 'small' stories (Phoenix, 2013) Rita described and dramatised at great pace – feeling ourselves to be completely overwhelmed, almost invaded by the violence, and yet intensely present in the moment – we were struck by her repeated use of the adjective 'useless'. It seemed to be a kind of keyword in Rita's narrative about living with NRPF. 'Useless' was, in her view, the way her male partners perceived her: 'when you don't have paper, they [men] think you are useless'. This 'uselessness' characterised everything. 'Even if you have baby for them', she continued, 'you are still useless. Even if they like the child, it doesn't really make a difference. They know you are not useful to them.' It was this logic of brutal utility or hyper-instrumentality, she appeared to feel, that both produced and made possible the male violence she had experienced. Without papers, or even the possibility of getting them, she felt she had no value in the eyes of the men she had relationships with. Even motherhood, which Rita seemed to expect to be a place of value, was a site of erasure. Her reproductive labour did not matter, and her lack of status came to determine the value (or lack of) of her entire being – she became an object to be ruthlessly used, exploited and degraded. 'Once they realise you can't [help them get their paper sorted], they treat you like trash [...] They think you are their slave.' This knowledge (of having/not having status) was something Rita felt men could see and find out very quickly – 'They will sleep with you, and then they will know. Then they will be gone. You are useless to them.' As we alluded to in Chapter 2, Rita's powerful analysis of value from her subject position as an undocumented migrant suggests social reproduction theory needs to consider the ways in which bordering intersects with questions of psychic value in the context of reproductive labour. A psychosocial understanding of value asks not only what value labour power has for capital, and what exceeds or sits ambivalently within this calculation, but how psychic value intersects with social and material notions of worth – something often missing from discussions of reproductive labour. For Rita, the hierarchical system of value constructed by the UK's migration regime – what Bridget Anderson (2013) has termed 'the community of value' – was reinforced and reproduced at the level of the intimate, in her romantic and sexual life. The 'production of migrant illegality' (De Genova, 2002) rendered Rita 'useless' in the context of a punitive migration regime that denies the means of life to those it excludes. She experienced herself, then, by way of this process and her 'deportability' (De Genova, 2002), as something akin to 'dehumanised waste', entirely abject (Tyler, 2013) to the undocumented men with whom she had relationships.

The repeated acts of violence Rita was subjected to by her male partners, and the complicitly of the community that often accompanied them, revealed a kind of ethical abandonment on the part of the perpetrators towards Rita, whereby there was, in effect, 'no subject' with whom to have an ethical relation. The abuse was a way of denying Rita's subjecthood. But this interpersonal violence was shot through with the organised abandonment we described earlier. In Rita's words, 'They see there is nothing you can do. They see there is nowhere for you to go, no one who will help you.' Rita gestures to a state of psychosocial imprisonment and abandonment brought about through the intersection of border controls and patriarchal violence. We might think here of the slogan of the non-profit domestic violence organisation Southall Black Sisters, 'No Recourse, No Safety', used in their campaigns against the NRPF condition in the 1990s, or the well-documented ways in which women subject to NRPF are liable to become trapped in abusive relationships (Anitha, 2010). 'They see there is nowhere for you to go' is a statement borne out of the fact that there really was nowhere for Rita to go. No refuge she could qualify for because she had NRPF. No local authority homelessness assistance she could turn to. And no support from social services, even when she did have a child, until that child became old enough for her to have a legally recognised right to remain in the country. (Indeed, Rita's initial attempts to seek support from social services in relation to domestic violence resulted in her being told that she would have to go to what she termed a 'deportation camp'.) As Rita put it, if your child is 'the little one's age', pointing at John, 'you will just have to keep suffering. There is nothing you can do. They will think you are useless. You will be waiting, waiting, until they are 7.'

But in her conversations with us, we also felt that Rita was getting at something else. 'They see there is ... no one who will help you' seemed to hint at something far more extensive than the absence of state support. The postcolonial hierarchy of value that Rita described shaping her relationships with men was in fact a much more general feature of her interpersonal world. 'Anywhere you are', she told Eve, 'If you don't have paper, you are useless. They find a way to offend you. They look down on you' – an experience many of the other mothers we spoke to shared. Rita talked about how other people 'they always want to know if you have paper', explaining that she felt they wanted to know, so that they could feel that they were better than her, even if they had also been undocumented in the past. She described this happening at gatherings and launched into a story about being on a bus. When something got heated on the bus, people told her, 'I will call the police. Don't think I am scared, I have my paper.' Rita told us that they said this because they knew that she didn't have her papers and that she would be deported by the police if they were called. This threat, in her view, was made so that she could 'never speak up' and would always have to 'shut her mouth and keep quiet'. Rita said she felt 'very judged' by other people who had their papers. What Rita described to us seemed to be a feeling that she was constantly being subject to a process of violent classification by those around her – one of the ways in which the border regime had pervaded her day-to-day relationships with others and her own embodied sense of self. In contrast to the invisibility that may often be associated with the clandestine experience of 'illegality' – which requires, as the title of this book gestures towards, living in the shadows – Rita's status felt, to her, highly visible to those around her. Her body was profoundly marked by it. In particular, she seemed to feel that those who had known it themselves could see it in her. Jessica, another of our participants whom we met in the last chapter, described NRPF affecting 'the body from head to toe', feeling, like Rita, that its effects were visibly worn on the flesh. Equally, having or not having status came to structure Rita's own perception of other people. While telling us that she used to go to church on Sundays, but had stopped going, Rita described seeing all the women 'dressed up' for church, in their 'special clothes and with their powder on' and thinking, 'They must have paper. That is why they are happy.' Her 'paper-lessness' saturated her everyday interactions with others in a way that left her feeling inferior, immobile and unable to speak. She began to equate 'happiness' and 'looking nice' with legal migration status. Yet, as we see in the case of Destiny in Chapter 6, legal status is by no means a panacea in the context of welfare bordering, though nor is having access to public funds, something captured so beautifully by Mode Williams (2021) in *The Next Story*.

In Rita's descriptions of the everyday mistreatment she experienced, the potential for solidarity amongst those who had also experienced undocumented life in Britain appeared to be foreclosed. It seemed as though this foreclosure was premised on a need these others felt to shore up their place in the hierarchy of the migration regime – a kind of securitisation of identity or process of disavowal by which they sought to situate themselves, as 'tolerated citizens', more firmly in the nation's 'community of value' (Anderson, 2013). As Valluvan (2019: 36–37) writes, the seductive power of nationalism 'is less a question of being moved by desires about who we are and more a question of being agitated by concerns about who we are definitely not [...] it is a social current that exceeds simple subject location'. At the same time as showing us the instability of citizenship vis-à-vis these notions of value, such psychic processes highlight the fragility of legal status and citizenship within this regime, which, as we have seen in recent years (Kapoor, 2018), may at any moment be violently withdrawn. Rita was, so to speak, the collateral of these psychic and legal mechanisms. But perhaps there may be something else at work here too. If we turn to Mbembe (2017: 7), we are reminded that 'the fierce colonial desire to divide and classify, to create hierarchies and produce difference, leaves behind wounds and scars'. In Rita's narrative, these formerly undocumented figures perpetuated the violent classification that they themselves were previously subject to – the violence was repeated, with the subject positions reversed. This is not to suggest a straightforward correlation or necessary slippage here, nor to deny the instances of conviviality or solidarity that occur in these contexts, which we highlight elsewhere (and for other examples see De Noronha (2022) and Back and Sinha (2018)), but to highlight that traumatic experiences of violence can, and sometimes do, result in a kind of slippery repetition – one that Rita seemed very alive to in her encounters with other formerly undocumented people.

Of course, the very idea of 'being legal' is dependent on someone else being 'illegal' – hence, as in Rita's description, the need for the kind of vigilant policing of what, in reality, are extremely porous and unstable categories. And such policing may indeed be a key mode of survival for these other subjects who – whether consciously or unconsciously – feel their precarity or 'provisional belonging' in relation to the ever-intensifying borders in contemporary Britain. As De Noronha (2022) writes, 'Borders get between people and follow them around; they have been internalised, and they are everyday and everywhere.' Rita's narrative interview reminds us that the constant and brutal (re)establishing of these categories may be experienced in a very intense way at an intersubjective level, leaving the subject feeling that everyone everywhere is out to classify and subjugate them according to the racialised logics of the nation state. This is an important dimension of 'everyday bordering' (Yuval-Davis et al., 2018) that may have received less critical attention than the extension of border controls into public services (e.g. healthcare, employment, schools).

Towards the end of our encounter with her, Rita reflected sadly on her life. She told us that because of her age, she felt she had lived half her life. 'What kind of a life?' she asked. She said she wasn't proud that she didn't go to school, but she also stated – in seeming defiance against the very logic of value we've reflected on above – 'I cannot say I have been useless.' This is an important statement of refusal, one that reminds us of the ways in which Rita, and the other mothers we spoke to, resist and counter the subject positions that they are forced to (also) inhabit. At the time that we met Rita, she was being supported by social services and was waiting for the Home Office to make a decision on her immigration application, now much stronger as her eldest son, Joseph, had turned 7. Despite having been refused support many times, Rita had determinedly managed to navigate the local authority's 'gatekeeping'. On one of her attempts, they had told her there was nothing they could do, that she had to go, but she had refused to leave the building. 'I'm not going to go,' she told us – describing the scene – 'I'm going to stay in the Council […] I called [the charity organisation supporting me] immediately. I said this is where we stand and they said just stay there.' The charity called her solicitor, who threatened to take the local authority to court. Rita's physical non-compliance was a kind of protest. She would not return to the violence she had endured for so many years, but insisted that her and her two children be given what they were entitled to. At four o'clock that day, they were given a key to a flat:

> That day I think it's over ... I escape all my violence, all my trouble, all the abuse from men. I escape it. What comes to my head that day is that I escaped ... And I took my son and I said, Joseph, they gave us key. Joseph was jumping up. We were jumping in the Council. They give us key. Today if I see the key, it's still like gold in my hand. I escaped violence in my life. I escaped from men.

Rita tried to impress upon Eve this feeling of being able to 'escape violence', repeatedly asking – 'do you understand me? Do you know what I mean?', evidently feeling that such understanding was not possible in the absence of shared experience. Reminding us of this limit was important – signalling what it was not possible for us to know because of the very different lives we had led. At the same time, Rita nonetheless endeavoured to communicate what this meant for her. She talked about the feeling of 'possibility' now that she knew she would get her papers. She would open a bank account for the first time in her life. She could study. She could travel. This is not to say that obtaining legal status is a remedy for those who are undocumented, but to show the hope and sense of future that Rita was able to keep alive – her perpetual struggle to stay alive, to have a life and a future for her and her children, to feel free. She was not defeated or 'worn out' – she was 'jumping'.

Reclaiming value

Rita's jumping, we want to suggest, like Ijeoma's 'as if', was part of a diverse repertoire mothers in our study employed to assert and reclaim their sense of value. These were their (un)conscious counterstrategies of resistance, which revealed that the processes of psychic erasure were never complete. While ethical and caring responsibilities towards others, especially children, were clearly troubling for our participants – often experienced as burdensome, taxing or impossible – they were also framed as a way of reclaiming value and weathering a punitive migration regime. In many instances, the mother–child relationship was articulated as a source of joy and faith, such as Abiola's representation of motherhood as a site of hope. She told us that her 10-year-old son Akin made her laugh, even when she felt like crying. In the starkest examples, children were positioned as bulwarks against suicide, heralded as the saviours of their mothers' lives. Some mothers had come very close to killing themselves and described thoughts of their children as the thing that had held them back. Hurting or killing oneself was framed as 'transfer[ring] the problem' to the child, which functioned as an imperative to stay alive. The need to survive was also articulated in terms of a responsibility to the child-as-dependant and as a form of parental love. These other-oriented narratives were not exclusive to the parent–child relationship but extended to other family members being supported. Ijeoma, for example, spoke of the support she provided to her mother, father, 18-year-old daughter, and her deceased sister's children – all of whom were living in Nigeria. As in the case of her maternal role to her children in the UK, the work of making and sustaining the lives of others served as a constant reminder of the necessity to weather the effects of NRPF. In Ijeoma's words, 'Back in Nigeria, a lot of life depend on me. I don't need to break. I need to be strong.'

Others talked about wanting to 'break cycle[s]' of abuse that they understood themselves to be caught up in, identifying connections between their experiences of abuse as children and adults. These mothers felt that through their children they could disrupt the repetition of abuse. Ijeoma spoke about her son Enofe giving her 'the power of mother', locating a kind of strength in the practice of mothering, particularly in the sense of its capacity to imprint upon and shape another life:

> We mother[s], we have a lot of impact in the grain of your children ... It's what I impart on him, and he will just renovate it and become a man ... boy, you can do more than me. You can do more than me.

As Ijeoma began to talk about this 'power', she brought her hand up and stretched out her palm, almost as though showing that the power was too big for her hand. The interview tone shifted from being full of struggle and suffering to having energy, possibility and excitement. We could feel the power as Ijeoma spoke – it suffused her voice with life and movement in a way that disrupted the more exhausting narrative of destitution. Children were understood both as lives 'to live for' and sources of agency insofar as they were imagined to offer their mothers a way of impacting or influencing the social world (e.g. through the reproductive power of producing other subjects). In Ijeoma's case, the power to shape the subjectivity of her child was deeply gendered. Reminding us that she had been trapped in an abusive marriage with a man, she spoke of telling her 6-year-old son Enofe every morning, 'You are not going to maltreat any woman.' This desire coexisted with others that sought to compensate for the injustices of Ijeoma's life, such as fantasies of prosperity, wealth and success, which were projected on to the child. These imaginaries around children's futures were common amongst the mothers we met, operating at once as a significant pressure *and* a source of hope and futurity that allowed them to keep going in the face of the impossible. The figure of the child frequently offered an imaginative, redemptive (future) counter to the impoverishment and hardship of the present. As we glimpsed in the previous chapter with Serwah, Miriam, Luke and Joshua, these fantasies were often intergenerational, functioning as collective dreams shared amongst family members. Indeed, as we go on to discuss further in the next chapter, many of the children we met were deeply invested in these narratives of redeeming the untenable present through their futures.

Deferred desires for oneself also worked as modes of weathering enforced destitution and debt. For all the families who participated in our research, the prospect of regularised immigration status was in sight, however unclear the timeline. Their claims for legal status rested on their children having lived in the UK for seven or more years, or on their children's British citizenship, which had mainly been established on the basis of ten years of continuous residence in the UK. Children were, in this way, implicitly positioned as the legal mechanism through which regularised life could be achieved. It's important to note that while we met families when they were at a stage of being highly likely to have legally recognised claims for belonging, or were at least close to such moments, our participants had been waiting for these points in time for extended periods – sometimes a whole decade. Fantasies of future selves tended to be orientated around independence (e.g. not being reliant on state or third-sector support), education and employment-as-contribution-to-society, such as hopes of becoming nurses, social workers, teachers and care-workers. These dreams positioned mothers as part of a future 'community of value' (Anderson, 2013), no doubt an important way of countering governmental and media representations of their 'undeservingness' and 'undesirability', such as the ones we saw in Chapter 1. Alongside these concrete hopes, we encountered more abstract desires, such as Ijeoma's imaginary of 'nobody disturbing' her, presumably a way of holding on to an idea of a future where one would not be subject to the policing and surveillance of the Home Office and social services.

The bigger strategies we have discussed thus far were complemented by tactics that operated in more of a minor key. By this we mean the more invisible, but no less significant, everyday gestures and practices that mothers implemented as ways of keeping going or asserting their value. We think here of Rita telling us about changing the hat she wore to a bright red one so that other people would not think she was depressed; Abiola smiling all the time so that her son and others around her would not know what she was going through; or daily coping strategies, such as listening to music to stay calm. Likewise, the mutual support Ijeoma offered to other mothers with NRPF through telling her own story of endurance:

> Sometimes when I see people depressed, I'm just like, let me talk to you. Most of the people in the hostel, they know my story. [...] I don't hide it. It's because when I tell you my story, you will know that if Ijeoma can do it, you can do it as well.

Here, Ijeoma understood the power and value of her own narrative for others as part of a more collective project of surviving life under duress. This sense of a more collective struggle to survive against the conditions imposed by the border regime often punctuated the accounts of our interlocuters and the desire for long-term, structural change – envisioned as helping to improve the circumstances of other families in the future – motivated many of the mothers to participate in our research. Given the pervasiveness of the radical aloneness we discussed earlier, the persistence of an ethos of common or shared survival in the face of hostility was all the more remarkable. Such sentiments, as we see in the next chapter, were also present in our encounters with children, who often spoke of the need for systemic change and, in some instances, imagined themselves as part of collective efforts to bring about such transformations.

Conclusion

This chapter put the concept of weathering to work in relation to the psychic lives of mothers, building on our analysis of material practices of sustaining everyday life in Chapter 2. Our use of weathering spoke to the deep roots of enforced destitution as it takes hold on the subject. Following our interlocuter's narratives of 'uselessness', feeling radically alone in their impoverishment, jettisoned by the state and unable to seek support from those around them due to the extremity of their hardship, we conceptualised the experience of enforced destitution as a form of psychic precarity and erasure. We traced the ways in which a sense of being cast aside and rendered valueless pervaded relationships with the state and others. Through our use of weathering, we examined the ways that mothers translated between narratives of abjection, loss, abandonment, value and toughening. We showed how welfare bordering produces a radical responsibilisation of the individual or family unit and creates fertile ground for hyper-exploitation, subjugation and usury of migrant mothers as workers, friends and partners.

At the same time, we emphasised how for many of our participants, reclaiming value lay down a path of ethical and caring responsibilities towards others, particularly as relational modes generative of meaning, value and futures – however far deferred – even as these responsibilities were simultaneously experienced as burdensome. As we gestured towards in this chapter, children play a central role in desires, hopes and dreams for a redemptive future. In the next chapter, we consider questions of childhood more fully, documenting the role of children in the labour of fulfilling embodied needs, caring for themselves and others, and making lives meaningful.

Note

1 Rita's third child lived in Nigeria and had been born much earlier than Joseph and John, but they were not mentioned by Rita beyond this moment. The spectre of such children beyond the boundaries of Britain's borders was present in several of our research encounters with families, as we discussed briefly in our introduction to this book.

4

Childhood in the shadows

If the labour and love of motherhood is viewed as a source of value in the face of unrelenting interpersonal and state violence, where does that leave childhood? Children in families with NRPF may be loved and cared about, but they also occupy an ambiguous position in policy, welfare contexts and in families. They are simultaneously the object of state interventions, their presence offers potential access to support and their unique status promises a route to settlement and even citizenship and belonging. How do children in families with NRPF grapple with familial desires and societal imperatives that they embody hopes and dreams for the future (Rosen and Suissa, 2020), and thereby give the difficult present meaning? What sort of life-making labour is called for in the context of childhoods' ambiguities and NRPF's enforced destitution? Taking forward the analytic of weathering we have been developing so far, we argue that children are not just emblematic of familial dreams but are co-participants in their families' present-day life-making practices. Yet this is often obscured when advocacy and support are framed within exceptionalist narratives of the iconic child-in-need.

In some ways, we can understand 'child-in-need' as a redundant term. In the UK (as elsewhere), childhood is often imagined as essentially, and even fully, encompassed by the notion of need. This term condenses a host of meanings about dependence, helplessness, inability to provide for oneself, deservingness of support and pan-cultural requirements for survival and flourishing 'as if they were intrinsic qualities of children's own psychological make-up' (Woodhead, 2015: 64). But there is a more specific way in which this iconic figure inhabits the lives of families with NRPF. The only way these families can potentially access support from the local state is through Section 17 of the Children's Act, which is activated if families or their advocates successfully make the case that a child is 'in need'.[1] The figure of the 'child-in-need' not only shapes the terms for presenting families' requests for support from local authorities, but the 'child-in-need' has become one of the primary discursive frames for analysing, critiquing and contesting the imposition of NRPF (Benton et al., 2022; Dexter et al., 2016;

Jolly et al., 2022). One problem with the child-in-need formulation offered by the state is that it exceptionalises the child as *the* subject deserving of protection and support, regardless of whether that support materialises, effectively justifying its abandonment of adults (Rosen and Dickson, 2024). But a child-in-need frame also serves as 'a powerful rhetorical device' more broadly, entrenching 'protectionist adult–child relationships in which adults are dominant providers and children are passive consumers' (Woodhead, 2015: 66–67). In so doing, the 'child-in-need' framework advances particularised notions of childhood and forms of care (typically middle-class and Euro-American) as universal prescriptions, while pathologising others. This is evident in the suggestion that migrant children are 'adultified' when they take on ostensibly 'adult roles' (Burton, 2007) or that migration leads to a 'role reversal' that is 'linked to parents' general inability to function in the new culture and environment' (Puig, 2002: 88).

In contrast, by paying close attention to the practices and narratives of our young interlocutors, here we explore their efforts at withstanding, contributing and fortifying as part of their commitment to family survival in the shadow of the UK's welfare state. Our young interlocutors were clear that reproductive labour undertaken by children is possible, important and even valued morally, not simply an aberration caused by the extreme conditions of NRPF. Indeed, the practical and emotional labour shared between mothers and children is essential, but – from children's perspectives – it also often represents a shared family project for weathering NRPF and constructing homeplace. In this sense, the stories we share in this chapter may seem to contradict those in the previous, where many of the mothers' narratives reverberated with what we have referred to as a form of 'radical aloneness'. As we go on to discuss, the socio-political positioning of childhood is different than that of adults, helping to explain why many of our young interlocutors may have had distinct perspectives from their mothers. Their narratives spoke to a feeling of common cause *with* those in their family – a form of togetherness in the face of enforced destitution. Yet, as we go on to show, the determination to collectively forge meaningful lives is never straightforward nor assured. It is fragmented by the violence of welfare bordering, but also by the ways that mothers and children are both connected and split by their generational locations (Rosen and Newberry, 2018) and their differential positioning vis-à-vis the nation state.

Life-making practices of childhood under NRPF

As we have already seen in Chapter 2, Miriam and Luke were intimately involved in their family's everyday life-making practices. Miriam was an active and necessary partner to her mother Serwah in the ongoing and intricate process of removing water from a kitchen sink that would not drain, carrying buckets of sink water to the toilet, and enabling Serwah to wash the dishes without flooding the kitchen. Luke and Miriam carried, cuddled and engaged with their baby brother Joshua, ensuring that Serwah could prepare the meals or the other could complete their homework. Participation in the often messy, typically intensive, sometimes fulfilling, but always necessary, task of sustaining life, was commonplace among our young interlocutors.

Sam was 8 years old when we met him and had been in London all his life, living with his mother Samantha, who is from Nigeria. The two spent a lot of time together and seemed very close. In our conversations, they constantly reminded each other of shared memories, told stories in tandem and laughed as they chose matching pseudonyms – examples of nurturing 'homeplace' (hooks, 2014) as we suggested when we first introduced Samantha in Chapter 2. They were undocumented when we met them but had recently been able to secure local authority support which included the provision of a small, two-bedroom house. Although they showed us the house with evident pleasure, they had initially been reluctant to accept it. The house was outside of London where they had been living, Sam had been going to school and all their carefully nurtured social networks were located. As they displayed their home with pride, it became evident that they had never had somewhere like this to live before and had never previously been able to invite people round. Things had been very difficult for many years, Samantha explained, but had eased up a bit now that they were receiving support from the local authority and living in a quiet house, despite its extended distance from everyone and everything they knew. In their old home, Sam was often kept awake well into the night by loud drumming and building works, but they had been unable to move until now.

Sam pointed out the hoover he used to clean his bedroom and explained his daily routine which involved tidying up his room and making his bed. He needed new chores, he commented, explaining 'on the old house we … I washed the dishes and … now that chore is gone for me, right mummy?' Samantha explained that the kitchen tap sprayed water everywhere, making it difficult for Sam to use properly and agreed that they needed to find other things for Sam to do in the new house. Although their interaction took the form of a discussion and mutual agreement, Sam's distancing from the change in chores using the passive voice, commenting that dishwashing was 'gone' for him, nods to ways that the two were differently positioned in relation to decision-making about the labour of life which – despite being infused with love and care – does not evade adult–child power relations as they articulate in neoliberal capitalism.

As critical childhood studies scholars point out, in the contemporary period, children, as a social group are largely positioned as 'human becomings' rather than human beings (Qvortrup, 2009). Characteristics such as dependency, irrationality and immaturity are assumed as essential and universal characteristics, read off the young body through frameworks of age and developmental stages. Positioning children in a zone of non-being has been used to justify paternalistic interventions to induce maturity (Rollo, 2016), violence enacted in the name of protection (Mills and Lefrançois, 2018; Rosen et al., 2021), expulsion from decision-making and enfranchisement (Wall, 2021), and objectification. In saying this, we point to general trends in the positioning of children rather than suggesting that this is what the individual mothers we engaged with thought or did. Our point is a more general one: family projects of common cause or homeplace are not void of power relations, be this of gender, status or – as we suggest here – generation.

That said, a sense of the household as requiring the labour of all its members pervaded families' narratives and practices. The expectation of many of the mothers in practice was that children could and should contribute, albeit that such expectations were differentiated between families, the age of the child(ren) and in relation to the task at hand. Serwah, for example, expected Miriam and Luke to help with cleaning, caring for younger children and – of course – draining the sink that would not drain. Cooking, on the other hand, was viewed as Serwah's role, linked to the perceived capacities of adulthood. Most of our young interlocutors embraced this sense of the necessity and indeed the importance of their role in the effort of sustaining life. Many found this labour rather unremarkable, only elaborating on their involvement in cooking, cleaning and caring when explicitly asked to do so. In many ways, this marks a clear distinction from dominant idealisations of contemporary childhood in the UK as a time of precious dependence where children's active engagement in household activities for the family is typically viewed as unusual or extraordinary, especially when they are younger. This is not to say that children do not participate in household life, so much as the way that 'good childhood' is hegemonically imagined and represented. But in West Africa, where the vast majority of the mothers we spoke with came from, children's participation in life's work is not only more common, but it is often viewed as central to 'good childhood', where respect for elders and contributions to the household are viewed as acts of reciprocity for the 'strenuous' provision of financial and other resources and 'vigilant' care and socialisation emblematic of 'good' parenthood' (Twum-Danso Imoh, 2022). This is not to reduce what happens in households with NRPF to simplistic cultural explanations, however, but to point out that ideas about 'good childhood' are culturally and socially produced and, in this case, butt up awkwardly against the 'needy child' of neoliberal welfare policy and the openings it can produce for families otherwise bordered from its protections.

Where children did remark upon their reproductive labour, it was in relation to more intense, unusual or extreme moments, rather than the banal every day. For example, Shanice spoke extensively about the latest move she and her mother Jessica had made to a room on the fourth floor of the large, multi-occupancy house with the deep bathtub where Jessica would do her laundry. Shanice explained that she had lived with her mother in single rooms in a series of houses 'literally as long as I've been able to remember, like, we've always shared the same room together, even sometimes the same bed'. She described being shown the bigger fourth floor room and saying, 'Let's go right now because, you know, I want to get to this room as soon as possible. I started moving the stuff at, like, 11 and we finished at, like, 7pm.' The long hours it took to move multiple and often heavy items up three flights of stairs, including her mom's 'load of stuff' kept safely to send to 'her [other] children back home in Ghana', were the material of Shanice's rich account of the move. 'When I'd finished, my back, my back felt like someone had stepped on it. My back was so … I was in pain, stuff like that. Like, yeah, it was horrible, but … I wasn't angry about it, but it was just too much, you know.' Less remarked upon, however, was that this move was one of many she had contributed to during her sixteen years of life, a byproduct of their precarious immigration status.

Children's gender seemed to matter less than age in determining tasks or responsibility for reproductive labour, with older children typically expected to take a greater role in caring for their siblings or contributing to the household. In many ways, a highly gendered division of tasks would simply have been impossible, given that families' destitution meant that the labour of daily life was intensive and extensive. Weathering grinding poverty and precarious immigration status meant that even small tasks required careful calculation and demanding labour, with no possibility to outsource to others and limited means to mechanise tasks. The possibility to share tasks among only female family members was also curtailed by family structures, particularly in the case of several families where the children were all boys. The division of reproductive labour may have also related to shifting ideas about gender. For instance, as 16-year-old Mobo spoke passionately about learning to cook from his Nigerian mother, he explained that his parents were 'liberal'. His mother 'was the one that introduced me' to cooking as he helped her in the kitchen. Mobo continued:

> It's kind of funny because like, I'm not the oldest, but it was like, I've been in the kitchen more than my older brother. Also, it's like, I feel because obviously

traditionally, it will be like, expected that oh, if you have like, a girl, then the girls will be in the kitchen. But I feel like because it's all boys, and that's kind of changed. Even like, the way my mum will see things and all of that. She just feels that everyone should know how to cook. And that's, she's always said she just feels like everyone should know how to cook. Like, it's not a thing to do whether you're a boy or a girl.

Should we understand the 'un-gendering' of reproductive labour as a reflection of the concatenation of women-and-children into a singular unit in contexts of welfare bordering, wherein both are infantalised and their relations to each other and reproductive labour are naturalised (Rosen and Newberry, 2018)? For instance, Olga Nieuwenhuys (2020: 131–132) reminds us that 'a majority of women and children' inhabit the 'global womb' engaged in 'producing abundant life for free'. Nieuwenhuys writes about the ways that labour in the Global South supplies life to the North, which we complicate here through attention to the lives of postcolonial subjects living in the shadows in the Global North. While highlighting the importance of attending to the intersections of gender and generation, she focuses primarily on girls who – in her account – seem to bear the greatest burden of reproductive labour in the global womb as both child and incipient woman. Can we understand from Mobo's account something akin to a temporary reprieve of the gendered burden of reproductive labour in the Global North, at least among children, and birthed by necessity? Certainly, as we wrote about in previous chapters, it was largely mothers who stayed with children in single-parent families. Or might we see this as productive of deeper, potentially long-standing, shifts in gendered social orders? Regardless of our answers to these questions, they highlight the importance of giving due attention to generation – understood here as the everyday and structural processes which create the relational and historical possibilities for what a child (or youth or adult) is imagined, allowed and required to be. Childhood and the socio-political positioning of children vis-à-vis adults has been largely missed until now in theorisations of stratified social reproduction (Rosen, 2023).

(Re)producing labour power

While mothers often balanced the exhausting reproductive labour of the household with some form of paid labour, be this Serwah's weekend shifts in social care or Rita's informal waged reproductive work for members of her church, children all combined their familial labour with schoolwork. School attendance is compulsory in England, with families risking fines for non-attendance. But children did not attend under threat of penalty as much as because school was generally viewed by families as an important commitment to their collective futures. As we heard in Chapter 2, Serwah advised Miriam and Luke over and over 'finish school, get a good job,' and Miriam took up the challenge in an effort 'to do her proud'. Regardless of how children individually felt about their experiences of school, we never heard it dismissed as unimportant or not valuable. Commitment to schooling is often so strong that, when families are moved out of their local area as a condition of receiving housing support, they travel back, often for long hours, on a daily basis in order to maintain continuity. As Samantha explained, they had been living in Southeast London and were moved to a different county (Kent), but she had initially continued taking Sam to his original school despite the hardship it produced: 'That was costing a lot of money. It was physically and mentally draining. I was starting to feel the effects physically.'

While valued by families, at the same time, we recognise that schooling represents a key modality of late capitalist reproduction of labour power. As a site where students labour alongside teachers in the development of their skills, knowledge, capacities and subjectivities, schools are productive, among other things, of citizen-cum-workers (Newberry and Rosen, 2020; Rosen and Newberry, 2018) and, we might add, their constitutive outside. In this sense, children's social reproduction in schools enhances labour power *quality*, thereby allowing a more concentrated workforce, one of the contemporary techniques mobilised by capital in its quest for profit (Rikowski, 2003), albeit that there is often a 'temporal lag' before it is appropriated (Rosen and Newberry, 2018). At the same time, schools are productive of stratified bodies, including those whom Gargi Bhattacharyya (2018) might refer to as the 'edge populations' of racial capitalism, a less dehumanising way of representing those deemed 'surplus', 'disposable' or 'reserve labour' on capital's terms.

It is possible to see how the production of edge populations via the schooled reproduction of labour power may trace its roots to the ways that dreams of the future are deeply raced, classed and gendered (Rosen and Suissa, 2020). Among the families we spoke to, even anticipatory imaginaries were constrained by the futures children could project themselves into. Mobo's older brother Kevin, for example, spoke about striving to achieve good grades necessary for university entrance at the same time as asserting that he preferred 'learning by doing'. Grappling with the awareness that not 'having a passport' meant he would have to pay international fees to attend university, Kevin made peace with his decision to do an apprenticeship in the finance sector rather than applying to university. The latter ultimately remained outside his imaginary, with NRPF haunting possible futures. Many of the girls we spoke to dreamed about being able to work in waged reproductive labour like their mothers, albeit in more formal sectors. Miriam fantasised about fulfilling her mother's dream and becoming a nurse, while Shanice described wanting to work in health and social care. Although these dreams were articulated decades after Bev Skeggs's (1997) seminal study *Formations of Class and Gender*, they are reminiscent of her compelling exploration of the ways that working-class girls' striving for moral value and secure incomes led them into one of the only sectors available to them: the respectable, but low-wage, and highly physically and emotionally demanding, care industry.

In a sense, then, waged work acquired a redemptive tint for these families, despite – or perhaps because – mothers with NRPF are largely denied the right to paid work due to their immigration status or are excluded from childcare services that might enable them to take on paid work while raising young children. While destitute mothers with NRPF may occupy an edge terrain, perennially excluded from exploitation as waged workers, instead trapped in the informal spaces of unfree labour or casualised surplus, or even relegated solely to serve capital as consumers (Bhattacharyya, 2018), the same – it was hoped – was not true for their children. For example, in response to his request to buy 'piggy points' for a video game, Samantha told Sam: 'If you want it, work for it. So, find a job. I'll give you a chore in the house that you do and then you can earn that 90p.' The logic here seemed to be that while Sam's participation in the everyday activities of life's work – such as vacuuming, bed making and dishwashing – were to be expected as part of his unremunerated contributions to family life, 'luxuries' had to be worked for, with 'work' standing for paid labour. We see something of adult–child power relations at play here, with Samantha determining what constituted luxuries and what, in contrast, were things which made life and made it meaningful. In some ways, this is reminiscent of the way that social services proscribe allowable spending for those applying for or receiving Section 17 support, reviewing mothers' expenditure to ensure that it is only used for what they consider to be necessities. At the same time, we hear Samantha's valorisation of wage labour as a route to self-determination, even though – or perhaps because – she herself was not allowed to work and had to rely on the local state for support. Incorporation into the stratified wage economy of racial capitalism via the next generation remained a practical strategy for weathering the effects of NRPF and an idealised imaginary of the future.

It would be too simple, however, to view dreams of the future as passing smoothly from mother to child, generation to generation, or the result of the psychic limits of an individual's imaginary. The future and its possibilities are profoundly rooted in the material inequities of the present.

Like the intensive labour of the household demanded by 'destitution economies' (Coddington et al., 2020), children's reproductive labour in the context of schooling is deeply stratified. Not all schools, nor children, have access to the same infrastructures or supports to reproduce labour power. In England, students attending schools with the greatest proportion of disadvantaged children face the largest constriction on funding. Budget cuts and increasing costs meant that spending fell by 12 per cent between 2010 and 2021 in these schools, compared with 5 per cent in schools in the most affluent areas (Drayton et al., 2023). Further, inadequate housing does not just mean that practices of sustenance and replenishment become so tough as to be virtually impossible, but it impedes and incumbers schoolwork, as Isaac pointed out.

Isaac was 13 years old when we met him. He lived with his mother Destiny who was from Nigeria. Destiny had Limited Leave to Remain with NRPF but had managed to obtain support from social services due to their destitution. When asked to rank a series of points including housing, immigration status, respect, family and friends in terms of their importance, Isaac was clear that 'number one [is] to have somewhere to live' because of his desire for 'somewhere I could study properly'. He explained that 'doing my homework is kind of a mess since, like, I can't, like, really organise myself. That I have to do everything like in one like small, cramped space. And considering that um, my mum was here as well …' Their small, shared room in a hostel sat under the sloping eaves of the roof. With the blackout curtain closed and laundry hanging on the walls, because 'especially in this COVID, you don't just leave your things around', Destiny explained, the room felt particularly small and claustrophobic. It was filled with their two single beds and a protruding wardrobe containing all their possessions. At the end of the small room was a shelf with food and a fridge that Destiny had purchased to keep their provisions safe and clean – something not guaranteed in the hostel's shared kitchen. A small TV sat on top of the fridge facing the bed. 'I can't really concentrate,' Isaac continued, 'Because she's, it's not that she's noisy. It's just that she has calls to take and going downstairs trying to do my homework is also a pain because there's 8-year-old children like running around and making a lot of noise.'

Isaac's experiences mirror those of many of the children we talked to, who spoke about the ways in which precarious and inadequate housing and enforced destitution impacted their schooling. Miriam spoke about struggling to complete schoolwork on the family's mobile phone – a situation intensified by the Covid pandemic and rise in home schooling and online learning: 'I do maths sometimes and I do research. And I can't always use the phone for that. I need a big screen and I don't have that … So, it's quite hard.' Like Isaac, Shanice longed for her own space, explaining,

If you're constantly sharing a room with someone, you can't get time to always be yourself and just do what you want to do because we're both different people and we both move at different paces ... Being by myself just means a lot. Like, it means a lot to me just to have my own time to reflect ... And it's not like I can't do that with my mum in the room, but, you know, it's a different sort of vibe I feel when I'm doing it by myself.

What we see in these children's experiences is akin to what Coddington et al. (2020: 1428) describe as part and parcel of destitution economies: 'destitute migrants ... face expectations of behaving as eventual citizens even as they are stripped of the ability to do so'. But we also see the way that life in close, confined spaces can cause stresses in families' fragile projects of everyday existence, and this is compounded by competing demands on mothers and children – on children to go to school and mothers to care for their children financially, practically and emotionally, including to enable their school attendance. In this sense, children's life-making practices under enforced destitution are affected in both immediate and long-term ways. Their production of anticipatory labour power in schooling is shaped by their experiences as well as social expectations and the limits surrounding life as an edge population. At the same time, children weather NRPF through acts of sustenance, replenishment and fortification of everyday family life. Their efforts in school reproduce labour power potential in the form of skills, capacities and subjectivities necessary for making lives in the present, not just as future workers or for capital, and this includes navigating British bureaucracy.

Navigating bureaucracies

It was not unusual, especially for older children, to be involved in negotiating institutional bureaucracies on their family's behalf. We caught glimpses of this as Miriam often answered the mobile phone for the family, arranging the research activity and coordinating between us and her mother. As we got to know the family, it became clear that this was because Serwah was not comfortable using digital technology like email. Yet many processes involved with navigating state bureaucracies from immigration to welfare, and indeed communication with advocates, is done online. Children often stepped in to act as technical, and therefore administrative, intermediaries for their mothers. For example, when Eve explained the research to Shanice and her mother Jessica, Shanice provided Eve with their full address, and they asked for all the documents to be sent to Shanice. All documents they received, no matter from whom, went through her phone, Shanice explained. 'It's a bit annoying, but it's ok.'

Children's labour to navigate bureaucracies may have had to do with their mothers' comfort levels with English, and this was the case particularly with Jessica who seemed more fluent in Twi. When children who speak the dominant language better than parents act as linguistic and cultural translators, this is often termed 'language brokering'. The term 'brokering' speaks to the complex decision-making that takes place in the act of translation: this is not simply about words, but contexts, cultural assumptions and navigating intimate information and even interpersonal conflicts as a deeply involved translator (Crafter and Iqbal, 2021; Reynolds and Orellana, 2009). In the families that we met, however, children's labouring seemed to be less about differentiated linguistic proficiency, not least because the mothers were English speakers from Britain's former colonies. Instead, children's labour seemed to be about navigating the technology necessary for engaging with the British state and about interpreting the demands of its bureaucracy. At one point during a research activity, for example, Jessica requested: 'Here, Eve, come tell Shanice and she will explain it to me.' Shanice came over, and evidently familiar with the process of supporting Jessica to make sense of institutional guidelines, listened to Eve repeat what she had been telling Jessica about the 'right to withdraw' from research before reiterating it back to her mum, in English. Isaac, for his part, did not present himself as currently playing such a role so much as indicating it was something he aspired to do. Speaking admiringly about his friends, also in families with precarious migration status, he explained, 'They also like help their parents when they don't understand things as well. And, it's like somebody I want to be. I want to be like someone who helps other people when they don't kind of really understand like, uh, what to do.'

Although we only glimpsed children's interventions in institutional processes like this in fleeting moments, we had the sense that many were familiar with translating between bureaucratic regimes embedded in the UK's neoliberal welfare state and their mothers, who remained largely excluded and in its shadows. We suspect that the specificities of schooled reproduction of labour power afforded children a particular set of resources for forging their way through British bureaucracy which their mothers may not have had due to their extreme marginalisation. This immediate enaction of schooled labour power seemed quite central to their family's sustenance and survival in precarious circumstances, and certainly navigating state bureaucracies was pivotal for weathering welfare bordering. Yet this was profoundly constrained by the stratifying circumstances of schooling in which labour power was (re)produced and the complexities of adult–child power relations within the family but also with the frontline workers they encountered (Reynolds and Orellana, 2009).

In an absurd twist, however, children's contact with institutional bureaucracies often stopped at the point families were in contact with social services, despite the impetus for potential support under Section 17 of the Children's Act 1989 being a 'child-in-need'. As Mobo explained, 'I haven't directly [had contact with Social Services], but I know my mum has and, obviously, she shared her experience. We've become quite close.' Mobo was born in Nigeria, but had been living with his mum, Martha, and three brothers for seven years in the UK. The family was undocumented and got by with a patchwork of support from their extended relations. The four children and their mother shared a single room in their cousin's house, while an auntie paid for telephone and lunch fees for the children. Members of their church provided them with foodstuffs, and friends from 'back home' sent Martha clothes. It was during the lockdowns of the Covid pandemic when the family hit an unmanageable crisis point. Their strategies to sustain themselves and weather NRPF began to flounder as precariously positioned members of their support network also began to struggle. Having heard that charities might be able to help, Martha made the decision to approach one and was in the process of applying for support under Section 17 with the charity's help. However, despite being framed as determining support for children-in-need, Section 17 assessments often take on a punitive and racialised tenor, emphasising potential fraud or inadequacies on the part of the parent rather than direct contact with children. This was the case for Martha, Mobo and her other sons, echoing the experiences of other children in families with NRPF where the credibility of the parent takes precedence (Dickson, 2019; Dickson and Rosen, 2023).

Reparative work

Mobo's words 'we've become quite close' gesture to his deep grasp of his mother's struggles and the state violence she was enduring. A similar awareness permeated our encounters with other children. Miriam and Luke's shared narrative of wanting to make Serwah 'proud' because 'she's struggled a lot for us', which we introduced in Chapter 2, is given significance by Miriam's imperative question to Eve when they first spoke: 'How ... how can we help my mum? ... She really struggles. ... I worry that we don't have enough money ... for food and stuff.' Shanice similarly spoke about doing well in school to offset the struggles her mum had faced:

> Doing well in my exams means so much because it would make, it would not only make me happy, but also my family, um, especially as I've only got my

mum. ... I see the way that she always is, like, struggling and working, like, twenty-four hours a day, like, you know. And to, kind of, like, share that joy with her.

Meanwhile Kevin talked about his efforts to achieve financial stability, motivated by a dream of helping his mother by providing for his severely disabled brother. We can see in these narratives children's efforts to embody the high-stakes hopes for the family future which condense in mother's stories about their sacrifices and struggles for their children, a difficult if willing take-up of an intergenerational family project of weathering present-day hardship through anticipatory action. Yet this is a fundamentally fragile dream, rarely able to escape the grinding violence of enforced destitution, the wearing burden of racialised debt and the wearying pressures of state exclusions constantly emphasising these families' unbelonging.

Gargi Bhattacharyya (2018: 44) reminds us that affective burdens of welfare bordering are not confined to futures: 'The degradations and depletions of racial capitalism require someone else to remake undervalued bodies and to soothe broken psyches' in the here and now. This resonates with Black feminist literature which presses against critiques that reduce family, understood broadly in terms of kinship, to sites of capitalist exploitation and co-option. This literature highlights the importance of family as a potential site of sustenance and regeneration in the face of capitalist alienation and the violence of state racism. In this light, we are probably more accustomed to thinking about the labour of repair as that done by mothers for children, or women for their partners. But who soothes those single mothers whose experiences of radical aloneness we elaborated in the previous chapter? Maybe an old riddle can offer some clues: 'When the child is taken in for an operation, the doctor says: "I cannot do the surgery because this is my son." How is this possible?' The enigma here, of course, is that the surgeon is a woman and the boy's mother. This simple answer is a possibility rendered sufficiently unthinkable by gendered imaginaries that the riddle has continued to puzzle multiple generations. Likewise, although less familiar and dare we say less imaginable, is the emotional labour of healing depletion caused by welfare bordering that is accomplished by children, and not simply as symbols of future redemption.

As we described in the previous chapter, Rita performed her narrative interview in a very dramatic way – using dynamic gestures, altering her voice according to what she was describing and sometimes treating Eve as the other person in the story. She paused after very heavy disclosures, as though to allow the heaviness to permeate and settle. Her trail of talk was punctuated only by occasional laughter or tears and to display the physical signs of abuse she had endured. But it also shifted when her son John intervened.

John was 3 years old at the time. He was present during the interview, watching TV and playing with toy cars nearby. He interrupted Rita's narrative a few times, always impishly, grinning and sometimes pretending to hide – a game he and Rita had laughingly played earlier in the day.

We suspect that John's presence might typically be read as a failure of protection, his mother subjecting him to accounts of horrific violence well before he was 'prepared' developmentally to receive them. But John, like the other children we met, lived the violent effects of enforced destitution regardless of whether this was spoken about. Even in those families where mothers endeavoured to keep their stories of hardship away from children, these secrets were impossible to completely maintain in the close and labour intensive life-making practices compelled by NRPF, even if such silences were viewed as desirable (something we discuss further in Chapter 5). John's interventions might also be read as evidence of the egoism of childhood, demonstrative of a lack of awareness of Rita's grief and struggles. But we suggest that there is something very different to be intuited from John's responses to the painful intensity of Rita's account.

The effects of John's interventions were that Rita paused her account and took a breath before moving on. This seemed to provide a temporary lightening of a moment permeated by the heaviness of the narrative. The interventions brought John's love and care for Rita to the fore, and likewise hers for him, as well as operating as a reminder that Rita's dreams for better futures were embodied by her sons. Do we know that John's actions were born from the act of attending to Rita's discontent and or that his intention was to soothe her psychic distress? No. But we can see the effects of his actions, which in any human interaction is really all we can know for sure. Some mothers even commented on their children's comprehension of the family's situation and their efforts at soothing and repairing. In a context where mothers bore heavy responsibilities but had limited to no options for achieving the unmeetable demands of intensive motherhood (Rosen and Faircloth, 2020), the relief of such reassurance and reparation was crucial. For example, commenting about her son Isaac, Destiny reflected, 'When he was, 12 plus, he was like, mommy, I can take care of myself, don't worry. So, that make me better. He really understands what is going on and was able to cope with it, so.'

We also know from the children who verbally articulated their own accounts that they had a deep understanding of their mothers' struggles and an attentiveness to their distress and sacrifices, as exemplified by Miriam's question: 'How ... how can we help my mum? ... She really struggles.' Children's efforts in the process of weathering NRPF were not simply anticipatory embodiments or practical reproductive labour but can be seen as emotional care and 'soothing broken psyches'. Mobo's comments encourage us to see reparative work as simultaneously about regeneration and replenishment:

> Something that really helps me ... [are] things that I do to help others. I feel like the most people surrounding me that need help with are probably like, my young brother and like, Mum. Obviously, like, being by herself and having to do things by herself ... So, I feel like I do, I do try to help my mum a lot, and I do help my little brother. It's just little things. Like, obviously like, I've learnt to cook so that if she's obviously been cooking and doing stuff, I'll just like say oh, I'll help. I'll make whatever. Or like, I don't even know. It's just like little things that make her feel ... There was one time. It was like, her birthday. I bought her flowers. It's just like little things like that. I think that it just makes a difference ...

Mobo's reference to his mother's need for help is not just an abstract comment on people's essential interdependence and therefore necessary reliance on others for care and sustenance, a point well elaborated by feminist ethicists of care (Tronto, 2011). Mobo's comment speaks to the very specific conditions in which this sustenance occurs, namely the deep and enduring depletions caused by the extensive and intensive labour demanded of single mothers in the face of welfare bordering. Mobo marked a difference between himself and other young people who may not have to undertake such efforts, commenting that it 'kind of prepares you for the reality of the world earlier than probably like, other people', at the same time as asserting its importance. His positive reference to his efforts for his mother and brother offer a glimpse of the value placed on his labour for both them *and* him, regardless of any difficulties it may have caused. This allows us to suggest that children in families with NRPF do not just engage in the emotional and practical labour of making lives because they have to, but that it potentially offers them a sense of meaning and value as protagonists in family projects, fragile and depleting as they may be in the context of enforced destitution. It also serves as an important reminder that we seek to keep in play with the concept of weathering: that fundamental duality of reproductive labour where depletion and regeneration coexist, marked by the effort of wearing, fortifying and sustaining on an unequal terrain with stratified outcomes.

And yet ... If the reproductive labour of women is masked by persistent associations with natural and essentialised characteristics or euphemised as a labour of love, even when it takes the form of exploited wage labour, children's reproductive labour tends to be erased altogether. The caring labour that the children we met narrated and practised often goes unnoticed in much of the literature and advocacy which rely on ideas of passive 'children-in-need' for their potency. We return to the famous riddle and the unimaginability of children's reproductive labour. For despite decades of effort to evacuate reproductive labour from obscurity and point to its centrality to both life and capital, here the protagonists of such labour are erased simply because they are children – essentialised as fundamentally dependent, immature and even burdensome. Perhaps more surprising, though, children's attentiveness and emotional endeavours are not narrativised by mothers as breaking the sense of the radical aloneness we described in Chapter 3. How might we account for the evident importance attributed to children in mother's accounts at the same time as observing that children's psychic and practical labour of life-making is nonetheless largely shrouded, even by their most intimate others?

Our sense is that this paradox may occur not only because children positioned their mothers as the protagonist of the family's struggle in keeping with mothers' representations (as we discussed in Chapter 2), but because children often obscured their own practical and emotional labour as a caring response to their mother's travails. We suspect this is part and parcel of their efforts to embody hope to address their mothers' evident and justifiable distress, a form of reassurance that mothers' struggles for the future of their children were worth it. While this may have been a performance of success, in the sense that good futures are hardly guaranteed, it served to fortify many of the families, making the grinding violence enacted by the state more possible to bear. At the same time, however, this also meant that children's own struggles and fears, and experiences of lives of duress, emerged only fleetingly. These did not seem to form part of the collective family narrative or often even to be speakable in the presence of others.

Miriam haltingly explained how hard it was to need something (shoes, clothing, food, a laptop for homework) but to know that asking for it would place immeasurable pressure on Serwah. Repeating 'really' to emphasise the depth of the impact, Miriam continued: "It's really, really hard. It's really difficult for me and Luke especially because she thinks of us first before she does herself. If we want a top, she needs a top too, but she gets it for us as well before she will get it for herself.' She described having to 'manage for now' when 'the only shoes I have is one trainers and that one's broken'. Aware of the burden her request would put on her mother, she described holding off and only asking for a new pair of trainers for Christmas, commenting carefully and quietly 'so hopefully she can get that'. Miriam's efforts to minimise or even curtail demands on Serwah are suggestive of a line of hopeful thought that: 'If I don't ask for something, if I don't make my suffering apparent to my mother, I put less pressure on her when I know she is already dealing with so much.'

Absorbing or containing their own needs can be understood as a form of caring labour children undertook for their mothers and siblings. But this is not to say that mothers did not feel the burden of their children's needs weighing heavily, marking their bodies and psyches. 'Maybe they forgot, or she pretends, I don't know, and asks for something that I can't afford. "I've seen these shoes," something like that,' Serwah commented about Miriam and Luke. Serwah's depiction of her children's requests as an unfair expectation or 'trying to disturb me' suggest a mismatch between children's and mothers' experiences of such discussions. It is possible, however, that both describe different aspects of the situation. Every little request would loom large for mothers as they would have to say 'no', not because they wanted to but because of the conditions of destitution: 'Because you can't afford something for your own children,' Serwah explained. At the same time, children's efforts to minimise demands pervaded their narratives, even if they sometimes 'slipped up' and asked for something. Without income of their own, yet expected to perform as 'eventual citizens', the impossibilities of going without may have simply felt uncontainable at times. For others, the wearying effect of being consigned as an edge population, excluded as children and potentially as future adults, consumption of needed and even high-status items may have felt one of the only routes into 'full humanness' in the context of racial capitalism (Bhattacharyya, 2018). Engaging in reparative work, including through containing one's own desires, was a delicate effort then, made by many of the children we spoke with, appreciated by mothers in some moments and obscured in others – all part of the families' fragile efforts to weather NRPF.

Aid and its refusals

The fact that many children we spoke with were reluctant, or simply did not, share their struggles produces a sort of paradox given that the only potential source of support available from the state was through the figure of the child-in-need. While citizenship is certainly no guarantee of material security or the easy ability to occupy the idealised footsteps of neoliberalism's *homo economicus*, Coddington et al. (2020: 1426) argue that precarious status, which is amplified by the 'enforced destitution' of NRPF, constitutes migrants 'as distinct economic subjects: destitute recipients of aid ... producing value for others through the grinding labor of living in poverty'. Their point is that circuits of capitalist value do not only operate through wage labour, but through the destitution produced by exclusion from wage labour. This exclusion, they suggest, renders destitute migrants dependent not just on the (local) state but on charities and outsourced private providers who in turn rely on migrant destitution for their own existence and enhancement. Indeed, the previous chapters have alluded to the ways that mothers weathered enforced destitution in part through support from charities or local authorities, resonating with Coddington et al.'s formulation of the ways that socio-legal migration categories border welfare provision to produce 'destitute recipients of aid'. For mothers, receipt of aid was often narrated as a turning point, providing some relief to the grinding precarity they were forced to endure, even as it required frustrating and hostile encounters with a punitive state.

The children we spoke with, however, seemed keen to resist incorporation as the subject of aid, despite awareness of their family's situations, or what Miriam referred to more pointedly as the fact that her mother 'really struggles'. Isaac was somewhat of an outlier in this regard, remarkable for his role in obtaining support for Destiny and himself. 'I was worried that we didn't really have food, if I was going to eat the right amount of food or if I was going to starve,' Isaac explained. 'I talked to my Head of Year. she helps us out with food banks or whatever. So we don't have to stress about food.' That Isaac was worried about *starving* certainly serves as an indictment of NRPF. His concern was not, unfortunately, unusual, laying bare the severe impact of enforced destitution. What was unusual was that Isaac was the one who articulated the family's need more publicly, inhabiting the space of the recipient of aid.

In contrast, describing her difficulties doing homework with a broken laptop, Miriam commented, 'I don't really talk to people about my problems. I just keep it to myself', explaining that rather than seeking assistance she did homework in the school's computer room during lunch or on the family's mobile phone. For Shanice, despite the challenges of sharing a series of tiny rooms with her mother for as long as she could remember, it was preferable to act as though 'everything's fine'. Asking for help, she explained, 'makes me feel like I'm really poor', a psychic weight that seemed almost more unbearable than the experience of destitution itself. We hear in these stories less of what Gargi Bhattacharyya (2018: 4) refers to as the 'hope and hustle' of getting by, an endeavour present in many of the mothers' narratives which included informal and casual work combined with a patchwork of thread bare support, including aid. Instead, for the children we spoke with, weathering through social reproduction was more about efforts to fortify fragile family projects and minimise one's own desires – weathering by 'making do'.

Kevin's frustration with having to settle with what is 'thrown at you' perhaps offers a way to understand many of the children's emphatic reluctance to embody the position of aid recipient, regardless of the consequences to themselves. Kevin's metaphor evokes a sense of passivity and lack of control, rendering visible the dehumanising aspects of aid. While destitution economies rest on dependencies, and seek to convert these into economic value, Kevin's exasperation lends weight to the idea that aid does little to address the conditions that have produced suffering and, in contrast, further vulnerabilise (see e.g. Ticktin, 2011; Dadusc and Mudu, 2020). He provides us with an image of having to settle for someone's scraps, positioning the recipient as subordinate and indebted just as the giver is positioned as dominant and a 'good' person through their act of generosity. Although we don't hear any coding of support as an act of 'goodness' in Kevin's comments, many of the other children described wanting to be 'rich' in the future so that they could help people who are struggling with NRPF. Such dreams hint at recognition of injustice in their own situation but also the way that worthiness gets concatenated with 'helping' or 'providing aid', regardless of where the funds come from or the often performative and self-aggrandising aspects of displaying such 'generosity' (Briggs, 2003).

Perhaps, though, this is not enough to explain the children's 'refusal' (Simpson, 2017) – a turning away from the demands of making oneself recognisable as 'in need' by the state and charities. For if this was simply about dehumanisation and self-aggrandisement, the problematic couplet of aid relations, would not the mothers have responded similarly? That many of the children we spoke with were born in the UK or came at an early age may also have shaped their distinctive relation to aid. Being a multi-status family was not just a legal experience, but this seemed to infuse the ways in which (un)belonging was experienced. Mothers often seemed to feel like 'outsiders', hardly surprising in the context of virulent anti-migrant sentiments pervading policy and public discourse in the UK, framing migrants as 'illegal', little more than 'waste' and certainly 'undeserving' of the support ostensibly provided to the tolerated or good citizen. For the children, who felt much more embedded, if only ever partially included, in the UK, the dissonances of being othered as 'destitute migrant recipients of aid' may simply have been overwhelming. Perhaps the position of 'child-in-need' also offered children some room for manoeuvre which mothers did not have given their hyper-responsibilisation. Children's refusals to be positioned as subjects of aid can potentially evade detection and even castigation as acts of 'ungratefulness' given constructions of childhood as a time of non-responsibility. We might also look to the particularities of children's social positioning within their family's life-making project, which was often discursively constructed in anticipatory terms, regardless of their actual, present-day participation in the labour of everyday life. As such, they may not have felt the same pressures as their mothers to seek support from the state or charity representatives to alleviate their family's immediate immiseration.

In rejecting positioning as the subject of aid, in many of the children's narratives we hear an articulation of family as an island apart, separated from those others who 'should not or could not to be told' about the family's struggles. In some ways, this depiction is akin to the sense of radical aloneness we heard from some of the mothers, but for our young interlocutors this was a condition to be endured with kin, echoing hooks' (2014) notion of homeplace. It is perhaps not surprising then that children's relationship to aid had a very different tenor than their mothers, marking the fragility of the practical and psychic project of daily existence under welfare bordering where aid may have been the only means for mothers to secure life itself.

Conclusion

By engaging children as research interlocutors with keen insights about the impacts of precarious migrancy, we have learned about the multiple ways in which they sustain everyday life, develop skills and capacities for the present as well as in anticipation of achieving familial futures, and engage in careful reparative work in the face of the violence of border regimes. These practices and strategies both parallel and are distinct to those of their mothers, most noticeably in relation to aid. Welfare bordering makes this shared practical and emotional labour an essential, valued and yet fragile, family project of common cause.

In pointing to the complex and valued/valuable reproductive labour undertaken by children as they weather NRPF alongside their mothers and siblings, we do not advance the argument that NRPF 'adultifies' children or forces them into types of labour that are 'abnormal' and 'not meant for the young' (as implied by Puig, 2002; Burton, 2007). Instead, we have shown that it is the conditions under which life's work occurs – welfare bordering, adult–child power relations and so forth – which lead it to be stratifying in both accomplishment and outcome, and it is here that the problem lies, regardless of whether the labouring subject is a child or adult. Time and space are implicated in these stratifications of life's labour, as we have hinted at throughout the preceding discussion, and it is to the spaces in which families with NRPF live their lives that we now turn.

Note

1 In the Children's Act 1989, 'need' refers to the inability to achieve a 'reasonable standard of health or development' without support. In practice, however, 'need' is generally equated with destitution as defined by the Immigration and Asylum Act 1999.

5

Secrets and silences

While the chapters in the previous section developed the analytic of weathering as a way to comprehend the making of subjectivities and embodied lives under conditions of welfare bordering, this next set of chapters focuses in on the spatial-temporal shaping of life with NRPF. Taking up the question of space in this chapter, and time in the next, we consider the impossible yet imperative life-making practices occurring under duress.

How do the spatial constraints enforced by NRPF shape the life-making labour of families weathering its effects? In this chapter, we document families' experiences of homelessness, cramped shared accommodation, dependence on the 'hospitality' of friends and strangers, and exploitative private rentals, highlighting in the process the practices they engage to weather these spatial conditions and configurations. We argue that the enforced destitution of welfare bordering compels proximity and fraught intimacy, as well as a sense of dangerous physical closeness, whether because of the potential of sexual violence or ideas of impropriety around mixing of ages and genders.

Conlon and Hiemstra (2017: 1) describe the 'intimate economies of immigration detention' as 'the complex systems of micro and macro relationships that enmesh in the realisation of detention and lived experiences of being detained'. Like immigration detention, enforced destitution produces 'intimate economies' which demand attention at the micro-scale. Examining the microprocesses that make up these intimate economies in this chapter, we discuss the ways in which mothers and children with NRPF use secrets and silences as 'practices under duress'. These secrets and silences manifest in different ways, sometimes taking the form of families concealing their circumstances from non-familial others. But many mothers also seek to contain knowledge of hardship from their children, and some children refrain from articulating how much they do know or their own struggles, as we showed in the last chapter. In the context of enforced proximity, secrets and silences are both a necessity and, at the same time, multi-layered, contradictory, and always already impossible. A mother may voice issues that are seemingly unspeakable across generations when her child is present, while simultaneously maintaining that her child is unaware of their circumstances. In other families, physical proximity might be chastised and monitored, despite the impossibilities of keeping bodies separate or secret in cramped spaces. Secrets and silences, we argue, operate as efforts to weather acute proximity with dignity and to make lives liveable in unbearable circumstances.

Welfare bordering in/as space

We suggestively pose welfare bordering 'as' space here to draw attention to the spatial ways in which NRPF operates within Britain. The NRPF condition borders access to space both externally (at the border) and internally (within the nation). As an internal border, NRPF directly bars access to social housing, housing benefit and other housing-related support (e.g. welfare payments for winter fuel costs). It works alongside other immigration controls that restrict access to housing, such as the right to rent policy, which prohibits those without legal residence from renting accommodation and mandates that landlords must check the immigration status of prospective tenants or face extortionate fines. At the same time, NRPF works as a spatial control in much more insidious ways, hampering the living conditions of families and others who endeavour to make their lives despite the welfare borders they face. Welfare bordering produces a proliferation of scales of spatial control – from the external border to the home. Here, we focus on the intimate scale of spatial control. As a policy through which destitution and debt are *enforced*, NRPF produces homelessness and highly constrained living arrangements, leaving families hyper-responsibilised and forced to rely on fraught and often non-existent informal support.

Martha, who had come to the UK from Nigeria almost a decade ago, was staying with her uncle and cousin when we first met her. She shared one room in their two-bedroom house with her three sons – Kevin (18 years old), Mobo (16 years old) and their brother Tayo (14 years old). The four of them had been sleeping in the same one room together for seven years. Kevin talked of the 'whole family just cramped up in there', describing how some of them had to sleep on the floor. Martha spoke in more detail about the difficulties of this arrangement, explaining that they had no privacy and that she felt it was 'not appropriate' – a sentiment we discuss more as the chapter goes on – but explained that there was nothing she could do. She told us she cooked all the meals for everyone in the house and that her and her children had been staying there rent-free, but the relationships with her uncle and cousin were clearly strained, not least because her cousin's financial situation had changed when he lost his job during the Covid-19 pandemic.

Martha was undocumented and therefore had no right to work, as well as having considerable caring responsibilities for her youngest son, Tayo, who was visually impaired. She and her children had recently approached a charity organisation for assistance, which had referred them to the council for an assessment under Section 17 of the Children Act 1989. In relation to this, Martha described visiting a two-bedroom flat where social services were planning to house her and the children:

> The place is ... not safe for my son ... I was trying to explain to, I think it's the social worker, but he seems not to understand what I'm trying to explain to him ... he felt, I'm an ingrate, that they provided this ... and I'm still staying, you know ... That I have the mouth to say something about the place. ... Not that I'm ungrateful.

Martha's concerns about the size and safety of the property given the needs of her children appeared to be met with hostility by social services. As she went on to explain, the social worker had hung up on her before she was able to say what housing requirements were necessary to meet Tayo's highly specific needs. In this respect, Martha's case illustrates a wider issue, highlighting the ways in which, even with the provision of formal support, families with NRPF often continue to be trapped in confined living spaces for many years (Threipland, 2015). In Martha's case, the unsuitable accommodation on offer from social services prolonged their stay with her uncle and cousin, exacerbating the pressures they were already experiencing as a result of the overcrowding. Martha seemed highly aware of the tensions in the household, appearing to feel that she and her sons had overstayed:

> Yeah, it's been more difficult [since he lost his job]. He just got something now ... And I think ... I don't know, I think he's, um ... He feels he has done so ... He has, um, accommodated us for this long, and, um, that has made him ... I don't know how to ... He needs his life back. I don't know how to put it, you know ... He complains. He's becoming ... I know it's getting to him ... Let's just put it that way.

Martha's sense of the pressure of the housing situation for her cousin was palpable, yet her series of unfinished sentences and her struggle to articulate what was going on ('I don't know how to put it') suggested much remained unsaid. It was as though the silences or ellipses said more than the words themselves – gesturing towards something that was hard to say or could not be verbalised. We could speculate about the omitted content – for instance, why it might have been difficult for Martha to articulate how the relationships within the house were being affected or how the discontent manifested – but we suggest that it may be more fruitful to attend to form here. That is to say, the significance of ellipses. There was something specific, as we saw it, about the way in which silences functioned in such circumstances of enforced proximity, where living conditions were at once impossible and yet had to be weathered. Martha draws our attention to the unsayable. Her speech is rife with gaps, producing a pattern of half-said sentences. These silences say something, we suggest, without saying too much, as we discuss in more detail in the next section.

Other families in our research lived in similarly constrained conditions. Shanice, a 16-year-old living with her mother in a single room in hostel-style accommodation provided by social services, told Eve that her and her mother had always shared the same room, and at times even the same bed. Rita, meanwhile, spoke to us of a harrowing experience of renting a room informally from a landlady who extorted her undocumented tenants for money: 'That woman would not rent for you if you have got paper because she knew you would deal with her. But if you do not have paper, you cannot call the police.' Once Rita had paid her rent, her landlady started sleeping on the chair in the kitchen, telling Rita that she couldn't use the kitchen and that she would have to pay her for meals as well as rent. After eight days, Rita's landlady started banging on her door in the middle of the night and telling her that she and her son Joseph had to leave. The landlady had done this repeatedly, extracting rent and deposits from other tenants who she knew would not call the police for fear of being caught by the Home Office – profiting off her tenants' 'evictability' (van Baar, 2017). Frequent moves – what Watt (2018) has termed 'recurrent displacement' – were also cited by our participants, suggesting that families' lives were continually disrupted by spatial dislocation and precarity, often uprooting them from social networks and support.

Other mothers spoke of times when they were sharing rooms with non-familial others, having to absent themselves during the day to give space and privacy to cohabitants. For those with young children who shared accommodation, the needs of other residents were often constraining, making it hard for children to move around freely. As Ijeoma told us: 'The kids can't play. They can't be kids so that they won't disturb the other family ... Can you just sit down? Can you just minimise play? Can you just stop jumping? ... No. That is not life. That is not life.'

Ijeoma's answering of her own appeals to her children with a resounding 'no' highlights her awareness of the impossibility of what she was asking. While she recognised that, without being able to play, jump and move about, her children couldn't have 'life', she was equally caught by the demands of others with whom they shared their accommodation. These were, as she made clear, irreconcilable needs.

Enforced proximity I: the (un)said and (un)heard

While Martha, Shanice, Rita and Ijeoma describe very different experiences of spatial restriction, they each highlight ways in which welfare bordering operates at a spatial level, producing enforced proximity between family members, as well as between families, extended kin and strangers. These conditions of enforced proximity, our interlocuters intimated, created irresolvable situations in which needs could not be reconciled with material circumstances. What we call 'practices under duress' were ways in which we observed parents and children navigating these impossible conditions intergenerationally. Secrets and silences were two such methods, emerging primarily in relation to what could (not) be said and heard, and, secondly, with respect to bodies and the illicit. We examine the former before discussing the latter, situating the (un)said and (un)heard in three contexts: the relationship between the family and the outside world; relational dynamics between parents and children; and lastly, the research encounter itself.

Abiola was making Eve a cup of tea in the cramped bedsit she and her 10-year-old son Akin shared. They were living on the outskirts of South London. There was nowhere to sit apart from a double bed, which was squashed up against the only window in the room. The wardrobe with broken doors was right up against the bed, so only some parts of it could be accessed. Precariously enclosed within it was a pile of clothes that constantly threatened to fall on the floor. The contents of the room seemed like it was overflowing the limits of the space, with clothes strewn all over the bed and jars of peanuts, crisps and other snacks with nowhere to be put away. There was almost nowhere to store anything, so everything was forced to be on display. At the same time, certain objects, seemingly more prized, were displayed at greater height – Akin's recent school photograph, two football trophies he had won, his school certificate for achievement and a photograph of his elder brother in Nigeria. Images and light flashed rapidly from a TV, which dominated the room and was set to CBBC. Akin sat on the floor with his eyes fixed on the screen. An old freezer emitting an orange light stood opposite the bed, next to a kitchenette in the corner of the other side of the room. A doorframe coming off the main room denoted the bathroom – more a designated area for washing than a separate room – containing a toilet and simple shower. Later, Akin told Eve that a short shower caused the room to flood with water, a source of much discontent for him and his mum – a daily difficulty reminiscent of Miriam and Serwah's efforts to stop the sink from overflowing in Chapter 2.

Abiola asked Akin to put away an iron and a pink towel. It looked as though the towel, which had been sitting on top of the overcrowded shelving unit on the floor, had formed part of a makeshift ironing board.

Akin started putting it away. Then his mum put down a plate of semolina and Nigerian stew on the rug on the floor and gestured to Akin to start eating. (Later, Akin told Eve he would like to sit at a table to eat his meals and do his homework, but that the space was too small for that.) Abiola sat down on the bed next to Eve. She began to talk about how mothers in her situation protect their children from knowing what is going on as much as possible. 'We shield them, we don't want them to know.' She explained that the children don't really understand what is going on. But then she talked about when children ask for things and mothers have to say no. 'Can I sleep at my friend's house?' 'No, because then they will expect you to invite them to sleep here and there is no space for them.' 'Can I go round to my friend's house?' 'No, because then they will expect to come round here and we have no space.' 'Can I have a bike?' 'No, I can't afford it. Even if someone gave us a bike, where would we put it? I cannot have it in this room, no.' 'Can I have my own room?' She said Akin sees what other children in his class get and he doesn't understand why he cannot have the same or why some people have houses and they do not. She said he sees that they are in the same class at school, they speak the same language, they are the same age, but that they live in very different spaces. She described how sometimes she could not get the food Akin wanted because there wasn't enough money. She said it was important that the children don't know what is going on as they would show sadness and the difficulty of the situation to outsiders as they wouldn't be able to hide it. She explained that she smiles all the time for Akin, even when she is feeling bad inside because she doesn't want him to know what is happening to them. As she said all of this, Akin was sitting at her feet. We wondered if he was listening.

A few weeks later, the family received a possession order. They were being evicted by the council. They had been illegally subletting from the actual council tenant and the court had decided they had to leave within the next month. Abiola planned to take the eviction letter to social services, as the social worker had told her that she could not be rehoused without it. She told Eve she'd been feeling bad about it, that she was worried they might be housed far away, which would have a negative impact on Akin. She was really worried Akin would start to feel bad and that it would show at school. When Eve asked if Akin knew what was happening, Abiola told her that he had heard her talking on the phone about it so she had to explain that they would soon be leaving. She told him that they would be getting a better place, where they could each have their own room, which is what he dreamed of.

These two instances highlight what appears to be a complex field of secrets and silences in the context of enforced destitution and proximity. Abiola's desire to 'shield' Akin was something we came across in many of our conversations with mothers, who were often deeply concerned about their children 'knowing' about their situation. But as the description above shows, this was a contradictory and impossible desire. Akin sat at Abiola's feet while she told Eve that mothers in her situation shield their children from the circumstances they are experiencing and that the children don't know what's going on. As we discussed in the Introduction, conversations in the research were led by participants rather than directed by the researcher. Abiola seemed to want to have the conversation in that setting, appearing relaxed and at ease with the juxtaposition of her narrative of shielding and Akin's physical proximity to her. That is to say, this instance seemed part and parcel of the family's everyday life rather than a contradiction that occurred in response to the research – something confirmed by our subsequent observations.

The contradiction here may be partly attributable to dominant imaginaries of children, for example, the child as the historically quintessential 'innocent' subject of Western thought, unknowing and oblivious to social issues, who cannot fully understand what is going on around them or what the adults are talking about (Garlen et al., 2021). Yet we suggest that this would be too simple a reading of the generational dynamic between Abiola and Akin. Abiola, perhaps unconsciously, moves quickly from an imaginary of Akin as oblivious to a depiction of Akin as highly aware of the differences between him and his classmates. Along the way, she calls attention to the mismatch between his own desires (for space, forms of sociability, food and objects) and their predicament, which renders them unrealisable. Even if Akin were not physically present, her speech unravels her own initial representation of her son, as though she knows what she seems to (also) not know. One way of understanding this paradox might be through the psychoanalyst Christopher Bollas's (1987) concept of the 'unthought known', which captures that which is known, often in a very deep sense, but which cannot be consciously thought. Although Akin is certainly aware of their circumstances, and, as Abiola's second conversation with Eve shows, hears his mother's conversations about their situation, Abiola's narrative that he does not know is nonetheless significant. It suggests, perhaps, that even though Akin does 'know' something, the painful truth of that cannot be consciously acknowledged by Abiola. The knowledge that borders produce intimate anxieties for all those in their orbit, including children and young people, may be too much for her to bear.

At the same time, it is important to register the social anxiety contained in Abiola's words, which are laden with concerns about Akin potentially revealing their situation to others. This is the conscious reasoning she gives for why it is important that children don't know what is going on. ('They would show the sadness, the difficulty of the situation. They wouldn't be able to hide it.') Such anxiety is no doubt overdetermined, containing traces of shame, fears of stigmatisation and discrimination, the residual fears of living an undocumented life and concerns about being cast as a 'bad parent'. For the child to know, in this sense, may carry with it an implied failure on the part of the parent to 'protect' (or to 'shield', to use Abiola's word) them, a heavy burden in the context of the UK's protectionist culture around children and the increasing responsibilisation of parents (Rosen and Faircloth, 2020). Not talking to children about traumatic or distressing events is thus often understood by parents as a way of protecting them (Humphreys et al., 2006), as in Abiola's case, which was something echoed by other mothers in our study. Equally, migrant and other socially marginalised parents are often unfairly blamed for the harsh conditions they suffer, as we see in the moralising discourse around welfare and migration (Dickson and Rosen, 2021; Jensen, 2018), as though they have 'chosen' to be undocumented or destitute, rather than these conditions being created by hostile policies. Parents with NRPF commonly encounter this culture of blame directly at the offices of social services, where they may be reproached by social workers for having ('too many') children, seeking support from the state when they 'should' be supporting their children themselves and, where they have the right to work, not working 'enough', despite the constraints of childcare responsibilities (Dickson and Rosen, 2023; Dennler, 2018).

Secrets and silences were traversed by children as well as parents. In the case of Abiola and Akin, our impression was that Akin may also have been navigating what he was and was not supposed to know. During a photo-elicitation interview with Eve, Akin seemed very aware of his mum, conscious that she was listening to what he said. He glanced over at her several times. Abiola, meanwhile, came to sit near Eve and Akin when they were speaking, somewhat hovering over them, and seemed uncomfortable when Eve asked Akin about a photograph he had taken of their housing conditions, or when she asked him about the NRPF condition, although she had consented to Eve asking. At the point that Eve asked if Akin had ever heard of the term 'no recourse to public funds', Abiola knocked over a lamp, perhaps unconsciously attempting to disrupt the possibility of an answer. When Akin did answer, he said, 'I've heard my mum saying it a lot, a lot. I don't know why.' Initially he said that he didn't know what it meant, but then he asked, 'Wait, does it mean that we're not supposed to have money?' Like Abiola, Akin may 'know' and 'not know' at the same time. That is to say, these generational dynamics around familial knowledge are complex and contradictory, operating at both conscious and unconscious levels. Where circumstances were (partially) hidden from children, which was particularly the case with younger children, our sense was that they were still very conscious of their circumstances (see also Dickson, 2019; Rosen and Dickson, 2024), though they may have felt the (un)conscious need to conceal this from their parents. While older children in our research were sometimes involved in supporting parents to navigate bureaucratic and institutional processes, as we saw in the last chapter, younger children we spoke to articulated their knowledge of their circumstances more intuitively, which was sometimes interpreted as a lack of knowledge by mothers. For instance, Samantha was certain that her 8-year-old son Sam 'didn't know anything' about their situation and explained that she felt the research would be helpful in facilitating more direct conversations between her and her son about unequal access to social support – something that echoed the sentiment of other mothers in a previous study in which Eve was involved (Dickson, 2019). Yet, when asked about 'no recourse to public funds', it appeared that Sam knew more than she might have understood. He told Eve he thought it had something to do with 'not being allowed to move houses'. This understanding is intuitive rather than technical, but we suggest that it conveys a deep understanding of the policies which shape Sam's life. His own felt experiences were what he associated with the technical term we introduced, but his suggestion that the NRPF condition was to do with controlling mobility reveals an astute understanding of what the policy means in practice. Such intuitive understandings of the immigration condition were characteristic of mothers as well as children – something the narrative interviews in particular revealed. Yet, as one of our other research projects highlighted, such forms of understanding are typically regarded as inferior within the policy domain, with advocates supporting families often priding themselves on highly technical and bureaucratic knowledge of NRPF and its interaction with welfare legislation.

Although our focus in this chapter is on 'secrets and silences', we should also note that there were varying approaches to how immigration issues were articulated or acknowledged within families. Ijeoma, for example, spoke of praying every morning with her children, explaining that her 6-year-old son Enofe prayed for 'mummy [to] get paper so that we can have our car. We can have our house. We can have garden. We can have a toy.' In this instance, the family's struggle to regularise was openly acknowledged, with a lack of papers being explicitly tied to their unfulfilled desires and needs. Our point, then, is not that secrets and silences were consistent across the families we met, but that the spatial bordering and enforced intimacy of NRPF meant that variegated secrets became a way to navigate the impossible conditions our participants lived.

Indeed, desires and needs were also often subjected to attempted concealment. In some cases, this took a more concrete form – for example, Miriam's postponement of her need for shoes in Chapter 4 – but for other young people it seemed a more generalised relationship to what they were going through. For instance, Shanice described the challenging circumstances in which she and her mother lived, and the difficulties of doing all her online schooling on her mobile phone during the Covid-19 pandemic when schools were closed, as well as speaking at length about the things she wished she could have, such as her own room and her dream of the kind of Christmas her and her mum could have if they had the space and money. But at the same time, she tended to conclude her descriptions with statements that attempted the assertion of a very different narrative, such as 'but we're doing fine', 'everything was good', 'it's ok' and 'we're not really struggling'. These sentences were difficult to know how to respond to – on the one hand, it seemed important to acknowledge the difficult conditions Shanice and her mum were experiencing, but on the other hand, Eve worried that such acknowledgements might contradict Shanice's simultaneous narrative that things were 'fine'. Perhaps these endings represented something of the unbearability of the situation, a kind of quick negation of the feelings and experiences that were being disclosed. They may have been at once for herself (to avoid 'staying with' an all-too painful reality and the feelings it evoked) and for Eve (the interviewer), to thwart the possibility of any response resembling compassion – something, as our discussion of 'Aid and its refusals' in the previous chapter hinted at, some young people in our research may have wanted to foreclose to refuse 'feeling poor' (in Shanice's words) or being treated as such.

Equally, however, such verbal patterns may operate as ways of warding off potential charges of being 'ungrateful'. Both Shanice and her mum Jessica repeatedly emphasised the gratitude they felt for the support they received from social services, despite its evident inadequacy and our attempts to open up conversations around this. They seemed to want to convey that the support was 'fine' and that they were 'grateful' for it, even though at other moments they indirectly acknowledged its serious deficiencies. For example, Jessica, as we saw in Chapter 2, went to great physical efforts to wash their clothes by hand because the cost of a laundrette had not been factored into their subsistence payments from social services, despite the hostel having no washing machine. Shanice spoke of the need she felt to have her own room to experience the possibility of being 'herself'. Yet, if asked directly about the support they were receiving from social services or their experiences of it, their narratives were quite different. Jessica spoke of social services 'doing the best they could do', words echoed by Shanice in a different conversation: 'They're helping us in the best way they can, you know. Me and my mum are doing great, so I'm just, I'm just really thankful to them for that.' Shanice's insistence that her and her mum were 'doing great' was followed directly by her thankfulness to social services, suggesting the two were somewhat intertwined. Such performances of gratitude may represent attempts to fit into dominant social scripts of 'good migrants' (Aparna et al., 2020). In this sense, there may have been a perceived risk, whether conscious or unconscious, that asserting more clearly that their needs were not being met would indict social services, turning Shanice and her mother into 'ungrateful' (Moulin, 2012) and thus 'undeserving' recipients of state support.

Silences, then, may represent careful navigation of precarious terrain, operating as collective practices that attempt to make unbearable realities psychically bearable. Children and parents with NRPF attempt to manage needs and desires rendered impossible by enforced destitution and proximity through the (un)said and (un)heard, endeavouring to hide these from themselves, from each other and, collectively, from the outside world. But as such needs and desires simultaneously burst forth, as we see in moments above, these practices under duress are always revealed as contradictory, confusing and impossible in themselves. Secrets and silences, as we understand them, were not practices that occurred specifically during, or in response to, the research encounter, but were ongoing practices we observed to be part of broader strategies of survival.

Enforced proximity II: bodies and the illicit

Alongside navigation of what could (not) be said or known, families were often contending with fraught physical intimacy. Concerns around the proximity of bodies was a frequent complaint from mothers sharing rooms with their sons, who spoke of the numerous problems such cohabitation created or threatened to create. Abiola, for instance, spoke of the difficulties she and Akin experienced as a result of having to share a bed and room. 'He's 10 years old now, and it's not easy, especially morally for the two of us. [Him] being a boy, and I'm a woman. And I'm trying to dress ... It's so hard.' This worry about the 'morality' of their living arrangements went hand in hand with fears about the psychological impact the lack of privacy might be having on Akin:

> Sometimes I have to give him his own privacy as well. When he wants to dress, sometimes I'll ask him to go to the toilet and dress ... Not every time you have to drop your towel, because I have to let it be in his brain that you can't just be in the midst of people and just drop yourself like that. You have to try and cover yourself up. So, that part is a bit hard for me as well. When he was a baby, yes, he didn't know anything. But now things are in his brain. I can't be exposing myself to him anyhow. And then, it can affect him mentally as well.

Where above we saw Abiola struggle with Akin's desires for his own room – something it was impossible to realise in their circumstances – here we can observe an anxiety about the seeming absence of a desire for privacy on Akin's part as he gets dressed. The lack of physical boundaries between them, Abiola suggests, confuses his understanding of social codes around nudity. She implies that her constant presence in the space – an unavoidable product of their overcrowded and inadequate housing – has normalised the idea that others might be there when Akin gets dressed. Concealing oneself in the context of enforced proximity is difficult for Abiola too, by her own admission ('that part is a bit hard for me as well'). Elaborating on this, she explains:

> Especially when I'm dressing up. That's the worst part. I can't say I'm so perfect that every time I keep to myself. Sometimes, I'll just get up and I'll forget myself, and I'll expose myself to him. It's not as if he's showing me he that he doesn't like it. But I know that morally it's not good for him. He doesn't really like it. And it makes him feel as if he doesn't really experience what children are experiencing. The life children are living. It looks as if he's just tied up in this tiny space in his life. He can't spread anything. I think that's the way he feels.

There is something difficult, it seems, about the way in which bodies get mixed up in such close quarters, perhaps particularly over time, as Abiola's reference to the increasing urgency of the situation as Akin gets older alerts us to. Physical and sexual boundaries become less clear, as the other (parent/child) is always there, close by. Abiola appeared concerned with their shared lack of propriety, as though they were perpetually breaching a moral order through an over-familiarity with one another's bodies. This was intermixed with an implicit but lurking unease around sexual development and thus illicit heterosexual desire, as suggested by Abiola's emphasis on Akin's age and gender, and her tacit reference to his sexual maturity ('When he was a baby, yes, he didn't know anything. But now things are in his brain'). For Abiola, it is these 'things in his brain' that necessitate clearer physical boundaries. Without them, there is a risk that her own physical exposure may become somewhat dangerous, crossing over into the realm of sexual desire. It is this latent anxiety, perhaps, that prompts Abiola to state 'He doesn't really like it', indicating potentially less about what Akin feels (though we are not making any suggestions about that either) and more about what she wishes to be the case. While Abiola's narrative constructs Akin as a sexual subject only at the point that he approaches adolescence, reflecting dominant imaginaries of children's innocence, children's sexual subjectivity – as Ijeoma alerts us to below – begins much earlier (see e.g. Rose, 1984; Freud, 1977; Blaise, 2013). We note this not to make normative claims about nudity and cohabitation within family life, but to point towards one of the ways in which the concerns we encountered were shaped by hegemonic conceptions of childhood sexuality and innocence, at the same time as addressing them in hegemonic modes was a spatial impossibility in the cramped quarters the families were compelled to occupy. Like Akin and Abiola, Destiny and her 13-year-old son Isaac were sharing one room. They were living in a hostel in East London, which was provided by social services after a lengthy battle to prove they were entitled to support. Destiny relayed similar anxieties to Abiola, explaining that as she tried to get ready quickly in the morning, she'd suddenly start 'thinking in my mind, his eyes is open and I'm changing'. She seemed surprised that social services expected them to share one room: 'So I had to tell [the social worker] ... we're trying but at the same time, this is not right for me to sleep with a 13-years boy ... you don't expect me to begin to expose him to what he doesn't know.' The social worker, however, appeared to pass over her concerns, simply telling her that she needed to try and find her own accommodation – something well beyond her means as a part-time relief worker at the hospital. Accommodation arrangements like this contravened statutory definitions of overcrowding contained in the Housing Act 1985, which state that children over 10 of a different sex to other family members should have a separate room to sleep in. While this legislation, at least in theory though often not in practice, determines accommodation standards for social housing, accommodation provided under Section 17 of the Children Act 1989 occupies a much vaguer position in law, and is currently not subject to any minimum standards.

Destiny's remark about the challenges of sharing one room brings us back to the question of what the child does (not) know. Where earlier this arose in relation to children's knowledge of their social conditions, here the perception of lack of knowledge, and its dangerous Other, emerges in relation to the sexual. Bodies and their sexual parts are at once concealed and revealed by mothers – seemingly impossible secrets in the conditions of enforced proximity. While mothers with sons approaching adolescence were particularly troubled by the bodily dimensions of cramped accommodation, fears around the blurring of sexual boundaries also occasionally emerged in other family configurations. Ijeoma, for example, who shared one room with her sons Enofe (6 years old) and Wale (4 years old), told us that 'staying in one room for more than five years is a life I never wish for my enemy'. Their living arrangements brought back traumatic memories of her own childhood, evoking acute anxieties around the dangers of sharing a single space: 'What you think they are not seeing, they are seeing a lot. Because it's right in their face. That's why I don't like one room. I don't want them to grow up in one room. I don't like it because of my experience, what happened between me and my brothers.'

Ijeoma was painfully aware of what children 'see' when people think that they aren't seeing. This is an involuntary kind of seeing ('it's right in their face'), borne of the conditions of destitution. Reminded of her own experiences as a child, when she shared one room with seven other family members in Nigeria, she was fearful of what she felt was an inevitable outcome of 'one room':

> Now, I was always on lookout ... If I'm sleeping, I have to run downstairs to go and see. I believe you're not touching each other. I believe you're not doing this. Because it's one room. It's bound to happen. It happened to me, between me and my brothers when they are sleeping with me.

Here and above, Ijeoma repeatedly emphasises 'one room', drawing our attention to the dangers of the proximity they are forced to endure. Ijeoma's past experiences of sexual trauma were overlayed onto the present, necessitating a practice of hypervigilance to avoid the possibility of generational repetition. This was a torturous present, where the dangerous blurring of sexual boundaries in the form of incest and sexual abuse were a constant threat. In Ijeoma's psychic reality, bodies in the room were therefore to be policed and monitored, continually reminded of what they should not be doing to each other ('I believe you're not touching each other'). Her description of sleeping and seemingly having to compensate for her own lapse in vigilance upon waking ('I have to run downstairs and go and see') shows just how intense a fear this was for Ijeoma, who was haunted by the trauma of her own early experiences. She felt she had to be constantly on high alert. Ijeoma explained that sometimes her sons would ask her, 'why are you saying all this thing', when she'd chastise them and tell them what was 'not allowed' physically. She clearly articulated the origins of the practice: 'Because of where I'm coming from ... I'm trying to protect him.' As we discussed in Chapter 3, some mothers we spoke to, including Ijeoma, were intent on breaking generational cycles of abuse through their own mothering, keenly aware of the harms they had suffered themselves.

It is worth noting that Ijeoma presented a very different picture of childhood than some of the other mothers in this chapter, highly aware of the ways in which children see what is going on around them, experience sexual desire and have early sexual experiences, some of which are abusive. She seemed all too aware of these realities of childhood, which weighed heavily on her and compelled a kind of hypervigilance in her day to day. Ijeoma was intimate with the dangers of enforced proximity – these were not potential threats in her psyche nor latent anxieties, but very present, real happenings. Bodies, in her family, needed to be kept secret from one another through constant policing.

As with Abiola and Destiny, Ijeoma articulated these dangers in terms of the harm they posed to her children. Speaking more generally about their lack of space, she explained: 'Psychologically, you are hurting the child. You are damaging the child without knowing it. The child is going through a lot.' Bearing in mind that Ijeoma and her children's accommodation was provided by social services, we may understand this as an invocation of the very discourse that is meant to guide local authority decision-making around support for families with NRPF. Support for families is, after all, premised on 'the child in need'. Parents, as we repeatedly heard from mothers, were not what mattered in the eyes of the local state. They were more often treated as appendices of their children. Ijeoma's repetition of 'the child', then, may be an attempt to articulate the family's needs in these terms, as well as representing her own sense of needing to protect her children. We heard less about mothers' needs for space and privacy, perhaps for these reasons. Their needs and desires were largely hidden, kept secret, even in their narratives. When Eve prompted Abiola on this point specifically, asking how she felt about not having her own privacy, she said:

> It's hard. Like I said, I feel really sad and I feel like maybe I'm going to affect my son in a way. Him being exposed to what he shouldn't be exposed to ... Mentally, I feel like I hope this will not affect him. I hope it's not going to tell on him in the future or something. And me not having my space, especially when my boyfriend is around, that time, it's so hard.

Abiola's answer focused primarily on the impact of enforced proximity on Akin, demonstrating the ways in which mothers often concealed their own needs and desires around space and privacy. Yet, Abiola's invocation of 'the future' and her worries about the long-term impacts of their living conditions on Akin may also reveal something of the significance of children's futures in mothers' hopes and dreams. Such futures may hold out a redemptive quality for mothers. The small space Abiola gave to her more immediate needs and desires, when she referenced her boyfriend, suggests she may understand these as secondary to Akin's. But what she did say is telling of the ways in which 'one room' renders romantic relationships impossible or constrained, something that posed difficulties for other mothers, even if it remained largely unspoken. For Samantha, the spatial constraints of NRPF were such that they foreclosed romantic relationships entirely: 'Try having a relationship with a child in a bedroom when ... It's affected a lot of things. It's meant I couldn't have a relationship.' In this sense, then, we can see the ways in which borders dictate the possibilities of intimate and sexual life not only through the external border – e.g. by barring entry in the case of racialised transnational marriages and partnerships (Dickson et al., 2023a;

Turner, 2015) – but also by way of welfare bordering, marking romantic relationships as off-limits for those subject to the spatial restrictions of immigration conditions like NRPF.

Conclusion

This chapter has examined how mothers and children use secrets and silences to weather the impossible conditions of enforced proximity. Developing our analytic of weathering, we highlighted how families employ these practices in their efforts to make and sustain meaningful lives with dignity – attempts to withstand the hostile climate that constantly threatens to wear them down. In the context of involuntary intimacy and physical closeness, these are practices under duress, always already contradictory, multi-layered, and impossible. They are attempts to navigate an absolute lack of privacy, manage impossible needs and desires, and counteract the dangerous over-familiarity of bodies. Operating both consciously and unconsciously, mothers and children use these practices to hide these things from themselves, from one another and from the outside world. On the one hand, secrets and silences make possible the ongoing practices of homeplacing within the family that we observed. Yet, on the other hand, secrets and silences set limits on such projects of common cause through their foreclosure of certain intimacies and knowledge, seemingly working simultaneously as potential undercurrents.

Here we have highlighted two key dimensions of enforced proximity: the (un)said and (un)heard, and bodies and the illicit, showing how these unfold across generations, creating a complex field of secrets and silences which are collectively produced. While knowing and seeing tend to be normatively understood as desirable, positive and advantageous traits, this chapter has shown how such characteristics can take on dangerous and problematic qualities in the conditions of enforced destitution, with families cultivating practices of not-knowing and not-seeing to withstand these perceived dangers of life in the shadows. Indeed, occupying the position of the one-who-knows may work against families in other contexts, as we saw in the case of the 2012 changes to the family migration rules in Chapter 1 where parents were constructed as 'gaming' the immigration system, or, as discussed above, with respect to the hyper-responsibilisation of mothers in social services, or more generally vis-à-vis racist assumptions of ignorance (Fanon, 2008).

Within this shadowy field, knowing and seeing are paradoxical, with secrets being both known and not known at the same time, as in what we have referred to in terms of the 'unthought known' (Bollas, 1987).

Hidden bodies, moreover, are at once seen and not seen, as physical and sexual boundaries are simultaneously blurred and policed. Such paradoxes represent the necessary but always impossible nature of secrets and silences in the conditions of enforced proximity. Life in the shadows is at once highly exposing and replete with obscurity.

While our focus in this chapter has been on the spatial, drawing on ethnographic material to call attention to the ways in which welfare bordering operates in and as space, as well as the ways in which these spatial restrictions are weathered by those they target, in the next chapter we seek to complement our understanding of space with a focus on time and NRPF. As we go on to argue in Chapter 6, these represent two intersecting dimensions of welfare bordering, shaping how and in what ways lives can be made and NRPF weathered.

6

Doing time

'I began to file in the ... the applications,' Destiny commented during Eve's conversations with her. The single word 'applications' in her narrative condensed a multitude of forms she had filed and bureaucratic processes she had engaged with over the years: applications for permission to stay in the UK, for British citizenship for her son Isaac, for financial and accommodation support from local authorities and to remove the NRPF condition from her visa because she was destitute. 'It was like, they throwed, they just throwed the case on you, back to you,' Destiny continued. 'Apply, apply, apply, they apply, they apply. It was like, I'm so fed up. I just, I just give up,' her litany of struggles weighing and reverberating in the exhausting repetition of the word 'apply'. When we met Destiny, she had succeeded in regularising her status. She had been given 'limited leave to remain' with NRPF and was in receipt of minimal local authority support while waiting for the outcome of her 'change of conditions' application to remove NRPF from her current 2.5-year visa. She had come to the UK from Nigeria years before we met her. Isaac had been born in the UK, but we heard little about Isaac's father except that he was around and helped occasionally – any financial support was sporadic and couldn't be counted on. When Destiny first started applying for permission to stay in the UK, her friends had warned her: 'Don't worry, you're going to come into a money issue. We'll lend you money ...' They had indeed lent her the money and 'then start 13 years that the things turn over' Destiny explained. Although Destiny punctuated her narrative with a finite number of years, her time enduring precarious immigration status and conditions of extreme destitution were not over when we spoke with her. Thirteen simply marked the number of years *thus far* that she had been weathering NRPF.

Destiny told her narrative in fits and starts, filled with repetitions: 'So, I summed all my courage. And I went back. I went back again. I went back.' These reprises in her narrative echoed and gave life to those in her everyday life. She not only spoke of untold applications to what appear in her narrative as a monolithic state bureaucracy – divided by neither scale nor speciality. She also spoke about having to repeatedly juggle impossible decisions about whether to stay and care for her young son or leave him with sitters so that she could take on work and, if so, how much income they needed to survive. Our encounters with her were replete with calculations detailing the number of work hours she combined by putting together different part-time jobs, the length of time it would take her to get between home and various workplaces, and the length of time she and her son Isaac would be apart. She spoke of a catalogue of 'bulk' debts she had accrued over time, and to multiple people, which she tried to repay 'monthly by monthly' but was never able to fully discharge as she remained trapped in deep immiseration.

Destiny's story, which we will return to throughout this chapter, draws our attention to the temporality of NRPF – the 'temporal injustices' (Meier and Donà, 2021) it produces and the temporal practices of those it affects. While the previous chapter considered the impact of spatial constraints enforced by NRPF on the life-making labour of families, in this chapter we turn to questions of time. Indeed, weathering is fundamentally a temporal analytic, and here we explore the use of time delayed as a tactic of state power, and we ask how this shapes families' impossible, yet imperative, life-making practices in and across time.

In conversation with the growing body of literature on migration time, we begin by tracing the specific ways that time articulates as a border technology through NRPF. Between enforced destitution, punitive debt and the challenges of completing official routes to settlement while subject to NRPF, it is evident that the UK's 'hostile' migration regime operates in the long durée. For mothers and children in precarious migrancy, this is a cumulative process where the promise of some form of inclusion through permanent settlement status is constrained so much as to be impossible. Yet, in conversation with our interlocutors, we argue that while time, including in its interface with space, is harnessed as a border technology, this is never a smooth and seamless process. Time can be, and is, mobilised as a 'weapon of the weak' (Scott, 1985). We trace the ways that migrant families not only come to terms with time as a technology of bordering, but in weathering with fortitude, persistence, planning and even love, put time to work in aid of making a legal case for status and in claims to belonging. Families' temporal practices under duress are imbued with hope and a sense that, one day, things will be different. We argue, however, that families' refusals of NRPF's existential erasure through 'doing time' to regularise or remove the NRPF condition is both critical and ultimately insufficient in addressing the profound and 'slow' violence (Mayblin, 2020) that lies at the heart of welfare bordering.

Welfare bordering in/as time

In the previous chapter, we wrote about the ways that NRPF operates spatially, not only bordering space externally, or at the border, but internally within the nation. NRPF, we demonstrated, bars access to affordable spaces to live as well as liveable spaces to inhabit, enforcing involuntary intimacies and physical closeness with kin, friends and strangers. Yet, despite the seeming impossibilities of life under conditions of enforced proximity, we showed how secrets and silences became ways of weathering NRPF. Spatial borders, in other words, are not, and cannot be, so total that they exhaust the conditions of life, livelihood and sustenance. Necropolitics may be an apt descriptor for the lethal actions of bordered ethno-nations in response to their constructed others (Bhattacharyya, 2018; Mbembe, 2019), but to accept this as a complete description of a complex empirical reality would involve a complicity in their operations, a smoothing out of the inevitable instabilities and fissures in spatial borders. Indeed, ethnonations themselves recognise this fragility, introducing temporal bordering when spatial borders fail to work as intended, Tazzioli (2018) argues. Here then, we pick up on the previous chapter's provocation – welfare bordering in/as space – to attend to the ways that welfare borders are also ones *of* time and *in* time or, to be more precise, time-space.

Above, Destiny draws our attention to a key point in relation to welfare bordering *as* time: the protracted, potentially endless, experience of life under NRPF. Her description of weathering 'the things turning over' for a drawn-out period was not unique amongst our interlocutors. In part, this reflects the nature of the UK's family migration rules, which mean that many undocumented parents in the UK cannot even begin the process of applying for regularisation until their child had been resident in the UK for seven years, although some – like Destiny – (have to) wait until their child is 10 and can apply for British citizenship. There is no progression through a bureaucratic process during this time, nor even the opportunity to 'wait well' (Drangsland, 2020) or perform 'good' migranthood (Griffiths, 2014) by recalibrating to the demands of the state and formal labour market. Families in this position live in the shadows. Destiny explained:

> You have to be counting the days and the years come. I will let waiting days lie you know because ... we need to stamp the yard ... It was just possible [because] of hope: waiting, waiting, waiting. When he [Isaac] is 10, two days to that, I was like, I think, I can't wait. I started filling the forms just like ... I just wanted to be clear us of this business ...

But the only punctuation or reward for this long wait is entry into another extended and expensive temporality through incorporation into the bureaucratic time of the migration regime. Undocumented families seeking to regularise their status typically must enter the UK's most arduous and costly route to settlement: the ten-year route. In other words, even if a previously undocumented family manages to submit each expensive and complicated application as demanded, they are likely to still spend years, often over a decade, under NRPF's conditions of enforced destitution. This prescribed temporal horizon takes root in families' everyday lives, extending over virtually the entire childhood of a young person growing up with NRPF, as in the case of Destiny's son Isaac and others we have introduced in these pages. And this is in the best of situations: presuming that escape from NRPF lies at the end of a set time period, such as the twenty years which Destiny and Isaac face, assumes that nothing will go wrong during this prolonged period. Yet, the possibility of roadblocks is always present, whether due to lack of funds for visa renewals or the short period of time given to submit payment if an application for an immigration fee waiver (in principle available to those on a family route to settlement) is turned down. And, as we have been at pains to point out, these long years of enforced destitution do violence to the subject and even the quality and tenor of hope and dreams that far outlasts any formal application of NRPF.

The omnipresence of NRPF, with its temporal horizon blurred by its indefinite end, shapes life's labours. This is not simply about the extended life of NRPF but of the everyday temporalities it imposes, staccato rhythms of rapid demands interspersing with grinding slowness. We hear from Destiny, as with other families, about the rush of time when their precarious strategies for weathering NRPF fracture. When Destiny and Isaac were asked to urgently vacate the home of a friend with whom they had been staying for many years, Destiny explained: 'I had to lodge myself into a hotel that very day. Even though I … begged things, he said, "No, no, you had to go because I am giving you that."' She clarified that she was compelled to move out at such short notice not only because it was not her house but for the sake of preserving the close connection she and Isaac had with their friend: 'As someone has been faithful for [a] good many years, I don't want to spoil the relationship, you know.' With limited time or options, and desperate to avoid street homelessness, Destiny checked herself and Isaac into a hotel, depleting the small savings she had managed to accrue from her part-time work. Bureaucratic time can also feel hurried. Destiny described how encounters with social workers about their living situation were rapid and superficial: 'How can you do assessments in just that way? Just, just a little bit talks that way, you were just saying, oh, just to check on Isaac. "Is he coping?" And then that's it.'

Yet other assessments feel long and drawn-out, such as decisions about whether Section 17 support or access to public funds will be awarded.

In one of our other research projects, an advocate referred to this as 'the dance', an extended and ritualised negotiation between local authorities, families and advocates even when everyone knew Section 17 support would eventually be awarded (Rosen, 2022). It is not just assessments but everyday life where time seems to come to a standstill. For Destiny and Isaac, time slowed immeasurably as they ended up spending weeks in the hotel when the local authority refused to support them, telling Destiny she could use her small savings for payment. Destiny and Isaac were only able to obtain temporary hostel accommodation from the local authority after finding a lawyer to help with their Section 17 application. As Isaac explained, it was not just the waiting without a known end that was insufferable, but the totality of the unknown that this created: 'There were so many frightening things, during that time when nobody was really helping us … I think that in general that um, they should speed up like the process of like helping other people, because who knows what could have happened between those few weeks, like nothing really happened.'

Time is also extended as families like Destiny and Isaac are placed in what is meant to be *temporary* hostel accommodation for drawn-out periods of time. Temporary accommodation had stretched over a year, Destiny explained, grumbling that 'since we are in third, top floor, over a year, we have to go to second floor for [the shared] toilet'. These drags on decision-making have their roots in the state's efforts to introduce a multitude of tests and conditionalities on social support for migrants based on ethno-nationalist ideas about deservingness and 'prioritising' citizens. But they also reflect the impact of neoliberal austerity policies leaving local authorities cash-strapped but financially responsible for supporting destitute people – whether they are positioned as 'non-citizen' or 'failed citizen' (Anderson, 2013). This is compounded by the limited social housing stock following its mass-scale sell-off in the 1980s, largely in the service of Britain's rentier capitalism (Harvey, 2003).

Whatever the causes, the rhythms of NRPF – whether frenzied or delayed – produce 'uncertain temporalities' (Griffiths, 2014). But the demands of socially necessary labour do not stop in the face of such uncertainties. Life's labour must continue regardless of where one is living or what resources are available to support its achievement. It is not surprising then that the stories we heard from our interlocutors were less about boredom or the emptiness of waiting as it appears in much of the literature on the temporalities of seeking asylum (Khosravi, 2021; Jacobsen et al., 2021). For families with NRPF, welfare bordering in/as time is better understood as one of excess, or time overflowing. The labour required to sustain life in the conditions of forced destitution produced by NRPF are extensive and intensive. It is not just the prolonged, yet indeterminate temporal horizon of NRPF, but the insidious ways in which people's time is controlled, demanded and extended to the point of overflowing by this form of welfare bordering. We wrote about this in Chapter 2 when we described Jessica's time-intensive labours, doing laundry by hand in a bathtub in a shared accommodation with the closest laundromat an unmanageable bus fare away, and when we described Serwah and Miriam's tiring manual labour to empty the kitchen sink that would not drain. Similarly, Destiny described how having to take multiple part-time jobs in whatever part of the city she could find work meant that she did not just spend money on transportation, but her work hours became extended by long travel times:

> So, I started working with Costa Coffee in minimal wage at that time ... The distance was so far, you know, so I have to do travelling for almost one and a half journey for a number of days, and I always wanted more time in my hour because of home, because of Isaac. Then he was in probably in year six or year five.

Such long hours of work and travel compromised her health: 'Doing the first job in the morning. I was working, in fact, I was working, I was not even taking care of myself as well.'

As this suggests, temporality cannot be understood without reference to space: the distances between places of work and living or the conditions of accommodation available for destitute families with NRPF place time out of their control. These spatialities do not just overfill time but shape it: to engage in the necessary labour of life means operating with a schedule or tempo that is not one's own. Our interlocutors spoke about being compelled to generate and maintain schedules based on spatial constraints rather than social and bodily needs. For Destiny, who explained that she really loves to cook and enjoys the food she makes, cooking at 'home' was next to impossible. The local authority accommodation where she lived when we met her had one kitchen shared between five families. Destiny explained:

> If I see somebody cooking there, I will leave because I'm not going to stays ... I don't know, I might not like their food. They might not like my sauce. I have to leave the kitchen for them to do whatever they wants to do. Because if I'm doing to cook maybe certain food that they don't like and the smelly was all over. And the same also, if they were cooking some of the food and the smelly was all over the place.

Sometimes, she explained, she would wait until they were finished, postponing her own meal with Isaac. At other times, she would 'rather go to my friend's house to do some of my food, who ... I know they really love what I'm cook'. Between spatial constraints and time that was not their own, Destiny and Isaac sometimes went to a low-cost takeaway, reluctantly parting with precious resources. It was partly for this reason that Destiny made the decision to invest in a small fridge and microwave to keep in the tiny room she shared with Isaac in the temporary hostel. They were able to heat food up when they were hungry without having to go down multiple flights of stairs, a travail when she was tired from long hours of working and travelling. They both commented that this meant Isaac did not have to interact with strangers in the shared kitchen when Destiny was out. 'He doesn't want to bump in, because they are, you know, they are ladies and he's 13 and some of their children are just 3, 4,' she explained, echoing some of the concerns about the dangerous intimacies produced by enforced proximity which we discussed in the previous chapter. Despite the cost, in this way, Destiny endeavoured to make time, and space, even just a little bit her own.

Weathering in time: saving, deferring and borrowing for life's labour

If temporal uncertainty and the prolongation of temporal horizons are outcomes of welfare bordering as/in time, or tactics to put it more boldly, how do families with NRPF respond? We have already hinted at this by describing the careful calculus of time, money and need which families engage in. Here, we develop these ideas, arguing that while welfare bordering can be understood as a form of 'organised state abandonment' (Gilmore, 2007), our interlocutors detail, in both words and practices, a refusal of the existential erasure this implies. We refer, therefore, to families' labour of weathering such temporal injustices with the metaphor of 'doing time', a processual verb seeking to get at both the entrapping violences of the UK's border regime and families' refusals, resistances, strategising and dreaming. We view these as part of life's labour and, indeed, life-making acts. Time, as we suggested in the introduction to this chapter, may be a tactic of welfare bordering, but it can also be viewed as a weapon of the weak – a resource of resistance that has not (yet) been entirely commodified (Sharma, 2014) and placed out of reach of the destitute.

What temporal 'weapons' are possible for families given how far the horizons of NRPF stretch? Our interlocutors show us that weathering involves both patience and fortitude, outwaiting any timelines imposed by the state. But ensuring that the insistent labour of life-making continues while 'waiting out' in the shadows and 'doing time' in conditions of destitution is no easy task. Savings and loans are crucial our interlocutors insist, but the debts they produce – be these social or financial – are many, as we go on to discuss.

Abiola had been in the UK for twelve years when we met her, arriving from Nigeria. Like Destiny, Abiola became aware of the high cost of regularising their status in the UK when her son Akin, who was born in the UK, was young. While undocumented and living in the shadows, she nonetheless realised that she had to use the time to begin to save for Akin's citizenship application. 'Bit by bit, I opened a box. A shoebox. I made into something like a safe. And I started dropping money inside that place for four, five years.' She described how any support from her ex-boyfriend would go into the box as well as little bits of money she earned from her jobs:

> The least I'm dropping is £5. Because I didn't want to drop pennies in it. I didn't want to drop £1. I try that. Any time I'm dropping, I will make sure that I'm dropping £5 in it. But there will be times in a whole month where I might not even put anything in that box. I'm telling you. For five years, there will be months where I'm so broke, I can't even afford. And there will be months where I can drop £20.

The shoebox with her savings was not just a safe. Symbolically, materially, and haptically, it encapsulated her dreams. Abiola continued:

> I didn't touch it. Everywhere I go, I take that box with me. Everywhere I go, I didn't touch it. I kept it. Even if I'm starving, I didn't touch that money. Even if I was desperate need, I didn't touch that money. Because I was really desperate. This is the money that is going to save me out of this condition ... Everywhere I went, I took the box with me. Everywhere. Every moving the house, I took the box with me. I've moved four times or five times since I've been in this country. I've been taking the box with me. Because I was hoping. This is where the future is lying. You have to save for it and get out of this condition, and live a better life.

We might understand the shoebox and Abiola's commitment to saving for the future regardless of her contemporaneous circumstances as resisting the 'enforced' presentism of waiting time in migration regimes (De Genova, 2002). But somehow to put it like this minimises the strength of her affective persistence. We hear in Abiola's repetitions 'I took it everywhere' and 'I didn't touch it' a verbalisation of her resolve to withstand the prolongated temporal horizon made by NRPF, not just as an act of bare survival but as an act of fortitude. At one point, Abiola had to move the money to another box:

> But I made sure that when I even opened it that time, I didn't count it, because I don't want to know. Then, I created another box because I had to open it and cut it up. I created another box. I sealed it again with Sellotape. Bind it very hard with Sellotape. And I kept it again. That's what I did.

Here, we understand Abiola to be saying something akin to: 'There may be nothing we can do individually to change the temporal borders you violently impose on us, but we will persist.' For, in many ways, the prolonged, expensive and punitive ten-year route can be understood as imposed by the state because of frustrations that settlement of migrant parents with British children cannot legally be stopped (see Chapter 1) and a 'technique for synchronizing migrants' mobility' into state-produced rhythms (Drangsland, 2020: 1130). But Abiola does not 'recalibrate' herself in order to wait well, as understood from the perspective of the neoliberal border regime. She does the opposite, using the extended time to prepare for her desired futures. What this took from her, or what she had to sacrifice, are not part of her story here, although her struggles and forfeitures emerge during other conversations and interactions. Saving for her dreams, symbolised by the shoebox, however, is narrated as a story of strength and a story of her ability to wait out welfare bordering in/as time, turning its prolonged temporality back onto itself to save what she and Akin would need when they could come out of the shadows.

Abiola's recuperation of NRPF time, saving money bit by bit in this way, was something of an outlier amongst the families we met, hardly surprising given their destitution. However, other interlocutors spoke about saving in other ways, such as buying bulk items. This was a way of spending less per item in the present but also insulating themselves against tough times that might be on the horizon – a refusal of NRPF's denial of futures. Sam, for instance, insisted that his mother Samantha show us the bulk items filling their hall closet. Samantha explained that one time she was in the hospital for kidney damage and then had to take off extra time from work to recover:

> For a couple of months, it was hard. Rent was paid, childcare was paid, Sam was fed, but it meant I had to go without a lot. But the lucky thing for me was because I've always been a bulk shopper. I've always believed in buying in case that day comes when you can't afford it. You've always got something there to fall back on, so it wasn't too bad. We got through it.

Others spoke of saving through deferral of material needs: holding on to desires but deferring their fulfilment until an unknown time in the future. As Destiny explained:

> I feel boys grow faster that age ... So, you keep on changing their shoes, you know. And then buy clothes, buy all those things. He needs certain things that your friend got a hat, you say, 'Okay, don't worry, just take your time. You will get it, it may be later but, oh, I'll find a way out to just ...'

This echoes the stories in Chapter 4, where children spoke about avoiding making impossible requests on their mothers, using deferral to nonetheless keep dreams alive and stave off the exclusionary and dehumanising effects of welfare bordering in/as time. As its etymological roots suggest, to defer is not just 'to delay' or 'to postpone', but 'to bear' or 'to carry', indicative of the embodied and affective aspects of deferral. We can hear something of this stress and struggle when Destiny sighed as she described the ways she explained to Isaac the necessity of waiting for desired clothes. But, deferral, in our interlocutors' accounts, also points beyond material forfeiture – to a postponement of education, of life projects and even of family relationships.

Returning to Abiola's story, we learnt on an early visit that, although we only ever met Akin, she had a second son with whom she was very close and whom she missed intensely. Abiola had not seen him since he was 8 and he had just turned 20. He was at university in Nigeria, studying engineering, but they were hoping he could come to study in London. Their delayed reunion was not by choice but necessity, a deferral brought on by her precarious immigration and financial status. Coming to London on a student visa 'would sort the most difficult part' of their reunification, she commented, indicating that she could not bring him through family sponsorship rules. Although this decade long deferral weighed heavily on her, and offers a glimpse of the ways that the UK's border regime denies families with NRPF the right to have families of their choosing, we see here a refusal to let this define their futures. Abiola's efforts to sustain family life across national borders, talking 'too much' to her son in Nigeria and centrally displaying his photos alongside Akin's, are suggestive that children who have stayed in their mother's home countries are not simply spectators or spectral presences in family life in the UK. These family displays and acts of connection echo Jessica's ever-present boxes of items for her children in Ghana (Chapter 4), material reminders of the hope that deferred reunions can be transcended. That such reunifications in the UK rarely happen in practice, at least amongst our interlocutors, and that such reunifications may not offer longed-for happy endings (Pratt, 2012) in large part due to the enduring effects of welfare bordering, does not diminish these families' efforts to weather their deferrals and resist any sense of their permanence.

Borrowing, not just to weather the present, but to weather into desired futures was also commonplace, as Destiny highlighted at the beginning of the chapter. To be sure, taking on such debts, indeed being forced to take on such debts because of their destitution and being unable to gain mainstream welfare support, was never done by choice. It was not an easy decision to ask for or accept financial loans or other forms of support – be this accommodation, childcare, food and so forth – because of the twin worries of being compelled to repay while knowing that repayment may never be possible. In the case of informal debts, repayment was not always demanded as forcibly as it was with credit card loans, state-negotiated repayment schedules such as for healthcare or debts to private loan companies (Dickson et al., 2023b) where loans to enable necessary reproductive labour become 'immediate sites of capital accumulation' through regimes of interest recovery (Federici, 2014: 233). But a feeling of moral obligation to repay loans made by family, friends or community members was always present, yet not always possible to fulfil. As Destiny explained, one of the people who loaned her money 'in a bulk' expected a single repayment in full. To do this, Destiny was 'saving through allowing to stay with a friend'. Like Destiny, for many of our interlocutors paying off one debt was only possible through taking on another – an amplification of precarity. 'When the accommodation issue came,' Destiny continued in reference to being asked to leave her friend's house, 'that is when I knew it is so serious that I can't even afford for the accommodation and all,' the 'all' here standing for not just the 'bulk repayment' of her loans but all those items necessary for her and Isaac's immediate sustenance.

At the same time, we are not sure that Graeber's (2014: 387) argument that capitalism works by 'continually converting love into debt', making it 'possible to imagine a world that is nothing more than a series of cold-blooded calculations', is an accurate way of conceptualising the place of debt in enabling the labour of life for families with NRPF. Certainly, this conceptualisation falters in Destiny's case. She describes only taking on debts as a last resort and with reluctance, from carefully selected people. But rather than 'converting love' into a 'cold-blooded calculation', she experienced loans as a sign that she was not alone and, to use Graeber's language, that she had 'love'. She explained: 'People really, they really stood down their support then. They stood their support with us ... So, that helped me going, it helped me stand on, giving, keeping me hoping.' We might consider loans/debts as productive of calculative accumulation in the case of more financialised modes, which we note are typically not available to those with irregular status and indeed, for some mothers, even informal loans felt out of reach – given their sense of radical aloneness. When undocumented families did rely on loans from relatives, friends or community members, debts took on a slightly more ambiguous status, sometimes calculating and generating conditions of expropriation, at others a sort of communal practice of collectively weathering the effects of NRPF. Although, it is perhaps more accurate to suggest that it may always be a bit of both, instrumental and replenishing, a complexity that compounds efforts to weather NRPF.

To return more directly to the theme of the chapter, debt raises temporal questions as it involves 'a reworking of the relations of time' (Adkins, 2017: 449). Debt can be understood as a mortgaging of the future, a promise is made to repay at a point in time that has not yet arrived, whether 'monthly by monthly' or 'in a bulk'. The present then becomes directly implicated in the future, with debt enabling an entirely different relationship to temporality than the prolonged and impossible horizons imposed by welfare bordering in/as time. Loans, financial or otherwise, and debts represent a recalibration of these horizons, providing a small fount of material hope to allow families to imagine and nurture life beyond NRPF. Debt, Adkins (2017) points out, is productive of 'speculative time' – imaginaries and practices towards possible futures. For Destiny and Isaac, such speculations were focused on regularising their status and gaining rights to permanent settlement, but they were about more as well, as we discuss below.

To be clear, this observation is not intended as a defence of the conditions of NRPF which enforces debt and demands deferral by suggesting some sort of platitude along the lines that families are resilient and can survive no matter what the state throws at them. Nor do we want to romanticise the informal relationships forged through debt which often create conditions which allow for unbearable expropriation and abuse. We know too that debt operates in the long durée, meaning that – as Destiny pointed out – paying it off completely may be beyond the bounds of possibility, just as deferral can wind up being a permanent rather than temporary postponement. What we are highlighting here is that, by taking up informal, and even formal, loans to support their life-making labour, by saving and deferring, families with NRPF push back against welfare bordering in/as time. To mortgage the future through debt, to defer and save for an imagined temporal horizon of difference, implies that one has a future: we might understand this as one way that families reject, even implicitly, the dispensability and deportability built into the UK's migration regime. By insisting on the future and effecting to imagine and put this future into practice in the face of the most extreme of obstacles – whether this be through saving, deferring, borrowing or other means, our interlocutors not only weather NRPF, but they put time to work against welfare bordering.

Weathering as time: hope and dreams against welfare bordering

We might think of the temporal bordering of NRPF we have described so far, with its distant horizon and uncertain temporalities, as a way of rendering families in its wake as out of sync with a global temporal order forged through colonialism (Nanni, 2023) and a denial of 'coevalness' (Fabian, 1991) with their citizen others. This is not simply a case of discursively constructing Otherness via ideas of temporal aberrance or uncivilised irregularity (Nanni, 2023), but also an imposition of conditions of life which require families with NRPF to operate within temporalities overfilled with reproductive labour and interruptions, misdirection and delays of dreams for the future. At the same time, we have shown how families weather such material and discursive conditions, fulfilling the necessity of life's labour with persistence and planning, saving and borrowing, in ways which mobilise time against the temporalities of NRPF. But, and this is the point we will expand upon in what follows, this is not just a technical or practical act of subsistence, it is also about efforts to create conditions in which weathering exceeds depletion and slow wearing (Rai et al., 2013). For many of our interlocutors, weathering through life's labour was as much an affective undertaking of nurturing care and sustaining hope while facing the wearing down implied by 'doing time'.

The narratives of the mothers who we spoke to were often preoccupied with questions of care and concern for their children and their futures, an idea that we first introduced in Chapter 2, but which permeates the book. Although Destiny described in intricate detail her financial struggles and decision-making, it is her references to Isaac that spoke volumes about her motivations. 'Before we just sit, you know, lie down on the bed. So moody,' she gestured towards Isaac's single bed lying side-by-side her own, explaining how difficult it was for him to lose their housing and outlining the discomforts of the local authority accommodation. Her concerns were not misplaced, according to Isaac, who separately explained:

> Worrying, that puts like dark scenarios in my mind and that. You start thinking about the worst-case scenario and like it's not really, it's not, it's not, it's not a really good picture to look out, look out … When we first come here, … I thought that, if they didn't help us in time, they, they might kick us out or something like that. And I thought like the worst-case scenario would be like maybe living on the streets, and I wouldn't really go to school … That was a time where I felt like this could be like our downfall, in my life, or something could happen.

Destiny continued, 'I had to quickly make something for him to make him happy,' pointing out the small TV and games console she had bought for their shared room in the hostel. With palpable relief, she said that with this 'he was a little bit lively'. Her narrative was awash with similar explanations, rooting her decisions in concern for Isaac: whether for what work she had taken on or dropped, or what dreams for herself, such as education, she had given up to keep dreams for him alive. 'I spoke to a friend and the friend said, that's it, you can't just pop into something that you don't know because you are so excited. So, you know, that's a bit true. To further my son. Instead of me … I started looking for a job.'

Mother's self-sacrifice for their children is a familiar gendered story (Hays, 1996; Rosen and Faircloth, 2020), and risks romanticising 'motherhood as martyrdom'. We do not dispute such critiques, so much as draw attention to the profound care in evidence among so many of the families we spoke with in the face of the violence of NRPF with its denial of coeval subjecthood and the means of life. This care is clearly unequally demanded. Isaac's father, like others in this book, makes rare and unreliable appearances in their children's lives. This care is also undertaken in circumstances of profound enforced destitution and prolonged exclusion. This does not, however, minimise its importance – in this case both for Destiny as a motivation to keep going and for Isaac as a sense of having someone important in the world: 'I have my mum, she's a really good, she's more, she's a really good like, person, she's a really good friend and I love her.' Perhaps a less told story here then is the care, love and nurturing undertaken by children, something we discussed in depth in Chapter 4. Isaac, for example, describes deferral as a form of sacrifice, but also a practice of love: 'I feel that to be content with what you have, it's like the way to be. Like even though like sometimes where I feel like there's things that I want ... it's better to wait until like, you can, rather than demand and demand and demand, until the point where she feels guilty.' Rather than viewing these reciprocal concern and sacrifice as a problem, as they often are in more liberal valorisations of individualised personhood, in thinking with our interlocutors it appears that the problem lies in the conditions which cause such *extreme* sacrifice to be necessary not in the offerings themselves.

Returning to efforts to 'do time' in NRPF's uncertain temporalities, our interlocutors suggest to us that a grounding aspect of weathering is about nurturing – through care – the capacity to go on. In so doing, the capacity to hope is also cultivated. For Destiny, maintaining hope was a struggle – an acute and physically demanding, but necessary, challenge. 'I beat my own self, so I don't lose it,' she declared. The violence of this statement is striking, and we can pause here to consider what is at stake that would make hope feel so necessary and yet so destructive. Perhaps the answer in part lies in Destiny's references to the intolerable weight of repeated rejections as she attempted to regularise her status, an unreassuring constant despite NRPF's temporal uncertainties. These agonies were such that at one stage: 'I decided, you know what, I'm not doing. I'm not doing. I'm not doing.' In that moment, it was the support and care of others that helped her to 'stand up'. She explained: 'You see with people it is possible. So, people really, they really ... stood their support with us ... So, that helped me going, it helped me stand on, giving, keeping me hoping. That I see hope.'

Hopes and dreams also filled the narratives of the children we spoke with, many of whom articulated a desire for more just futures. Miriam and Luke spoke about providing a home and better transportation for their mother Serwah, a sense of a future filled with care and conditions which support life's labour. Looking even beyond his own family, Isaac echoed his mother's critique of NRPF as being 'unfair' saying:

> I brainstormed a bit and then I came to this conclusion that when I'm older, I want to like, help those people and like help my family. And help people who are in a situation that um, like living in a hostel, like really help with them. Help them with the things that they need so that they don't stress out about things that they shouldn't really be stressing out abut. Because, before this, we didn't have food. We didn't really have a lot of food that we like to eat …

The way we use it here then, hope is not an individual desire untethered from human action, nor is it a form of 'cruel optimism' (Berlant, 2011) that continually nurses impossible dreams in the context of NRPF's spatial and temporal injustices. Hope, as 'a form of futural momentum, a way of pressing into the future that attempts to pull certain potentialities into actuality' (Bryant and Knight, 2019: 134), is fundamentally about being able to imagine otherwise and acting in an effort to bring these potentialities into being. These may be small movements in the highly constrained conditions of NRPF, but in nurturing hopes and dreams through shared practices, we can understand families with NRPF acting to 'counter-temporalise' (Meier and Donà, 2021) or engage in 'insurgent temporalising' (Mitchell, 2022) against the insistence embedded in welfare bordering: denying futures by making the present untenable. The sense of the future as a collective endeavour, motivated by an awareness that things could and can be different, and more just, infused Isaac's narrative. He reminded us: 'It's not only about you, it's about other, other people. And humans should work together in order to help each other out, because we get through things better when there's more than one person involved in a job.'

While the UK's border regime seeks to use NRPF to make the conditions of life impossible for those it does not want, but cannot eject, by producing uncertainty and discordant temporalities and fractured temporal horizons, our interlocutors offer a way of seeing otherwise. Moments of care, love and dreams for themselves, their families and others who are suffering are not only a refusal of futures denied but a vision of what could be different. Albeit speaking of conditions of waiting linked to asylum, Khosravi (2021: 206) explains that 'approaching border waiting this way', by which he is referring to attending to migrant imaginings rather than consigning them to waithood, 'we can avoid the pitfall of reproducing the coloniality of power'. But hope is fragile, plagued by depleted material conditions and profound worries, as Destiny's comments remind us. It is always threatened by the risk of placing too great a demand on those who 'stand up' for and with families with NRPF or by the affective experience of radical aloneness. At one level, marking the simultaneity of contradictory feelings – such as collective hope and radical aloneness, which may come into greater or lesser relief at different points in time – is simply to recognise that as humans we aren't 'coherent' but awash with complexities and incongruities. Such contradictions necessitate labour for their management and navigation, just as hope's need for constant cultivation adds another layer of affective labour on top of the already overflowing time of life's labour for families with NRPF.

Conclusion

In this chapter, we have built on our discussion of welfare bordering in/as space through attention to time and its interface with spatiality. We have demonstrated the ways that NRPF works to prolong and blur temporal horizons, creating uncertain and overflowing everyday temporalities for families living in its shadows. By 'doing time' through saving, deferring, borrowing, hoping, caring and dreaming, our interlocutors show us how they weather with fortitude, effectively turning the imposed time of the UK's migration regime on its head. Whilst recognising the importance of families' refusals to accept the temporal injustices and existential erasures proffered by NRPF, we – along with our interlocutors – caution that this provides no simple panaceas for an austere welfare state, the precaritisation of labour and the UK's racialised borders – points we pick up in the following chapter.

7
(En)countering 'race'

In this final chapter, we take a step back from the close portraits we have been offering, learning from and with our interlocutors as they navigate life's labour in the context of the UK's welfare borders. We pick up on racialisation, indeed structural racism, which has had somewhat of a spectral presence thus far, seeking to make the case that NRPF is both symptom and technology of the UK's 'racial state' (Goldberg, 2002). In so doing, we refuse the assertion that NRPF is a race-neutral technique for managing migration, a proposition fronted most strongly by the neoliberal British state, but also apparent in the long-standing silences in much of the literature and advocacy about NRPF. Notwithstanding some recent shifts since the Black Lives Matter protests in 2020, racism has rarely been a focus of advocacy around NRPF, which has, at most, been treated as a form of 'indirect discrimination' based on 'race'. In our first engagements with our ethnographic material, we were also struck by what seemed to be a heavy silence about (state) racism, especially in conversations with mothers, and yet – as we develop below – we believe this seeming silence was not only about what was possible or impossible for our interlocutors to say in a research encounter with us. It was also about the ways in which neoliberal racisms, manifested by the proliferation of external and internal borders which we have been discussing, operate by so easily slipping out of grasp, away from articulation and (our own) infrastructures of hearing, despite the deep impact of racism on the lives of our interlocutors.

As De Noronha (2022: 164) argues, one of the risks of research on everyday and interpersonal encounters (the mainstay of ethnography) is that '"everyday racism" [is] too easily reduced to the interactional and the micro. State racism (policing, immigration enforcement, the punitive welfare state) or matters regarding housing, urban displacement and precarious work fall out of the picture.' Heeding his warning, in what follows, we move away from portraits that draw on only what is seen and heard directly in our interlocutors' accounts. Instead, we attend to silences in policy, advocacy and previous scholarship to understand how NRPF can be presented as 'raceless', with its racialised effects justified despite equality being an ostensibly legal obligation for services. We demonstrate that, in policies, institutions and everyday interactions, NRPF can be understood as imbricated in the racial logics and fabric of British society, operating through migration status and nationality as well as racially coded but seemingly 'race neutral' characteristics and competencies. The results, or impacts, we demonstrate are that the racist character of NRPF receives little attention or theorisation, at the same time as NRPF shunts negatively racialised families labouring under its burden into especially subjugated positions within an already stratified field of life's work, and ultimately renders them 'vulnerable to premature death', as Gilmore (2007) puts it in her provocative definition of racism. Developing understandings of how and why NRPF can be understood as a tool of state racism is thus important politically as well as intellectually.

NRPF and 'racial discrimination'

'The imposition of a NRPF condition does not discriminate directly,' UK Visas and Immigration (2023) stated in August 2023 in a *Policy Equality Statement (PES)*. This 36–page review engages in a series of verbal contortions to construct the case that the imposition of NRPF on families on the ten-year route to settlement is entirely compliant with the Equalities Act 2010. In UK law, 'direct discrimination' refers to policies, provisions and practices that *apply* differently to people with protected characteristics (e.g. race, gender, age) than those without. Given that 'race including colour, nationality, ethnic or national origin' is a protected characteristic in the UK it would seem self-evident that NRPF is discriminatory, since NRPF is applied solely to those with non-British national origin/nationality. Yet, in the *Policy Equality Statement*, UKVI argues that Section 29 (which focuses on the provision of services):

> [does not] apply to race discrimination, so far as relating to nationality or ethnic or national origins, in the exercise of functions exercisable under the Immigration Act or Immigration Rules. Nor does it apply to anything done pursuant to the Immigration Acts or Immigration Rules which discriminates against another because of the other's nationality.

In making this case, the state both links 'race' with nationality and ethnicity and delinks identification of and opposition to discrimination on these bases through exceptions which grant precedence to immigration law over equality law. Having excluded national origins and immigration status from consideration, and effectively rendered discrimination based on immigration status allowable, the statement goes on to assert that the policy applies equally to all, whether or not people have 'protected characteristics' under the Equalities Act. Such discursive and categorical acrobatics allow UKVI to state unequivocally that NRPF does not 'directly discriminate'.

The statement, however, does recognise the policy's 'disproportional impacts' on 'particular racial group[s]' in the sense that the majority of those given NRPF on the ten-year-route come from Nigeria (35.71 per cent), Ghana (14.29 per cent), Pakistan (9.24 per cent), Jamaica (7.98 per cent) and Bangladesh (6.30 per cent). However, having already concluded that the policy applies equally to all, this amounts to little more than a simple accident that cannot be accounted for. 'We do not know why the proportion of applicants granted recourse to public funds varies by region,' the statement asserts.

Further, UKVI argues that the disproportionate impacts of NRPF on the ten-year route cannot even be understood in the happenstance terms of 'indirect discrimination', where 'a policy which applies in the same way for everybody has an effect which particularly disadvantages people with a protected characteristic' (Section 19, Equality Act). UKVI achieves this defence, first, by reducing 'race' to 'colour' (as it has already been delinked from nationality, ethnicity and national origins). Because they 'do not collect data' about 'colour', the UKVI finds 'no evidence' of racial discrimination. This is little more than a case of denial by inaction and omission. Second, UKVI asserts that, even if there had been evidence of disadvantage because of 'race', 'the Policy pursues legitimate aims ... and is a proportionate means of achieving those aims'. Defences of policy-produced disadvantage like this are enabled by Section 19 of the Equality Act 2010 which sets out that any impact is ultimately acceptable if 'the person applying the policy can justify it', effectively limiting questions of indirect discrimination to that of 'who are we willing to sacrifice for net gain?' (Atrey, 2021: 25). In this case, UKVI justifies disproportionality through nothing less than 'the economic well-being of the United Kingdom'. This aim is presented as being at risk from 'third country nationals' who might become 'burden[s] on taxpayers' without 'sufficient resources to support themselves and their children', who potentially engage in 'benefits tourism', and who are in the UK 'unlawfully'.

In the *Policy Equality Statement*, UKVI indicates that the impetus for the revised 2023 statement, which was originally conducted in 2015, is not just changing immigration laws but 'the situation of British citizen children, and in particular black British children, of migrant parents under the Policy' – an issue UKVI notes has been raised frequently by third sector organisations. For example, in a detailed study for The Unity Project and Deighton Pierce Glynn, Woolley (2019) asks whether groups sharing protected characteristics are disproportionately impacted by NRPF: in other words, are they indirectly discriminated against? Compiling data from telephone surveys, interviews and contributions of demographic information from third sector organisations working with families on the ten-year route to settlement with NRPF, she responds in the affirmative:

> Most families with NRPF have a British child and nearly all of these families are black and minority ethnic (BME). NRPF is inherently more likely to affect BME British children than white British children indicating the indirect racially discriminatory impacts of the condition. (Woolley, 2019: 36–37)

In this respect, advocates who seek to make a case against the racialised effects of NRPF do not necessarily contest the premise that the NRPF policy itself is 'race-neutral' and that nationality is not relevant in considering whether something constitutes racial discrimination. Instead, the racialised impacts of NRPF become, even in some third sector research and advocacy, seemingly an unanticipated consequence. As such, UKVI's statement of its 'legitimate aims' linking provision of support and services to citizenship remain beyond question. As we have argued elsewhere in relation to campaigns for free school meals (Rosen and Dickson, 2024), a focus on British citizenship to leverage social support for families with NRPF is often used tactically for 'policy wins'. In so doing, however, this upholds, and even amplifies, a perception that welfare is and should be a right of citizens not – for example – all those who reside in a location, a form of reparation or an act of (transnational) solidarity.

In the case of the claim that NRPF is a form of indirect discrimination against Black British children, UKVI simply repeats their response that charges of discrimination are not relevant. First, they assert, Section 29 'does not apply to discrimination based on age (so far as relating to persons under 18)' – an ejection of children and childhood altogether from anti-discrimination legislation about services. Secondly, differential impact on Black British children is 'justifiable', the UKVI argues, because the policy 'applies' not to children but to their parents, which the UKVI had already rendered beyond consideration using provisions in existing discrimination law. Therefore, in one fell swoop UKVI dismisses the equalities impact of NRPF on children, as well as adults, by arguing it does not amount to prohibited discrimination.

If the UVKI can easily manoeuvre its way out of legal charges of racial discrimination, why do organisations supporting families with NRPF continue to pursue this line of advocacy? Beyond the limitations of equalities law, one of the challenges here may be about what is heard, or said, in advocacy and research encounters. For example, reflecting at an international migration conference in 2018 about her widely cited NRPF study with Jonathan Price, Sarah Spencer indicated that participants did not speak about 'race', meaning there was no 'direct evidence' of racism from interviews beyond demographics (Price and Spencer, 2025). Indeed, while the literature on NRPF is unequivocal that single-mother-headed families from Nigeria, Jamaica, Ghana,and Pakistan are hardest hit by NRPF, this acknowledgement primarily serves as a demographic descriptor. As with the *Policy Equality Statement*, the reasons these groups are most affected by NRPF are left largely unexplored and state racism is granted little explanatory purchase in discussions of the policy, although there are some notable exceptions. For example, Erel (2018: 6) argues that the lack of support for postcolonial families with NRPF is symptomatic of ethno-nationalist constructions of belonging depicting migrant families as a 'threat to the nation'. This is suggestive that there are processes at play whereby such differentiation is produced, enforced and experienced. However, overall, 'race' and racism remain at best undertheorised in relation to NRPF, but more often go unnamed, at most hesitatingly gestured towards in both theory and practice.

Yet we wind up in a different place altogether if we do not reduce racism to the liberal terms of individual attitudes or expressions of prejudices, but to its structural character, namely the ways that inequalities within and between nations rest on economic and political systems of racialised segregation, dispossession and exploitation. In other words, the fact that Sarah Spencer, or indeed ourselves, rarely heard narratives from participants about outwardly racist treatment vis-à-vis the nation state does not provide evidence that NRPF is raceless. Our point then in laying out the *Policy Equality Statement* in such detail is not to develop a legal case suggesting, for example, that the law has been incorrectly applied. Indeed, part of what we have gestured to above is that anti-discrimination law in and of itself provides grounds for defending discrimination against migrants, including through welfare bordering. Primarily though, we go into detail above as a way of entering a conversation about NRPF, welfare bordering and state racism. What is silenced or obscured in debates to date about NRPF in relation to 'race' and racism? What racialised effects do these erasures enable? If the definitions of 'race' and 'racial discrimination' prove ineffective for addressing NRPF's racialised impacts, how might we alternatively conceptualise the interface between 'race', racism and welfare bordering in the case of NRPF?

Racialising the migrant

One starting point, amongst others, in articulating a response to these questions is to focus on how 'race' is theorised and understood.

The definition of 'race' we are presented with by the British state suggests that there is such thing as a 'racial group' – a distinguishable bounded entity – characterised by predetermined features such as 'colour' or 'national origin'. Yet 'race', as a 'mode of categorisation that references the body, nature, an underlying and unchangeable essence that signals unpassable difference' (Bhattacharyya, 2018: 2), is an enduring fiction where phenotypic, anatomical and physiological differences are treated as natural rather than social fact. The result, De Genova (2018: 1770) argues, is that 'the pernicious power of racial distinction operates precisely through the naturalisation of social inequalities'.

Rejecting any essence to 'race', therefore, is not a rejection of the *impact* of racialisation. Instead, it is an invitation to attend to the ways race is produced: what differences come to matter and why, how these differences are stratified, and with what effects. The point then is about the importance of being attentive to 'race' as a relation of domination, segregation and enclosure, rather than a thing, which, by extension, demands attention to the dynamism and variation in modalities of racism (Virdee, 2019). To assert, for example, that Nigerians are a 'racial group', as UKVI does above, homogenises a varied and ethnically and religiously diverse region of the world, at best providing advocates with a neat, but ahistorical, story of 'race' to make a case about indirect racial discrimination. As Goldberg (2002: 109) points out, one characteristic of racial states is that they go through the process of amalgamating and categorising populations, placing them into 'racially identified groups, and they do so more or less formally through census taking, law, and policy … in and through bureaucratic forms, and administrative practices'. Contemporary immigration law, and the legal (and illegalised) statuses which have proliferated in its wake, are core to this process (De Noronha, 2019) as are those collated in the name of equality law.

One problem then of asserting indirect discrimination due to 'Black and Minority Ethnic (BME)' status or national origins is that this falls into the trap of reifying 'race', presenting these as self-evident categories such that those who are classed as 'BME' have always been the targets of racism. Yet this relatively new policy terminology brings together a disparate set of people and presents 'racial discrimination' as ahistoric, simply read off the body in unchanging ways. Our point here is not to disregard long-standing anti-Black racism linked to Britain's cross-Atlantic slave trade and colonial extractivism. Our point is that groups which are negatively racialised change over time and across place (Wacquant, 2023). Virdee (2019: 21), for example, points out that:

> In the first half of the 20th century, it was Jews who could not be imagined as British while in the second half of the century it was people of Caribbean

and Asian descent ... each time the boundary of the nation was stretched to encompass more members of the working class it was simultaneously accompanied and legitimized by a racializing nationalism that excluded more recent arrivals.

Now this sounds, perhaps, like we are venturing into a terrain of unfettered agency allowing for the everyday reconstruction of 'race' at will or, worse still, providing the grounds for a sickening reversal of logic to argue that whiteness is now the target of racism exemplified by notions of 'reverse discrimination' or 'great replacement theory'. This is categorically not the argument we are making. While we reject the idea that there are bounded pre-existing groups always already etched with a stamp of the negatively racialised, a form of 'ethnic absolutism' (Gilroy, 1993), racism is processes of reifying difference, enforcing segregation and the 'codified stratification of human worth and disposability' (Valluvan and Kalra, 2019: 2397). By moving away from the 'anaemic' (De Genova, 2018) liberal terms of discrimination, and instead attending to the ways that racism makes its object ('race'), we can – in Virdee's (2019: 7) terms – better consider 'what work racism accomplishes across time and space, as well as for whom and why'. This requires concentrating on how racialised social relations change, as well as ossify, over time and how these are forged at the intersections of class and gender. To this end, conceptualising racism in contemporary Britain – including the proliferation of external as well as internal borders and the logics which allow for the state's presentation of NRPF as race-neutral – requires attention to white supremacy and imperial nostalgia, which derive their continuing force from plantation slavery as well as (settler-)colonial projects and neocolonial divisions of the world. It also requires attention to exclusionary European narratives of belonging which have variously depicted Jews, Muslims and Roma as their constitutive outside (SSAHE, 2020).

That said, today's racisms are not vestiges of the past but represent reconfigurations of historical forms, most notably a shift from 'race' as a natural or biological category, ideas which inhabited the scientific racism of colonialism, towards 'new' forms of racism focused on culture understood as bounded, predetermined and immutable. Familiar frames of cultural racism include the way that speaking English becomes indexed to insideness or efforts to 'protect brown children and save brown women from brown men', to paraphrase Spivak (1988), draw on racist essentialisations which depict the Black, Brown or Muslim man as inherently misogynist. Such cultural characteristics are typically linked to 'blood and soil' (Hall, 2017: 126), with cultural traits read off the body via historical modes of meaning making (Alcoff, 1999). This suggests that biological logics of 'race' making have become entangled with the cultural, rather than being completely replaced – much as we see in the UK's definition of 'race' in terms of colour and nation origin.

The significance, according to Kundnani (2023), is important for understanding contemporary racism in neoliberal Britain. He demonstrates that, on the one hand, neoliberals' celebration of an untethered market lies in having an expansive and expanding set of buyers and sellers limited by neither 'race' nor nation. Capitalism searches out new markets wherever they may be. On the other hand, leading neoliberals such as Hayek and Friedman feared that their foundational values of competition and marketisation might be at risk from those 'cultures' or nations which neither embraced a competitive ethos nor had the capacity to cultivate, support or sustain the marketised order of capitalism's neoliberal variant. These ideas about inferior nations, unable to grasp market supremacy, were in part a reworking of colonial stratifications of 'race' and nation, and their elision (Rattansi, 2020). It was also a response to decolonial movements of the twentieth century which were agitating not just for an end to empire but for the redistribution of wealth through reparations or even ideas of welfare as an international, not just national, responsibility. The result, according to Kundnani (2023: 182) was that 'the logic of their political and economic project inexorably led to both liberal antiracism [as we see in equalities law] and new forms of structural racism, irrespective of the intentions or attitudes of its founding intellectuals'. Further, and crucial to what we discuss below, much of the infrastructure of the British racial state is so deeply embedded that racism no longer requires explicit articulation or violent enaction. This allows for everything from the 'war on terror' to the rewriting of human mobility as a crime to be presented in seeming race-neutral terms or for NRPF's advocates (including the UKVI in the *Policy Equality Statement*) to present themselves as non-racist or race neutral.

As this suggests, the nation and its borders modelled on the colonial division of the world has assumed great importance in neoliberal era racism. Distinctions based on national origin are presented in the *Policy Equality Statement* as a rational response to the 'problem' of migration and state security. This, in a nutshell, leads us to a moment where neoliberal states espouse a post-racial fantasy – exemplified by an ethnically diverse government – at the same time as the past decade has borne witness to the 'accumulation of dead black and brown bodies awash on the halcyon shores of the Mediterranean Sea' (De Genova, 2018: 1765) as well as the English Channel and Britain's immigration detention centres. Post-racial ideologies, like those we see in the *Policy Equality Statement*, suggest that while discrimination may exist, the explanations for 'premature vulnerability to death' do not lie in structural racism but elsewhere (Meghji and Niang, 2022), for instance smuggling and trafficking, so-called 'illegal' mobility and criminality including 'manipulation' of human rights law, and so forth.

In responding to this fantasy, much of the existing literature on the 'race-migration nexus' in Britain treats border regimes and racialisation as 'co-constructed' (Erel et al., 2016). The 1905 Aliens Act was designed to keep out Jews while the Commonwealth Immigrants Act (1968) effectively barred Black and Brown Commonwealth citizens from settling in the UK. Indeed, borders have a long history of being racialised, and this could be understood as their *raison d'être*: separating the national 'us' from the foreign 'them'. While seemingly contradicting neoliberals' dreams of mobility unshackled, and indeed their drive for securing ever cheaper labour, borders have proliferated in the contemporary period just as capital has become unmoored from place. Kundnani (2023) suggests that answers to this contradiction lie in Enoch Powell's legacy as the architect of Britain's racialised neoliberal project: winning consent for a market order relied on the creation of a new neoliberal subject brimming with a sense of individual ingenuity and self-responsibility. This required depicting Britain's (always exclusionary) welfare state and trade unionism as forms of 'un-English' dependency and slovenliness. Because migrants, with their 'communal values' and limited affiliation to Englishness, could not be won over in this hegemonic struggle, for Powell they would always be dangerous. As compelling a story as this is, it perhaps paints too simple a tale of the neoliberal fascination with borders. We might also turn to Andersson (2014) who calls attention to the 'business' of borders or Mezzadra and Neilson (2013) who argue that borders are not so much barriers but filtering devices of 'differential inclusion', effectively hierarchising labour power.

If we accept that borders do not do just one thing, and that there are different modalities of racism, we can begin to see that borders do not simply produce a singular form of racism against racially marginalised migrants (and indeed those long-standing citizens who are racialised as outsiders to the nation) as a 'them' to a fictive and exclusionary national 'us'. They produce distinct forms of differentiation and ranking both through the proliferation of immigration statuses (De Noronha, 2019) and racialised scripts – whether this is the Muslim migrant framed as threat to British values or the 'job stealing' Eastern European, an animating figure of the Brexit debate.

'Race', then, is made with and through migration status. But, in thinking with the claim of Erel et al. (2016: 1352) 'racialization produces various categories of migrants', we can also understand migration status as one form of racialisation in and of itself, or the migrant as a racialised subject. To make this case requires two moves. First, we need to recognise that the category of 'migrant' is not a category applied to *all* people on the move: it is not imposed on those ex-pats, entrepreneurs or indeed the 'brightest and the best' conjured and summoned by Damien Green in Chapter 1. In other words, the labelling of a person as a migrant is already a separation from the national 'we' as well as the larger group of people on the move, yet with the reduction of 'race' to somatic characteristics and the naturalisation of the nation state, 'the migrant' is often presented as a race-neutral figuration. We find the proposition of Mulinari and Neergaard (2023: 3–4) provocative here: writing about the Swedish context, they draw on Stuart Hall to suggest that 'migrant background is a central modality in which race is lived', an insight that resonates with the claims we make here about the UK.

Second, the case we make requires exploration of the specific techniques and logics of racialisation that operate on/as the seemingly de-raced figure of the migrant. The near-hysterical concerns about lack of integration and the fragility of community cohesion of the past decade (Valluvan, 2018) flag up the ways that supposedly immutable differences between migrants and the national 'we' have mobilised 'national cultures' to racialise the migrant as alien other. This is compounded by representations of the figure of the migrant as always already mobile (Silverstein, 2005). Such 'itinerancy' is rendered suspect in the context of assumptions about belonging as rooted or sedentary, with citizenship understood as loyalty to a singular nation. Racism here takes a nativist form which, following Newth (2021: 162), denotes 'a racist and xenophobic form of politics which discursively constructs (along antagonistic and horizontal lines) a "non-native", "foreigner", or even the "non-integrated co-citizen" against "the native people"'. The irony here, of course, is that mobility is one of the few constants in human history (Nail, 2015) and those 'native born' children of 'migrants' – including many of the children who animate these pages – are themselves often racialised as a generational extension of otherness. The 'native born' then, like other types of racialisation, is a myth rather than empirical reality. Autonomous mobility is treated as a particular threat to nativism, not least because it shows the limits of any effort to 'control migration' or impose borders on human movement. One consequence is that, while there are general ways that migration itself is racialised, how this happens is worked out in the particular: the situated context and the intersection of class, gender, national origins and immigration status. For example, one particularly menacing figure in the nativist litany is that of the fertile migrant woman, threatening to 'brown' the population, such that 'fecundity is itself a racial characteristic' (Bhattacharyya, 2018: 39; Erel, 2018). To take another example, the 'bogus asylum-seeker' is not racialised via the exact same terms and processes as the 'benefit tourist', the 'illegal' or the figure of the migrant family with NRPF (a point we return to below).

Taken together, the above discussion begs the larger question: why, or to what purposes, are such processes of racialised differentiation enacted? It is here that theorisations which attend to racial capitalism provide one of their most compelling interventions. For such differentiation is not a reflection of a timeless black–white, east–west or south–north bifurcation of the world – an always-already process of subjugation of the one by the other. Nor is it a holdover from 'traditional' racism, destined to fall away as capital reaches its apex of 'free' and abstracted labour power, an orthodox Marxist assertion which implies that, as capitalism advances, racism will inevitably decline. Instead, building from Cedric Robinson's (2000 [1983]) key insights about racial capitalism: capital does not proceed towards greater homogenisation of labour power, instead capital grounds its founding impulse for expansion on the production of unequal, differentiated and stratified labour power. It is worth quoting Kundnani's (2023: 141–142) development of these ideas at length here:

> Capitalism, on this view, constantly recreates itself through differentiation of labor: waged industrial workers, enslaved plantation workers, workers who migrate back and forth between temporary waged work in capitalist economy and work in other modes of production, and various kinds of 'surplus populations' ... These different labour relationships to the capitalist mode of production are correlated to differential regimes of rights and privileges, with boundaries between citizens and non-citizens, the free and the unfree, the protected and the disposable. Race, in turn, provides a conceptual framework to represent and legitimate these varied relations of workers to capitalism.

What this conceptualisation allows us to begin to come to grips with is an understanding of how capitalism 'sifts people into different categories, sometimes with an economic purpose, but always with an economic outcome' (Bhattacharyya, 2018: 59) and therefore why and how racism is so fundamental to capital's continuance. It offers resources to begin to consider links between historically and spatially situated constructions of 'race' and material aspects of life. Hall (1980), for instance, points to the indexing of Britain's racial division of labour to (neo)colonial stratifications of the world. As Africans, Caribbeans and South Asians were driven to migrate to Britain in the 1950s and 1960s because of impoverishment caused by dispossession and extraction, they faced hard labour, over-exposure to unemployment and sub-standard living conditions – fundamentally different relations to capitalism than white workers in Britain.

For Bhattacharyya (2018: 56) and others, however, there has been perhaps too much of an emphasis on waged labour in accounts of racial capitalism and they point also to 'differentiation of whether and to what extent [populations] may be part of any formal labour force'. Regardless of whether someone is rendered exploitable labour power or surplus population, in the UK we would be hard-pressed to find anyone who has not been brought into capital's orbit through the monetisation of life itself. For the UK's neoliberal border regime produces not just racialised migrant subjects but ones which may be compelled into forms of unfree labour (e.g. in detention centres or in the exploitative informal relations we discussed in Chapter 3) due to their pre-emptive illegalisation, while others are rendered disposable and 'costly', yet undeportable, and therefore ejected from even the most pitiful of welfare supports but still needing financial resources to live. Those who have the 'gall' to challenge their ascription as unvalued and abandoned, whether through autonomous movement or tactics of time, are not just abandoned or excluded but punished by the state through destitution and debt, in a not directly coercive but nonetheless violent manifestation of welfare bordering. And, for the purposes of the arguments we have been putting forward about weathering through social reproduction, this nods to the potential ways that the labours of life are steeped in racialised relations to capital and the racial state. As we pointed out in Chapter 3, a sexualised postcolonial taxonomy of value and the psychic life of immigration status (see also Dickson, 2023) mean that the racialisation of the migrant figure is both deep and enduring.

NRPF as symptom of the neoliberal racial state

With this groundwork in place, we return to the *Policy Equality Statement*, in which the UKVI performs a set of rhetorical contortions to render NRPF and its racialised outcomes a rational and acceptable way to meet its legitimate, and therefore justificatory, aims of protecting the UK's economy. But how have such aims come to be seen as legitimate in the first place? The answers to this question are key to demonstrating how and why NRPF can be understood as both symptom and technology of the neoliberal racial state and its racialisation of the figure of the migrant, not simply an unexplainable effect. When UKVI speaks about the risk to the UK economy from 'third country nationals', it is setting up a series of truth claims emanating from a depiction of the UK as a bounded nation state with little relationship, and certainly no imaginable obligation, to those outside its borders or indeed those deemed as outsiders within its nativist shores. It also puts a great weight of racialised responsibility on to the backs of migrants for economic conditions which are better understood as the result of capitalism's perpetual contradictions and crises (McNally, 2010), although we bracket off this latter point here.

This naturalisation of the nation state and its bordered frame has haunted welfare provision in the UK since its inception. Yet this is a fantasy. The British welfare state was founded and funded through colonial extraction.

As Bhambra (2022: 11) convincingly traces: 'Over half the money at the disposal of the government at Westminster came from the labor, resources, and taxes of those within empire and beyond the national state.' Although this story of the welfare state has been obscured in contemporary accounts, it was no secret at the time, with Winston Churchill explaining in 1929 that the provision of 'social services at a level incomparably higher than that of any European country' was precisely due to its colonies which 'constitute[d] the keystone ... of our economic position' (Bhambra and Holmwood, 2023: 170). In the post-Second World War period of welfare state building, this included both direct extraction from Britain's remaining colonies (notably including Nigeria and Ghana, where many families made destitute by NRPF come from) and cancellation or diminishing of its debts to newly independent India and Pakistan. Such imperial grooves continue to funnel resources from formally independent countries through foreign and local elite ownership of resources and wealth, as well as the conditions of sovereign debt servicing (Gilbert et al., 2023). In this sense, Britain can be understood as an imperial, rather than national, state. Yet, Bhambra (2022: 8) argues, welfare, which is a way to 'pool and redistribute wealth raised through taxation for the benefit of the members of the political community', is framed as a fundamentally national affair aimed at those recognised as citizens. We part ways with Bhambra's perhaps too simple assertion that 'metropolitan society as a whole benefitted' from colonial extraction, instead understanding the UK's neoliberal welfare system to be shot through with intersectional inequalities and punitive mechanisms of control and exploitation of benefit to the racial state and capital against those who have to 'hustle' (Bhattacharyya, 2018) or engage in paid labour for their sustenance (Anderson, 2016). However, her forensic accounting and claim that extraction was (and is) imperial and redistribution was (and is) national is crucial for making sense of NRPF.

Indeed, setting out those deemed to be naturally and rationally entitled – or not – to welfare via NRPF is an exercise of national imaginary grounded in racialised exclusion. NRPF is based on the logic that the 'public' entitled to the state's redistributive function – providing 'recourse to public funds' as and when needed – is constituted by only a portion of those present on British shores. With limited routes to enter and reside in the UK, many Black and Brown people on the move have been pre-emptively illegalised (De Genova, 2018: 1779) or restricted from indefinite residency rights in the UK – the point at which NRPF status is permanently removed. For Isaac, living with his mum in a single room due to her NRPF status and facing periods of extreme immiseration and hunger in the UK, this represented a fundamental contradiction between people saying 'England is a multicultural country' and NRPF 'basically screwing over those people who came from different backgrounds' as it 'only favours a certain type of people ... It doesn't favour the whole of Britain.'

Isaac went on to describe this process as akin to 'cheating you out of your country', reminiscent of El-Enany's (2020) diagnosis of the 1981 Citizenship Act as 'the final act of colonial appropriation'. The Act rendered impoverished Black and Asian people from former colonies outside the British polity and therefore not part of 'the public' which has 'recourse to public funds', despite being present in the UK and coming from countries which funded the development of the British welfare state. In this sense, we suggest, NRPF can be understood as symptomatic of the racial state, setting the limits of its (marginal) redistributive functions firmly within an ethno-national imaginary. This is not an unexpected or unexplainable consequence, as the state would have us believe. It is a welfare policy that rests on (ongoing) extraction of a neocolonial nature, but which overtly limits redistribution to a constructed idea of the ethno-nation. Yet Isaac's assertation of belonging reminds us that the stranglehold of the nativist logic of the state on subjectivities or imaginaries is never complete and that alternatives can be and are being nurtured in its shadows. 'I feel like everybody should help everyone, no matter where they come from,' Isaac continued. 'Because like discriminating just because of someone's like, race, or discriminating because of where someone comes from is really bad.'

NRPF as a technology of the neoliberal racial state

NRPF is not simply a symptom of the already existing neoliberal racial state, however, but it can be understood as a technology involved in its production. If, in British mythology, the welfare state is deemed to represent and care for the nation, determining who qualifies for social support is precisely an act involved in its construction. NRPF is a means for demarcating and differentiating migrants as the constitutive outside of the nation in increasingly microscopic ways. We wrote about this in Chapter 1 when we discussed how NRPF had moved from a general policy at the border to one targeted at people who had settled in the UK and how it was then extended to increasingly specific groups of people. In this sense, the growing plethora of legal statuses to which NRPF has been attached by default or design creates new forms of racialisation. Those granted a five-year-route to settlement with NRPF tend to be portrayed as 'good migrants', rewarded with a shorter and less costly route to settlement for their use of state-sanctioned routes and demonstrated financial security. This is not to valorise such a tenuous position which is, at best, a route to 'tolerated' citizenship, a moniker for partial entry into the 'community of value' providing access to a conditional, punitive and insufficient neoliberal welfare state (Anderson, 2013). Meanwhile, the wife portrayed in the suspicious language of 'sham' marriage or the mother exercising her rights to family life who is presented in terms of her 'human rights trickery' are typically given the more punitive and costly ten-year route to settlement with NRPF.

These differentiated and racialised NRPF routes produced through bordering – both legal and discursive – create multi-status families, with all the complexities and 'multifaceted exclusions' that entails (De Noronha, 2019: 2417). For Destiny, like many of the mothers we spoke with, the combination of differential status and the state's discursive, if not actualised, commitment to supporting children in need, meant that, 'probably the social worker ... cares about the sons ... They don't care about me anyway.' In what appeared to us as a resigned acceptance of a form of state abandonment, this did not however seem to lead to divisions between mothers and their children. Where such divisions seemed more pronounced were instances where there were extended family members present in the UK with differential statuses. In such cases, mothers' illegalised status or NRPF-produced destitution and debt often rendered them reliant on support from family members with more secure status. Yet these family members were often still precariously positioned financially and outside the 'community of value'. Supporting those racialised as migrants with NRPF was perhaps experienced as amplifying their impossibilities for achieving 'tolerated citizenship', a form of 'contingent acceptance' which turns on having to 'endlessly prove themselves, marking the borders, particularly of course by decrying each other to prove that they have the right values' (Anderson, 2013: 7).

In this sense, families are both split by their differentiated immigration statuses and yet family members are simultaneously concatenated, 'tainted' by the status of the most precarious and excluded amongst them. This is perhaps most evident in the case of children as they are denied the right to welfare in their own right, regardless of their citizenship, always subsumed by their mother's/parents' status. Thus, as the *Policy Equality Statement* asserts, even when children in families with NRPF are nominally recognised as citizens, their child status serves a rhetorical and legal justification for their racialised exclusion alongside their parent(s). Here child status reduces children racialised as migrants to a 'zone of non-being' (Fanon, 2008) or 'human becomings' (Qvortrup, 2009) not able to access rights of citizenship, with echoes of colonial infantilisation as it dovetails with developmentalism (Gagen, 2007). The point is not to assert false independence for children such as that embodied in the idealised neoliberal subject, but to understand the intersection of racialisation and the subjugation of childhood, where each fill in the gaps left by the other, with the effect of bolstering welfare bordering.

NRPF does not just serve as a technology for making the racialised neoliberal state through continuously demarcating and differentiating the migrant as the constitutive outside of the nation by status attributions, but also via its operationalisation. The reference to 'public funds' in state policy indexes a long list of social support and benefits, public services and tax credits. Each item on the list involves specialised institutions and different bureaucratic processes for applying and receiving support. Prohibitions due to NRPF, and exceptions when granted, are largely negotiated independently for each policy and on a piecemeal basis in practice. Free school meals, a key plank in the British state's 'poverty alleviation' strategy, is one such example. Until recently, children in families with NRPF were excluded from accessing free school meals, despite being some of the most destitute in Britain. Following nearly a decade of campaigning, in April 2022 a permanent expansion of free school meals to children in families with NRPF along the same lines as national children was announced. However, the change has been poorly publicised, meaning that schools continue to deny meals and parents are reluctant to demand their child's entitlements over concerns this might expose their status (Rosen and Dickson, 2024). It is hardly a surprise then that Miriam did not want to tell her school about her difficulties doing homework on the shared family mobile phone or that Mobo commented, 'People you talk to either don't really care, or you're talking to someone and they just, they're ready to use it against you. It's just like, I'd rather just suffer in silence.'

These fears, however loosely defined, likely pick up on mothers' concerns over any encounter with the multi-scalar state, from registering their child(ren) at a school to accessing healthcare. Each encounter is fraught with questions about whether the service constitutes 'public funds' and if accessing the support will have other repercussions. For instance, between 2016 and 2018, schools were required to collect data about children's nationality and country of birth – confidential and identifiable personal information which was then shared with the Home Office. Although children are allowed to go to school in the UK regardless of their immigration status, this demand for data sharing placed undocumented families in an even more precarious, and potentially exposed, position. The policy was only changed after a successful grassroots and legal campaign; although the data that were collected are still being held by the Home Office (Schools ABC, 2024). The impacts of such policies are concerns in and of themselves but our primary point in this chapter is that in each policy instantiation, and in each welfare encounter, the constitution of the ethno-nation – as defined by its racialised outside – is confirmed over and over to both 'citizens' and racialised 'migrants'.

In our interlocutors' accounts, such direct encounters were rarely imbued with explicitly racialised content. Yet, both mothers' and children's narratives were replete with descriptions of being treated with suspicion or as though they were ignorant. Samatha, for example, spoke numerous times about her 'controversial dining table' which 'caused all the trouble'. This simple wooden table, covered lovingly with a runner and flower vase, provided her and Sam an area to eat and doubled as a space for Sam to do his homework without having 'his food and stuff balanced on his knees'. The controversy, Samantha explained, came about because she had purchased the table with subsistence funds from the local authority, without receiving advanced permission. When the social worker saw that Samantha had spent £139 at a home store, she cut off the next subsistence payment, demanding that Samantha provide her with a receipt or return the table. Samatha's purchases, as with other families in receipt of local authority support, were monitored and controlled – implying that families may be taking advantage of the state or may not have the skills to manage money 'properly'. This combination of suspicion and infantilisation both justifies and reinforces practices of policing of daily spending, a pre-exemptive and invasive criminalisation of the intimate decisions and practices of social reproduction.

Similarly, Mobo, reflecting on his mother's experiences with social services, used the word 'disrespect' over and over, commenting on the ways in which his mother was treated as though she was 'stupid' and unknowing, but at the same time she was 'suspicious' or conniving because of 'stereotypes of what a needy person should look like'. The entire experience of seeking support from the local authority due to their destitution was 'deliberate', 'hurtful' and 'mean' and ultimately dehumanising. Mobo articulated a form of advice to their social worker and others: 'Like, it's not ... the family is this case number in this file that you've been assigned to ... Those are actual lives. Those are actual people that do also have their own stressful journeys and their own stressful periods.'

In our conversations, mothers never analysed the conduct of social workers and other street-level bureaucrats they encountered, or NRPF more generally, as a form of state racism, despite their evident frustration, anger and disbelief about how they were being treated. In many ways this is not surprising given the seemingly raceless language of encounters with the neoliberal state in combination with its proponents' post-racial fantasies. These proclaim an opposition to racism (equated with individualised acts intended to hurt or cause suffering) while allowing structural racism – including against the racialised figure of the migrant – to fester. We also do not discount the overdetermined whiteness of the research encounter as potentially contributing to this silence. We mean this in the obvious sense that both of us are racialised as white but also that social research has long been viewed by minoritised communities as an extractivist process akin to, or part of, colonialism and its racial logic (Simpson, 2007).

Perhaps even more relevant, however, is the limited nature of direct encounters between families with NRPF and the racial state despite its omnipotent force in their lives. For those who are undocumented, to come out of the shadows is to risk deportation. Even those families who enter the expensive and punitive ten-year family route to regularisation deal with a state that is obscured through digitisation, hidden by bureaucratic chains as applications are submitted by immigration advisers to unknown and anonymous readers, or mediated by private and third sector groups such as private accommodation providers contracted by local authorities. Section 17 assessments are at most fleeting and, particularly since Covid, faceless encounters. Taken together, and in combination with individualising discourses of neoliberalism which hold people uniquely responsible for their own suffering, structural and state racism may become obscured amidst the daily challenges of sustaining life under duress – even for those most affected.

Yet, as Mobo reminded us, it is not hard to draw a line from the 'negative stereotypes' which animated his mother's encounters with the state and racialised ascriptions drawing on ideas of Black criminality or long-held colonial stratifications of intelligence and competence: 'It's just African countries and like, black nations as a whole ... it's usually just like, the bad stuff that makes the news.' Mobo continued, making a link between the ejection of Black people from racialised national imaginaries of the British state and the sorts of degradations, humiliations and demands for 'gratefulness' they encounter when seeking support from the state. Street-level bureaucrats, such as those treating migrants with NRPF as though they are 'stupid' and 'suspicious', may view themselves as simply carrying out the demands of their job to ensure the efficient and effective redistribution of state resources. But these bureaucratic processes and state actors' ways of seeing, knowing and responding to families with NRPF are steeped in infrastructures born out of the racial state even if this is obscured by their implicit assumptions and technicist presentation. Crucially here, policy is not simply written and imposed by the state, but it is interpreted and enacted, and therefore also made, in practice. In other words, in the practice of interpreting NRPF and its exclusions through racialised scripts obfuscated by liberal anti-discrimination legislation and neoliberal multiculturalism, the decisions of state actors to deny support, investigate spending, report data and so forth constitute part of the everyday making of the neoliberal racial state through NRPF.

Conclusion

This chapter has highlighted the racialised differentiation and disproportionality of NRPF in demographic and descriptive terms, but that has not been our primary aim. Instead, we have drawn together existing theorisations of 'race', offering some initial ways to conceptualise NRPF in relation to state racism and, more broadly, racial capitalism – a relative lacuna in existing scholarship and advocacy on NRPF. We began by contesting the shaky empirical basis of charges of and defences against claims of NRPF's 'indirect discrimination', demonstrating how in both instances constructed national borders and socially produced depictions of bounded cultures and racialised figures masquerade as natural fact. Our larger point here is that impoverished conceptualisations of 'race' and racism (for example, those which reduce it to the liberal terms of pre-existing difference and individual maleficence or 'indirect discrimination') not only hamper analysis of the conditions facing families with NRPF but scholarship runs the risk of contributing to the British state's ability to mask the racialised character of welfare bordering and the injustices it produces.

In an effort to move away from the problematic of anaemic liberal formulations of racism, we sought to give flesh to De Noronha's (2022) challenge to think with our interlocutors both about their everyday lives and about the systems, institutions and borders they are embedded within. In so doing, we have demonstrated that NRPF is both a symptom and technology of the neoliberal state that works through the racialised figure of the migrant – not just an outcome of pre-existing racial nationalism and welfare bordering but part of its reconfiguration and (re)production. We have further shown how immigration status is not just a euphemism for race, but 'the migrant' – in its diverse instantiations including NRPF – has become a form of racialisation itself and an apologia for state racism. In our concluding chapter, we consider what this means for the ways in which we seek to understand NPRF's impacts on the life-making practices of those it most directly impacts and for how we contest and challenge NRPF and welfare bordering more broadly.

Conclusion:
Contesting welfare bordering

As we sit down to write the conclusion of this book, far right riots have taken place across the country under the flag of 'stopping the boats', a reference to illegalised cross-Channel migration utilised by the rioters and state alike, and 'protecting the children' from Muslims, migrants and people of colour – an unveiled, racialised attack. The new British government has cancelled an infamous treaty to deport to Rwanda asylum-seekers who were deemed to have entered the country 'illegally', instead using the commissioned flights to send people to Vietnam and East Timor and warning of a significant uptick in immigration raids at nail bars and car washes. Thousands of unaccompanied children were placed in hotels in the past two years, during which time their asylum claims were effectively paused, increasing the likelihood that they will be denied care-leaving support and instead become subject to NRPF. The immigration condition has also been extended to more recent European arrivals in the post-Brexit era, with contentious new immigration law (Nationality and Borders Act 2022 and the Illegal Migration Act 2023) threatening further expansions. At the same time, the news is full of reports of struggling local authorities, including six which have declared bankruptcy since 2021, with councillors from many others warning they are on the verge of the same (Kenyon and Clarke-Ezzidio, 2024). On the one hand then, the spectre, spectacle and practice of bordering – including through detention, deportation and welfare bordering – are intensifying in the UK. On the other hand, while NRPF has consistently enforced extreme destitution on precariously positioned migrants, the only possible, albeit minimal, support for families through the shadow local welfare state is being further degraded. In other words, the stakes for the families we have been writing about in this book could not be higher.

Since we began working on NRPF as researchers in 2018, and earlier in campaigning and advocacy organisations, we have seen NRPF come out of the shadows so to speak. Not only has it made inroads into mainstream public discourse through media coverage and governmental debates, but there has been a significant growth in organisations that are working on

NRPF, whether through the development of 'lived experience' groups or lobbying against NRPF provisions. NRPF has also made its way into the social sciences, with more researchers focused on the particularities of the immigration condition. These are important efforts, and we have witnessed some small gains won through efforts to challenge NRPF's pernicious effects, for instance the extension of free school meals to children in families with NRPF along the same lines as national children, as well as Section 17 support won for individual families like Destiny and Isaac thanks in part to advocacy on their behalf. Whilst we applaud these wins, it is simultaneously evident that the edifice of welfare bordering, of which NRPF forms a part, is growing. Indeed, as we have written elsewhere, the framing of advocacy and campaigns – often around a particular and seemingly 'sympathetic' figure like the 'British child' – 'can end up reproducing long-standing exclusions in efforts to achieve incremental policy gains' (Rosen and Dickson, 2024: 215), ultimately leaving the logic of NRPF unchanged while naturalising and ossifying the violence of welfare bordering.

To effectively contest NRPF then, it is important to understand the concrete conditions in which it plays out and its specific effects, but also why it persists, and where it is fragile and liable to be overturned. Our discussion thus far has primarily been an endeavour to address the first of these points. As we move the book to a close, we turn to the latter points, considering what our diagnosis thus far has to offer struggles against welfare bordering with its abandonment, punishment, and extraction through NRPF and other exclusionary technologies. Part of this effort lies in critique – building an analytic frame for identifying those structures and practices which we strive to abolish, by searching for points of weakness, fissure and contradiction.

In this regard, throughout the book, we have developed an understanding of NRPF as an aspect of welfare bordering, part of tripartite technologies states use in their drive to 'control migration', alongside detention and deportation. Welfare bordering, we have demonstrated, works against those who are embedded but excluded, rather than those who are enclosed and ejected – although the shifting nature of border controls means that individuals often move between these positions. Welfare bordering, we have also shown, is not simply an immigration policy but it lies at the interface of immigration control and welfare provision. This means that it is not so much a part of the spectacle and spectacular material violence of borders – as we see in the form of push backs of the 'small boats' that have formed so much a part of recent anti-migrant discourse in Britain or in the threat of deportation flights to Rwanda, Vietnam or other places.

Instead, welfare bordering operates in the register of the banal and routine (for a discussion of this in the context of the asylum system, see

Darling, 2022; Mayblin, 2020). Its material violences are profound incursions in everyday life – existential erasures and violations operating at the level of the subject as well as the missed meals, fears of starving, uninhabitable housing and intensive labour demanded for survival which we have written about in the pages of this book. In the face of NRPF's fundamental assaults on life and dignity, we have referred to families' practices under duress, including their efforts at making lives worth living, as 'weathering' through social reproduction. Our point in doing so has been to move away from framings of families with NPRF as victims or lack, as they often appear in advocacy and scholarly literature. Whilst such framings may have appeal in efforts to advocate for families, they move us towards a limited politics of humanitarianism and aid (Dadusc and Mudu, 2020), often based on moral arguments linked to ideas about children as deserving because of their essentialised status as vulnerable subject par-excellence. As we have pointed out, however, this neither reflects children's experiences nor practices, and it runs the grave risk of rendering mothers with NRPF as undeserving at best, and hyper-responsibilised and individually at fault for the family's predicament at worst. At the same time, we have pointed out that an emphasis on the reproduction of life under NRPF as either depletion or regeneration misses the ways in which our interlocutors seek to represent themselves, flattening the complexities of lives lived in the face of welfare bordering. In so doing, we have emphasised the important ways in which families persist, fortify and wear in their efforts to sustain meaningful lives.

As this suggests, welfare bordering is a slow, grinding and constant companion to life in the shadows – often hidden in plain sight. One point we make in concluding this book, then, is about the importance of attending to these obscured or invisible stories in the shadows alongside those of the (hyper)visible and the more immediate violences of bordering apparent in immigration raids; deportations; push backs; the gates, walls and biometric edifices bounding nation statues; and border externalisation. To do otherwise is to miss the quiet viciousness of welfare bordering as it works at the levels of sustenance, infrastructures of care, relationships and subjectivity that we have been writing about.

Ruth Wilson Gilmore (2023: 477) reminds us, however, that it is not enough to focus on negating structures of subjection and extraction, but about 'making something into something else'. What practices of presence, or more affirming structures of care and solidarity, are evident in everyday life in the shadows? What imaginaries and practices do families with NPRF illuminate which we might strive for and grow into? Weathering encourages us to be on the lookout for such efforts, attending to the ways – for example – that people use time as a weapon of the weak over and against the violence of time as it is put to work by welfare bordering (Chapter 6).

It has allowed us to pay close attention to the ways the discipline of hope (Kaba, 2021), however delicate and cruel, is nurtured in the shadows to work the cracks in the UK's border regime. We have learned about the importance of life's work for sustenance and survival, but not only for these as bare minimums or bare life. We have learned about the importance of reproductive labour in the sense of its value and meaning for nurturing (transnational) relationships of care and the reparative work of soothing damaged psyches as families engage in fragile projects of common cause in the face of the degradations of welfare bordering.

Throughout this book, we have been at pains to keep alive the duality of the labour of making lives through the concept of weathering, neither reducing these efforts to depletion nor replenishment, or a simple calculus between the two. At the same time, we have insisted that weathering is not an elixir. It does not magic up a solution – empirically or analytically – to a rapidly retrenching and outsourced welfare regime, intensifying inequalities and the precaritisation of migrant labour, or the UK's racialised borders. Yet the idea offers us, we hope, not only intellectual but political purchase. So, we turn once again to our points at the start of this chapter, asking what practices of weathering welfare bordering have to tell us that might help to explain the limitations of moral arguments against NRPF (Rosen and Dickson, 2024; Dickson and Rosen, 2021) and point out directions for taking up Gilmore's political calls to imagine and engage in practices of presence, alongside those of absence.

In drawing this book to a close, we ask ourselves: Why do moral arguments against border technologies like NRPF, such as those which draw their force from ideas about child exceptionalism and deservingness, seem bound to fail or at least do little more than rework the contours of welfare bordering? Why are border policies like NRPF sustained, even expanded, when they cause such extreme harms and so obviously do not meet their stated aims? As we outlined in the previous chapter, the defence being offered by the state as to the disproportionate effects of NRPF on racially marginalised families is mounted via contortionist claims of the state's 'legitimate aims'. Yet the imposition of NRPF has done nothing to meet its stated aim of protecting 'the economic well-being' of the UK – at least for the most marginalised. In 2022, rising levels of impoverishment in the UK have left 1 million children and 2.8 million adults in the UK in destitution – a 2.9 times increase from five years before – with relative child poverty increasing by close to 20 per cent between 2012 and 2021 (Marmot, 2023). As we have been at pains to point out throughout the book, these figures include families with NRPF who typically bear the most extreme levels of deprivation of all. Similarly, the 2012 expansion of NRPF to families who had previously been protected has not achieved the state's aim of 'reducing net migration'. The presence and persistence of families on the ten-year route to settlement with NRPF makes clear that the policy does not and cannot achieve its punitive aims. Autonomous human mobility and practices of weathering through social reproduction mark a steady refusal and consistent excess to neoliberal border regimes – both at the edge of the nation state and within its internal practices of welfare bordering. In nation states' negation, even criminalising, of rights to mobility and settlement, however, we see the creation of a strawman of sorts. Imogen Tyler (2013: 9) calls this figure the 'national abject', made via processes whereby 'public anxieties and hostilities' caused by the ravages of neoliberal capitalism 'are channelled towards those groups within the population, such as the unemployed, welfare recipients and irregular migrants, who are imagined to be a parasitical drain and threat to scarce national resources'.

The question still remains: if the state is not meeting its so-called 'legitimate aims' via NRPF, why does it persist with the policy and, indeed, propose to extend it to further groups of migrants? We do not pose this question in acceptance of the aims themselves, which we have shown to be based on problematic racialised national imaginaries, or with a face-value understanding of how the real intentions of policies may be articulated or unspoken. Further still, we do not imagine policies as 'rational' objects. Instead, we ask this to comprehend the logics and systems that allow welfare bordering to persist, and the implicit aims of policies such as NRPF, which may themselves lie in the shadows. As Andersson and Keen (2023: 2) point out: 'When policies fail (and fail persistently) we need to look not only at "what went wrong" but also at "what went right" – and at who is benefiting from these apparent failures.' Looking at everything from the war in Afghanistan to the 'fight' against international migration, they argue that such policies, and indeed the continuation of the purported problem 'routinely offers major payoffs and few costs for those who claim to be addressing it' (Andersson and Keen, 2023: 7). And, as scholars of racial capitalism remind us, capital and the racial state use tactics of classification, division and stratification into categories of deservingness, belonging and expendability with significant economic outcomes – not least, consolidating wealth for the few and expanding destitution among the rest. It behoves us, then, to consider what benefits NRPF generates for those pursuing the policy. We do so with some trepidation, wary of the risks of painting a dense partnership within and between factions of the racial state and capital or suggesting there is a coherent and consistent plan among them. Nonetheless, we engage here in some sociological speculation gesturing to the possible beneficiaries of a policy that does not achieve its stated aims and produces such profound harms for those it singles out, knowing that this is an important element for understanding and successfully challenging welfare bordering more broadly.

As we have argued throughout the book, and developed in more detail in Chapter 7, NRPF both reproduces and reconfigures the neoliberal racial state, amplifying the notion that welfare is a national preoccupation, regularly marking and enlarging those deemed to be outside the 'national we'. If this ethno-national imaginary brings together groups that have a purported common identity, nativity and so forth, in distinction to those who are deemed to be its outside, what other sets of social relations are minimised or obscured (e.g. class)? What do such erasures mean for efforts to articulate a politics of solidarity against (racial) capitalism – something which the production of national abjects mitigates against? In learning with our interlocutors about the frayed contours of their life-making practices, we bear witness to the degradations of enforced destitution produced by welfare bordering. Their production as the national abject works not only against them, it serves to drum up consent for the state's punishing and austerity-riven welfare reforms, Tyler (2013) reminds us. As families with NRPF are framed as 'illegals' rather than neighbours, friends and comrades for and by those currently rendered citizens, this serves to fracture or destroy possible solidarities across differences (Anderson, 2016).

We have also suggested that this ethno-national imaginary supports the political conditions whereby migrant destitution can be naturalised as 'someone else's problem', bolstering and justifying welfare bordering. One effect in the case of NRPF has been to reduce the national welfare bill, even while it increases local costs (via the Children's Act). Further, as others remind us, policies like NRPF which limit access to welfare provision for migrants can serve to embed a neoliberal logic of welfare retrenchment and conditionality more broadly (Anderson, 2013; Tyler, 2013; Guentner et al., 2016) – trialling models for retrenching social support and privatising aspects of the social that may not have previously seemed possible. This is certainly not to suggest that welfare bordering is important to contest and resist simply because it is a warning of what may happen to citizens, so much as an argument that the language of deservingness, desirability and national citizenry (the counterpoint to national abject) are slippery figurations. We can see this in the way the way that the policies purporting to support diversity and equality can easily be turned against the marginalised (see Chapter 7) or the language of bureaucratic fairness can serve as a justification for denying support to those who need it (see Chapter 2 and 3). Indeed, the broader discursive realm in which welfare bordering occurs shows how an idiom of protection (as in 'protecting our own') serves as a euphemism justifying policies that produce such remorseless impoverishment and indebtedness. While the families who have shared their lives with us in the pages of this book live the sharp end of enforced destitution, and make every effort to survive its most brutal and subjugating affects, the processes, practices and imaginaries of welfare bordering run deep, ultimately connecting diverse experiences within logics of exclusion, expropriation and exploitation. If it is not the women and children whose lives fill the pages of this book, then it will simply be someone else, another figuration of abjection, unless we challenge this underlying logic.

Our effort here then has not been to make a case of the deservingness and desirability of these families, but an effort to fundamentally disrupt such logics, which are so central to the practice of welfare bordering, in their entirety. The specific case of NRPF in this book is not intended to be read as an exception. This deep dive into the conditions which enforce and justify extreme destitution hint at how such forms of welfare bordering could be expanded further. So, we ask: what does this reduction of the redistributive function of the welfare state via the racialisation of migrants mean for public expectations for and actual practices of capital taxation? Or, to put this differently, in what ways might NRPF play a part in vindicating Britain's second empire – the free movement of capital within and beyond its borders without regard for marginalised people who are dispossessed or stuck in place?

Illegalised and precarious migration are themselves sites of income generation for the racial state and capital. For example, the Home Office openly identified the 'monetised benefit' arising from 'extending the time period to settlement' listing this as £200 million over ten years (in 2012 terms) (Home Office, 2012a: 1). Direct profiteering from precarious migration is also evident in the business models of platform corporations, or – to bring things more directly to the families we focus on in this book – the increasing number of (illicit) businesses involved in facilitating human mobility, processing bureaucratic applications to state institutions and operating outsourced housing for families in receipt of Section 17 support or allowing housing to fall into disrepair while making rental income in the private sector (as Serwah and Miriam showed us so powerfully in Chapter 2), to name but a few. For migrants themselves, precarious status effectively means living in the condition of deportability (De Genova, 2002), with the constant threat of deportation, alongside enforced destitution and debt, serving to create a sub-class of super-exploitable workers. We saw this in previous chapters when some mothers spoke about being compelled to take on work in conditions of extreme risk, low pay and often profound abuse in contexts which might be understood as unfree relations to capital produced through racial stratification.

We may then conceptualise these families as subject to 'organised state abandonment' (Gilmore, 2007) via NRPF – a racialised necropolitics which renders populations 'dying or for dead' because they are not even viewed as potential labour power for capital (Bhattacharyya, 2018: 20). Or we may think about these families as being constituted as reserve labour by NRPF, their subjection to punitive and degrading treatment used to justify their dynamic and stratified inclusion within an always exploitative capitalism (Mezzadra and Neilson, 2013). Here, though, we end by returning to those unwaged, everyday life-making practices we have been describing throughout this book. This labour – of both love and obligation, satisfaction and degradation, fulfilment and depletion, value(s) making and the site where value is 'scraped' by capital (Bhattacharyya, 2024) – is characterised by such dualities.

Our interlocutors have shown us throughout this book how welfare bordering constricts and contorts life-making practices, producing a profoundly uneven and highly racialised terrain for accomplishing the labour of life. For NRPF, as a symptom and technology of the racial neoliberal state, releases it and capital from supporting the social reproduction of an ever-expanding group of racialised 'outsiders' whilst still benefiting and accumulating from their presence as (future) labour power, consumers and debt-servicers. Although reproductive labour is necessary for families' survival, we can see our interlocutors' strivings towards meaning and value as an insistence, even if just in brief moments, that life exceeds racialised necropolitics. They remind us that social reproduction is a core site where struggles are waged over who we want to be and how we want to live in and with this world. We – which we mean in Jodi Dean's (1996) expansive and processual terms of creating a you and me, rather than us and them – must work carefully and systematically to understand and challenge the situated processes which produce racialised outsideness and rationalise welfare bordering. This is an effort to ensure that our analysis does not replicate assumptions about a golden age of the British welfare state, as though it were not always a détente with capitalism, or leave unquestioned racialised national imaginaries. We view such endeavours as part of a reaching towards the hope and promise of an enlarged solidarity embedded in ideas about dignity and liberation for all.

References

Adkins L (2017) Speculative futures in the time of debt. *Sociological Review* 65(3): 448–462.
Agamben G (1998) *Homo Sacer: Sovereign Power and Bare Life*. Stanford, CA: Stanford University Press.
Alcoff LM (1999) Towards a phenomenology of racial embodiment. *Radical Philosophy* 95: 15–26.
Anderson B (2013) *Us and Them? The Dangerous Politics of Immigration Control*. Oxford: Oxford University Press.
Anderson B (2016) Against fantasy citizenship: The politics of migration and austerity. *Renewal: A Journal of Labour Politics* 24(1): 53–62.
Andersson R (2014) *Illegality, Inc.: Clandestine Migration and the Business of Bordering Europe*. Oakland, CA: University of California Press.
Andersson R and Keen D (2023) *Wreckonomics: Why it's Time to End the War on Everything*. Oxford: Oxford University Press.
Anitha S (2010) No recourse, no support: State policy and practice towards South Asian women facing domestic violence in the UK. *British Journal of Social Work* 40(2): 462–479.
Aparna K, Kande O, Schapendonk J and Kramsch O (2020) 'Europe is no longer Europe': Montaging borderlands of help for a radical politics of place. *Nordic Journal of Migration Research* 10(4): 10–25.
Atrey S (2021) Structural racism and race discrimination. *Current Legal Problems* 74(1): 1–34.
Back L and Sinha S (2018) *Migrant City*. London: Routledge.
Balagopalan S (2019) Childhood, culture, history: Redeploying 'multiple childhoods'. In: Spyrou S, Rosen R and Cook DT (eds) *Reimagining Childhood Studies*. London: Bloomsbury Press, pp. 23–40.
Baldassar L and Merla L (2014) Introduction: Transnational family caregiving through the lens of circulation. In: Baldassar L and Merla L (eds) *Transnational Families, Migration and the Circulation of Care: Understanding Mobility and Absence in Family Life*. New York: Routledge, pp. 3–24.
Ball T (2011) Government consultation plans to aid migration: Points of view. *Brentwood Gazette*, 20 July.
Benchekroun R (2024) Mothers doing friendship in a hostile environment: Navigating dialectical tensions and sharing support. *Sociology* 58(2): 369–385.
Benchekroun R, Humphris R and Sigona N (2024) Mothering in hostile environments: Migrant families negotiating the welfare and immigration regime nexus. *Critical Social Policy* 44(2): 285–306.

References

Benton E, Karlsson J, Pinter I, et al. (2022) *Social Cost Benefit Analysis of the NRPF Policy in London*. London: LSE Centre for Analysis of Social Exclusion.
Berlant L (2011) *Cruel Optimism*. Durham, NC: Duke University Press.
Bhambra GK (2022) Relations of extraction, relations of redistribution: Empire, nation, and the construction of the British welfare state. *British Journal of Sociology* 73(1): 4–15.
Bhambra GK and Holmwood J (2023) The trap of 'capitalism', racial or otherwise. *European Journal of Sociology* 64(2): 163–172.
Bhattacharya T (2017) *Social Reproduction Theory: Remapping Class, Recentering Oppression*. London: Pluto Press.
Bhattacharyya G (2018) *Rethinking Racial Capitalism: Questions of Reproduction and Survival*. London: Rowman & Littlefield International.
Bhattacharyya G (2024) *The Futures of Racial Capitalism*. Cambridge: Polity Press.
Blaise M (2013) Charting new territories: Re-assembling childhood sexuality in the early years classroom. *Gender and Education* 25(7): 801–817.
Bollas C (1987) *The Shadow of the Object: Psychoanalysis of the Unthought Known*. London: Free Association Books.
Brennan D, Cass B, Himmelweit S and Szebehely M (2012) The marketisation of care: Rationales and consequences in Nordic and liberal care regimes. *Journal of European Social Policy* 22(4): 377–391.
Briggs L (2003) Mother, child, race, nation: The visual iconography of rescue and the politics of transnational and transracial adoption. *Gender & History* 15(2): 179–200.
Brown M and Booth R (2022) Death of two-year-old from mould in flat a 'defining moment', says coroner. *Guardian*, 15 Nov.
Bryant R and Knight D (2019) *The Anthropology of the Future*. Cambridge: Cambridge University Press.
Bulman M (2020) Coronavirus: The people left with nothing because of the lockdown. *Independent*, 12 May.
Burton L (2007) Childhood adultification in economically disadvantaged families: A conceptual model. *Family Relations* 56(4): 329–345.
Butler J (2016) *Frames of War: When is Life Grievable?* London: Verso.
Cameron D (2011) Speech on immigration. Available at: https://www.theguardian.com/politics/2011/apr/14/david-cameron-immigration-speech-full-text (accessed 12 June 2020).
Cameron D (2013) Speech on immigration and welfare reform. Available at: https://www.gov.uk/government/speeches/david-camerons-immigration-speech (accessed 5 December 2024).
Careja R and Harris E (2022) Thirty years of welfare chauvinism research: Findings and challenges. *Journal of European Social Policy* 32(2): 212–224.
Casas-Cortes M, Cobarrubias S, De Genova N, et al. (2015) New keywords: Migration and borders. *Cultural Studies* 29(1): 55–87.
Chakrabarti S (2005) Rights and rhetoric: The politics of asylum and human rights culture in the United Kingdom. *Journal of Law and Society* 32(1): 131–147.
Children's Commissioner (2020) Our letter to the Home Secretary regarding the crisis facing migrant families with children in the face of the Covid-19 outbreak. Available at: https://www.childrenscommissioner.gov.uk/news/our-letter-to-the-home-secretary-regarding-the-crisis-facing-migrant-families-with-children-in-the-face-of-the-covid-19-outbreak/ (accessed 5 December 2024).

Clarke S and Garner S (2005) Psychoanalysis, identity and asylum. *Psychoanalysis, Culture & Society* 10(2): 197–206.
Coddington K, Conlon D and Martin LL (2020) Destitution economies: Circuits of value in asylum, refugee, and migration control. *Annals of the American Association of Geographers* 110(5): 1425–1444.
Colen S (1995) 'Like a mother to them': Stratified reproduction and West Indian childcare workers and employers in New York. In: Ginsburg FD and Rapp R (eds) *Conceiving the New World Order: The Global Politics of Reproduction*. Berkeley, CA: University of California Press, pp. 78–102.
Conlon D and Hiemstra N (2017) Introduction: Intimate economies of immigration detention. In: Conlon D and Hiemstra N (eds) *Intimate Economies of Immigration Detention*. London: Routledge, pp. 1–12.
Cooper M (2017) *Family Values: Between Neoliberalism and the New Social Conservatism*. Boston, MA: MIT Press.
Crafter S and Iqbal H (2021) Child language brokering as a family care practice: Reframing the 'parentified child' debate. *Children & Society* 36(3): 400–414.
Crawley H and Skleparis D (2017) Refugees, migrants, neither, both: Categorical fetishism and the politics of bounding in Europe's 'migration crisis'. *Journal of Ethnic and Migration Studies* 44(1): 48–64.
Crossley S (2016) 'Realising the (troubled) family', 'crafting the neoliberal state'. *Families, Relationships and Societies* 5(2): 263–279.
Cuibus M and Fernandez-Reino M (2023) *Briefing: Deprivation and the No Recourse to Public Funds (NRPF) Condition*. Oxford: COMPAS.
Dadusc D and Mudu P (2020) Care without control: The humanitarian industrial complex and the criminalisation of solidarity. *Geopolitics*. 27(4): 1–26.
Darling J (2022) *Systems of Suffering: Dispersal and the Denial of Asylum*. London: Pluto Press.
Davies T, Isakjee A, Mayblin L and Turner J (2021) Channel crossings: Offshoring asylum and the afterlife of empire in the Dover Strait. *Ethnic and Racial Studies* 44(13): 2307–2327.
Davis AY (1971) The black woman's role in the community of slaves. *The Black Scholar*. Available at: https://www.freedomarchives.org/Documents/finder/DOC46_scans/46.RoleBlackWomenSlavery.pdf.
Davis AY, Bhandar B and Ziadah R (2020) Angela Y. Davis. In: Bhandar B and Ziadah R (eds) *Revolutionary Feminisms: Conversations on Collective Action and Radical Thought*. London: Verso, pp. 171–182.
Dawar A (2011) Bid to cut influx into UK doomed. *The Express*, 21 June.
De Genova N (2002) Migrant 'illegality' and deportability in everyday life. *Annual Review of Anthropolology* 31: 419–447.
De Genova N (2018) The 'migrant crisis' as racial crisis: Do Black Lives Matter in Europe? *Ethnic and Racial Studies* 41(10): 1765–1782.
De Noronha L (2019) Deportation, racism and multi-status Britain: Immigration control and the production of race in the present. *Ethnic and Racial Studies* 42(14): 2413–2430.
De Noronha L (2020) *Deporting Black Britons: Portraits of Deportation to Jamaica/Luke de Noronha*. Manchester: Manchester University Press.
De Noronha L (2022) The conviviality of the overpoliced, detained and expelled: Refusing race and salvaging the human at the borders of Britain. *Sociological Review* 70(1): 159–177.

Dean J (1996) *Solidarity of Strangers: Feminism After Identity Politics*. Berkeley, CA: University of California Press.
Deighton Pierce Glynn (2023) *Major Home Office Concession on NRPF Policy*. Available at: https://dpglaw.co.uk/major-home-office-concession-on-nrpf-policy/ (accessed 5 December 2024).
Dennler KT (2018) Re/making immigration policy through practice: How social workers influence what it means to be a refused asylum seeker. *Migration and Society* 1(1): 82–95.
Desmond A (2018) The private life of family matters: Curtailing human rights protection for migrants under Article 8 of the ECHR? *European Journal of International Law* 29(1): 261–279.
Dexter Z, Capron L and Gregg L (2016) *Making Life Impossible: How the Needs of Destitute Migrant Children are Going Unmet*. London: The Chilkdren's Society.
Dickson E (2019) *Not Seen, Not Heard: Children's Experiences of the Hostile Environment*. London: Project 17.
Dickson E (2023) Bordering subjectivities: The psychic holds of Britain's asylum system. *Ethnic and Racial Studies*. DOI: 10.1080/01419870.2023.2292641. 1–21.
Dickson E and Rosen R (2021) 'Punishing those who do the wrong thing': Enforcing destitution and debt through the UK's family migration rules. *Critical Social Policy* 41(4): 545–565.
Dickson E and Rosen R (2023) *Policy Briefing: Section 17 Support for Families with 'No Recourse to Public Funds' (NRPF) in London*. London: Solidarities Project.
Dickson E, Redclift V and Rajina F (2023a) Attacking transnationalism and citizenship: British Bangladeshis, family migration, and the postcolonial state. *Critical Social Policy* 44(1): 45–66.
Dickson E, Rosen R and Sorinmade K (2023b) Hunger or indebtedness? Enforcing migrant destitution, racializing debt. In: Gilbert P, Bourne C, Haiven M and Montgomerie J (eds) *The Entangled Legacies of Empire: Race, Finance and Inequality*. Manchester: Manchester University Press, pp. 131–140.
Dines N, Montagna N and Ruggiero V (2014) Thinking Lampedusa: Border construction, the spectacle of bare life and the productivity of migrants. *Ethnic and Racial Studies* 38(3): 430–445.
Dowling E (2016) Valorised but not valued? Affective remuneration, social reproduction and feminist politics beyond the crisis. *British Politics* 11(4): 452–468.
Doyle J (2011) Ministers target migrant abuse of 'right to family life'. *Daily Mail*, 4 July.
Drangsland KA (2020) Bordering through recalibration: Exploring the temporality of the German "Ausbildungsduldung". *Environment and Planning C: Politics and Space* 38(6): 1128–1145.
Drayton E, Farquharson C, Ogden K, et al. (2023) *Annual Report on Education Spending in England: 2023*. London: Institute for Fiscal Studies.
Dudley RG (2017) Domestic abuse and women with 'no recourse to public funds': The state's role in shaping and reinforcing coercive control. *Families, Relationships and Societies* 6(2): 201–217.
Education Committee (2012) *Minutes of Evidence*. London: Hoiuse of Commons.
El-Enany N (2020) *(B)ordering Britain: Law, Race and Empire*. Manchester: Manchester University Press.

Erel U (2018) Saving and reproducing the nation: Struggles around right-wing politics of social reproduction, gender and race in austerity Europe. *Women's Studies International Forum* 68: 173–182.

Erel U, Murji K and Nahaboo Z (2016) Understanding the contemporary race–migration nexus. *Ethnic and Racial Studies* 39(8): 1339–1360.

Erel U, Reynolds T and Kaptani E (2017) Migrant mothers' creative interventions into racialized citizenship. *Ethnic and Racial Studies* 41(1): 55–72.

Esping-Andersen G (1990) *The Three Worlds of Welfare Capitalism*. Princeton, NJ: Princeton University Press.

Fabian J (1991) *Time and the Other: How Anthropology Makes its Object*. New York: Columbia University Press.

Fairclough N (2003) *Analysing Discourse: Textual Analysis for Social Research*. London: Routledge.

Fanon F (2008) *Black Skin, White Masks*. London: Pluto.

Federici S (2012) *Revolution at Point Zero: Housework, Reproduction, and Feminist Struggle*. Oakland, CA: PM Press.

Federici S (2014) From commoning to debt: Financialization, microcredit, and the changing architecture of capital accumulation. *South Atlantic Quarterly* 113(2): 231–244.

Fernández-Reino M (2020) *Children of Migrants in the UK*. Migration Observatory Briefing. Oxford: Uniuversity of Oxford.

Freedman D (2010) Media policy silences: The hidden face of communications decision making. *International Journal of Press-Politics* 15(3): 344–361.

Freud S (1977) *On Sexuality: Three Essays on the Theory of Sexuality, and Other Works*, tr. from the German under the general editorship of James Strachey; this vol. ed. Angela Richards. Harmondsworth: Penguin.

Gagen EA (2007) Reflections of primitivism: Development, progress and civilization in imperial America, 1898–1914. *Children's Geographies* 5(1–2): 15–28.

Garlen JC, Chang-Kredl S, Farley L and Sonu D (2021) Childhood innocence and experience: Memory, discourse and practice. *Children & Society* 35(5): 648–662.

Ghorashi H, de Boer M and ten Holder F (2018) Unexpected agency on the threshold: Asylum seekers narrating from an asylum seeker centre. *Current Sociology* 66(3): 373–391.

Gilbert P, Bourne C, Haiven M and Montgomerie J (2023) Introduction. In: Gilbert P, Bourne C, Haiven M and Montgomerie J (eds) *The Entangled Legacies of Empire: Race, Finance and Inequality*. Manchester: Manchester University Press, pp. 1–38.

Gillies V, Edwards R and Horsley N (2017) *Challenging the Politics of Early Intervention: Who's 'Saving' Children and Why*. Bristol: Policy Press.

Gilmore RW (2007) *Golden Gulag: Prisons, Surplus, Crisis, and Opposition in Globalizing California*. Berkeley and Los Angeles, CA: University of California Press.

Gilmore RW (2023) *Abolition Geography: Essays towards Liberation*. London: Verso.

Gilroy P (1993) *Black Atlantic: Modernity and Double Consciousness*. London: Verso.

Gilroy P (2005) *Postcolonial Melancholia*. New York: Columbia University Press.

Goldberg DT (2002) *The Racial State*. Malden, MA: Blackwell Publishing.

Gonzales RG, Sigona N, Franco MC and Papoutsi A (2019) *Undocumented Migration*. Cambridge: Polity Press.

Graeber D (2014) *Debt: The First 5,000 Years*. Brooklyn and London: Melville House.

Green D (2011) Family migration. Available at: https://www.gov.uk/government/speeches/immigration-damian-greens-speech-on-family-migration (accessed 5 December 2024).

Green D (2012) Making immigration work for Britain. Available at: https://www.gov.uk/government/speeches/damian-greens-speech-on-making-immigration-work-for-britain (accessed 5 December 2024).

Griffiths MBE (2014) Out of Time: The Temporal Uncertainties of Refused Asylum Seekers and Immigration Detainees. *Journal of Ethnic and Migration Studies* 40(12): 1991–2009.

Guentner S, Lukes S, Stanton R, et al. (2016) Bordering practices in the UK welfare system. *Critical Social Policy* 36(3): 391–411.

Gunaratnam Y (2020) The violence that sustains us: Plantations, care and the pandemic. In: *The Politics of Social Reproduction, Migration and the Hostile Environment, SSAHE webinar*, Social Scientists Against the Hostile Environment. https://www.youtube.com/watch?v=a7XPK4hF1ZY (accessed 5 December 2024).

Hall S (1980) Race, articulation and societies structured in dominance. *Sociological Theories: Race and Colonialism*. Paris: UNESCO.

Hall S (2017) *The Fateful Triangle: Race, Ethnicity, Nation*. Cambridge, MA: Harvard University Press.

Hamilton JM, Zettel T and Neimanis A (2021) Feminist infrastructure for better weathering. *Australian Feminist Studies* 36(109): 237–259.

Hartman SV (1997) *Scenes of Subjection: Terror, Slavery, and Self-Making in Nineteenth-Century America* New York; Oxford: Oxford University Press.

Harvey D (2003) *The New Imperialism*. Oxford: Oxford University Press.

Harvey D (2007) *A Brief History of Neoliberalism*. Oxford: Oxford University Press.

Hayes D (2002) From aliens to asylum seekers: A history of immigration controls and welfare in Britain. In: Cohen S, Humphries B and Mynott E (eds) *From Immigration Controls to Welfare Controls*. Abingdon: Routledge, pp. 30–46.

Hays S (1996) *The Cultural Contradictions of Motherhood*. New Haven, CT, and London: Yale University Press.

Heidbrink L (2014) *Migrant Youth, Transnational Families, and the State: Care and Contested Interests*. Philadelphia: University of Pennsylvania Press.

Heidbrink L and Statz M (2017) Parents of global youth: Contesting debt and belonging. *Children's Geographies*. DOI: 10.1080/14733285.2017.1284645. 1–13.

Hollway W (2016) Emotional experience plus reflection: Countertransference and reflexivity in research. *The Psychotherapist* 62: 19–21.

Home Office (2011) *Family Migration: A Consultation*. London: Home Office.

Home Office (2012a) *Impact Assessment: Changes to the Family Migration Rules*. London: Home Office.

Home Office (2012b) *Statement of Intent: Family Migration*. London: Home Office.

Home Office (n.d.) Apply to the EU Settlement Scheme (settled and pre-settled status). Available at: https://www.gov.uk/settled-status-eu-citizens-families/ (accessed 5 December 2024).

hooks b (2014) *Yearning: Race, Gender and Cultural Politics*. New York: Routledge.
Humphreys C, Mullender A, Thiara R and Skamballis A (2006) 'Talking to my Mum': Developing Communication between Mothers and Children in the Aftermath of Domestic Violence. *Journal of Social Work* 6(1): 53–63.
Isin EF and Nielsen GM (2008) Introduction: Acts of Citizenship. In: Isin EF and Nielsen GM (eds) *Acts of Citizenship*. London and New York: Zed Books, pp. 1–12.
Jacobsen CM, Karlsen M-A and Khosravi S (2021) *Waiting and the Temporalities of Irregular Migration*. London: Routledge.
Jacobsen CM and Karlsen M-A (2021) Introduction: Unpacking the temporalities of irregular migration. In: Jacobsen CM, Karlsen M-A and Khosravi S (eds) *Waiting and the Temporalities of Irregular Migration*. London: Routledge, pp. 1–19.
Jensen T (2018) *Parenting the Crisis: The Cultural Politics of Parent-Blame*. Bristol: Bristol University Press.
Jolly A (2018) No recourse to social work? Statutory neglect, social exclusion and undocumented migrant families in the UK. *Social Inclusion* 6(3): 190–200.
Jolly A, Singh J and Lobo S (2022) No recourse to public funds: A qualitative evidence synthesis. *International Journal of Migration, Health and Social Care* 18(1): 107–123.
Jolly A, Thomas S and Stanyer J (2020) *London's Children and young People Who are Not British Citizens: A Profile*. London: Greater London Authority. Available at: https://www.london.gov.uk/sites/default/files/final_londons_children_and_young_peope_who_are_not_british_citizens.pdf.
Kaba M (2021) Hope is a discipline: Mariame Kaba on dismantling the carceral state. Available at: https://theintercept.com/2021/03/17/intercepted-mariame-kaba-abolitionist-organizing/ (accessed 5 December 2024).
Kapoor N (2018) *Deport, Deprive, Extradite: 21st Century State Extremism*. London: Verso.
Katz C (2002) Stuck in place: Children and the globalization of social reproduction. In: Johnston RJ, Taylor PJ and Watts MJ (eds) *Geographies of Global Change: Remapping the World*, Oxford: Blackwell, pp. 248–259.
Kaur S (2020) Thousands of migrants denied help in the pandemic. *BBC News*, 18 August.
Kenyon M and Clarke-Ezzidio H (2024) Council bankruptcy tracker: Authorities under increasing financial strain. *The New Statesman*. Available at: https://www.newstatesman.com/spotlight/economic-growth/regional-development/2024/01/council-bankruptcy-tracker-local-government-authorities-finances#:~:text=Councils%20in%20financial%20distress,debt%20relative%20to%20their%20size.
Khosravi S (2021) Afterword: Waiting, a state of consciousness. In: Jacobsen CM, Karlsen M-A and Khosravi S (eds) *Waiting and the Temporalities of Irregular Migration*. London: Routledge, pp. 202–208.
Kilkey M (2017) Conditioning family-life at the intersection of migration and welfare: The implications for 'Brexit families'. *Journal of Social Policy* 46(4): 797–814.
Kirkup J and Winnett R (2012) Theresa May interview: 'We're going to give illegal migrants a really hostile reception'. *The Telegraph*, 25 May.
Kirkwood S, Goodman S, McVittie C and McKinlay A (2016) *Destitution, Detention and Forced Return: The Language of Asylum*. London: Palgrave Macmillan.

Kofman E (2012) Rethinking care through social reproduction: Articulating circuits of migration. *Social Politics: International Studies in Gender, State and Society* 19(1): 142–162.
Kundnani A (2023) *What is Anti-Racism? And Why it Means Anti-Capitalism*. London: Verso.
Lambie-Mumford H and Green MA (2017) Austerity, welfare reform and the rising use of food banks by children in England and Wales. *Area* 49(3): 273–279.
Larkins C (2013) Enacting children's citizenship: Developing understandings of how children enact themselves as citizens through actions and acts of citizenship. *Childhood* 21(1): 7–21.
Leon L and Rosen R (2023) Unaccompanied migrant children and indebted relations: Weaponizing safeguarding. *Child & Family Social Work* 28(4): 897–1234.
Levitas RA (2010) Back to the future: Wells, sociology, utopia and method. *Sociological Review* 58(4): 530–547.
Lewis G (2005) Welcome to the margins: Diversity, tolerance, and policies of exclusion. *Ethnic and Racial Studies* 28(3): 536–558.
LGA Asylum and Refugee Task Group (2009) *NRPF 'Cost Implications for Local Authorities Report'*. London: LGA.
Lisiak A (2017) Other mothers: Encountering in/visible femininities in migration and urban contexts. *Feminist Review* 117: 41–55.
London Councils (n.d.) No Recourse to Public Funds (NRPF). Available at: https://www.londoncouncils.gov.uk/our-key-themes/asylum-migration-and-refugees/no-recourse-public-funds (accessed 16 November 2022).
McGovern F and Devine D (2015) The care worlds of migrant children: Exploring inter-generational dynamics of love, care and solidarity across home and school. *Childhood* 23(1): 37–52.
McKinney C and Sumption M (2021) *Briefing: Migrants on Ten-Year Routes to Settlement in the UK*. Oxford: COMPAS.
McNally D (2010) *Global Slump: The Economics and Politics of Crisis and Resistance*. Oakland, CA: PM Press/Spectre.
Marmot M (2023) Britain's hunger and malnutrition crisis could be easily solved – yet politicians choose not to. *The Guardian*, 27 Dec.
Marsh S (2020) London councils call on government to suspend NRPF immigration status. *The Guardian*, 8 July.
Marx K (1976) *Capital: A Critique of Political Economy – Vol 1 (1867)*. Harmondsworth: Penguin Books.
May T (2011) Speech to the Conservative party conference. Available at: https://www.politics.co.uk/comment-analysis/2011/10/04/theresa-may-speech-in-full (accessed 5 December 2024).
Mayblin L (2020) *Impoverishment and Asylum: Social Policy as Slow Violence*. London: Routledge.
Mbembe A (2017) *Critique of black Reason*. Durham, NC, and London: Duke University Press.
Mbembe A (2019) *Necropolitics*. Durham, NC: Duke University Press.
Meghji A and Niang SM (2022) Between post-racial ideology and provincial universalisms: Critical race theory, decolonial thought and COVID-19 in Britain. *Sociology*. 56(1): 131–147.

Meier I and Donà G (2021) Micropolitics of time: Asylum regimes, temporalities and everyday forms of power. In: Bhatia M and Canning V (eds) *Stealing Time: Migration, Temporalities and State Violence*. Palgrave Macmillan, pp. 39–64.
Mezzadra S and Neilson B (2013) *Borders as Method, or, The Multiplication of Labor*. Durham, NC, and London: Duke University Press.
Mills C and Klein E (2021) Affective technologies of welfare deterrence in Australia and the United Kingdom. *Economy and Society* 50(3): 397–422.
Mills C and Lefrançois BA (2018) Child as metaphor: Colonialism, psy-governance, and epistemicide. *World Futures* 74(7–8): 503–524.
Mills J (2020) Boris Johnson 'surprised' to hear about his own immigration law. *Metro*, 27 May.
Mitchell K (2022) Migration, memory, and the insurgent temporalities of sanctuary. *Geografiska Annaler: Series B, Human Geography* 105(2): 179–192.
Mitchell K, Marston SA and Katz C (2003) Introduction: Life's work: An introduction, review and critique. *Antipode* 35(3): 415–442.
Mitton L (2009) The British welfare system: Marketization from Thatcher to New Labour. In: Schubert K, Hegelich S and Bazant U (eds) *The Handbook of European Welfare States*. London: Routledge, pp. 478–494.
Mohdin A (2019) More than 70% of UK immigration fee waiver requests by destitute are rejected. *The Guardian*, 4 Apr.
Morgan B (2024) *Destitute Migrant Families' Experiences of Approaching Social Services for Support: A Report Based on the Accounts of Volunteer Accompaniers*. London: Solidarities research project.
Moulin C (2012) Ungrateful subjects? Refugee protests and the logic of gratitude. In: Nyers P and Rygiel K (eds) *Citizenship, Migrant Activism and the Politics of Movement*. London: Routledge, pp. 54–72.
Mulinari P and Neergaard A (2023) Trade unions negotiating the Swedish model: Racial capitalism, whiteness and the invisibility of race. *Race & Class* 64(4): 48–66.
Nail T (2015) *The Figure of the Migrant*. Stanford, CA: Stanford University Press.
Nanni G (2023) *The Colonisation of Time: Ritual, Routine and Resistance in the British Empire*. Manchester: Manchester University Press.
Narotzky S and Besnier N (2014) Crisis, value, and hope: Rethinking the economy. *Current Anthropology* 55(S9): S4–S16.
Newberry J and Rosen R (2020) Women and children together and apart: Finding the time for social reproduction theory. *Focaal* 86: 112–120.
Newth G (2021) Rethinking 'nativism': Beyond the ideational approach. *Identities* 30(2): 161–180.
Nieuwenhuys O (2020) Women and children in social reproduction and the global womb. *Focaal* 2020(86): 129–132.
NRPF Network (2022) *NRPF Connect Data Report 2021–2022*. London: NRPF Network.
NRPF Network (2024) Cost to councils of supporting people with NRPF rises to £77.6 million. Available at: https://nrpfnetwork.org.uk/news/nrpf-connect-data-report-2022-23 (accessed 30 January 2024).
O'Neill M and Roberts B (2019) *Walking Methods: Research on the Move*. London: Routledge.
O'Neill M, Erel U, Kaptani E and Reynolds T (2019) Borders, risk and belonging: Challenges for arts-based research in understanding the lives of women asylum

seekers and migrants 'at the borders of humanity'. *Crossings: Journal of Migration and Culture* 10(1): 129–147.
Oliveri F (2012) Migrants as activist citizens in Italy: Understanding the new cycle of struggles. *Citizenship Studies* 16(5–6): 793–806.
Parrenas RS (2000) Migrant Filipina domestic workers and the international division of reproductive labor. *Gender and Society* 14(4): 560–580.
Parrenas RS (2012) The reproductive labour of migrant workers. *Global Networks* 12(2): 269–275.
Phoenix A (2013) *Doing Narrative Research*. 2nd ed. London: SAGE Publications.
Pinter I, Compton S, Parhar R and Majid H (2020) *A Lifeline for All: Children and Families with No Recourse to Public Funds*. London: The Children's Society.
Pratt G (2012) *Families Apart: Migrant Mothers and the Conflicts of Labor and Love*. Minneapolis, MN: University of Minnesota Press.
Price J and Spencer S (2015) *Safeguarding Children from Destitution: Local Authority Responses to Families with 'No Recourse to Public Funds'*. Oxford: Compas.
Puig ME (2002) The adultification of refugee children. *Journal of Human Behavior in the Social Environment* 5(3–4): 85–95.
Qvortrup J (2009) Are children human beings or human becomings? A critical assessment of outcome thinking. *Rivista Internazionale di Scienze Sociali* 117: 631–653.
Rai SM, Hoskyns C and Thomas D (2013) Depletion. *International Feminist Journal of Politics* 16(1): 86–105.
Rattansi A (2020) *Racism: A Very Short Introduction*. 2nd ed. Oxford: Oxford University Press.
Reynolds JF and Orellana M (2009) New immigrant youth interpreting in white public spaces. *America Anthropologist* 111(2): 211–223.
Rikowski G (2003) Alien life: Marx and the future of the human. *Historical Materialism* 11(2): 121–164.
Robinson CJ (2000 [1983]) *Black Marxism: The Making of the Black Radical Tradition*. Chapel Hills, CA, and London: University of California Press.
Rollo T (2016) Feral children: Settler colonialism, progress, and the figure of the child. *Settler Colonial Studies* 8(1): 60–79.
Rose J (1984) *The Case of Peter Pan, or, The Impossibility of Children's Fiction*. London: Macmillan.
Rosen R (2022) Welfare statecraft and the reproduction of migrant destitution. In: *Solidarities: Negotiating Migrant Deservingness*. Available at: https://solidarities.net/welfare-statecraft-and-the-reproduction-of-migrant-destitution/ (accessed 5 December 2024).
Rosen R (2023) Childhood in and through social reproduction theory. In: Balagopalan S, Wall J and Wells K (eds) *Handbook of Theories in Childhood Studies*. London: Bloomsbury Academic, pp. 280–294.
Rosen R and Dickson E (2024) The exceptions to child exceptionalism: Racialised migrant 'deservingness' and the UK's free school meal debates. *Critical Social Policy* 44(2): 201–221.
Rosen R and Faircloth C (2020) Adult–child relations in neoliberal times: Insights from a dialogue across childhood and parenting culture studies. *Families, Relationships and Societies* 9(1): 7–22.

Rosen R and Newberry J (2018) Love, labour and temporality: Reconceptualising social reproduction with women *and* children in the frame. In: Rosen R and Twamley K (eds) *Feminism and the Politics of Childhood: Friends or Foes?* London: UCL Press, pp. 117–133.

Rosen R and Suissa J (2020) Children, parents and non-parents: To whom does 'the future' belong? *Families, Relationships and Societies* 9(1): 125–141.

Rosen R, Baustad S and Edwards M (2017) The crisis of social reproduction under global capitalism: Working class women and children in the struggle for universal childcare. In: Langford R, Prentice S and Albanese P (eds) *Caring for Children: Social Movements and Public Policy in Canada*. Vancouver: UBC Press, pp. 164–185.

Rosen R, Crafter S and Meetoo V (2021) An absent presence: Separated child migrants' caring practices and the fortified neoliberal state. *Journal of Ethnic and Migration Studies* 47(7): 1649–1666.

Sainsbury D (2012) *Welfare states and Immigrant Rights: The Politics of Inclusion and Exclusion*. Oxford: Oxford University Press.

Sayer A (2011) *Why Things Matter to People: Social Science, Values and Ethical Life*. Cambridge: Cambridge University Press.

Schön D (1993) Generative metaphor: A perspective on problem-setting in social policy. In: Ortony A (ed) *Metaphor and Thought*. 2nd ed. Cambridge: Cambridge University Press, pp. 137–163.

Schools ABC (2024) *Against Borders for Children*. Available at: https://www.schoolsabc.net/ (accessed 7 February 2024).

Scott JC (1985) *Weapons of the Weak: Everyday Forms of Peasant Resistance*. New Haven, CT: Yale University Press.

Sharma S (2014) *In the Meantime: Temporality and Cultural Politics*. Durham, NC: Duke University Press.

Shilliam R (2018) *Race and the Undeserving Poor: From Abolition to Brexit*. Newcastle upon Tyne: Agenda Publishing.

Shropshire Star (2020) Dame Emma Thompson calls on Priti Patel to allow migrants to access support. 24 Apr.

Shutes I (2017) Controlling migration: The gender implications of work-related conditions in restricting rights to residence and to social benefits. In: Hudson J, Needham C and Heins E (eds) *Social Policy Review 29*. Bristol: Bristol University Press, pp. 243–257.

Silverstein PA (2005) Immigrant racialization and the new savage slot: Race, migration, and immigration in the New Europe. *Annual Review of Anthropology* 34: 363–384.

Simmonds DM, Coyle NM, Farron TM and Butler P (2020) Covid crisis demands 'safety-net for all'. Politics.co.uk, 3 Dec. https://www.politics.co.uk/comment-analysis/2020/12/03/covid-crisis-demands-safety-net-for-all/ (accessed 5 December 2024).

Simpson A (2007) On ethnographic refusal: Indigeneity, 'voice' and colonial citizenship. *Junctures* 9: 67–80.

Simpson A (2017) The ruse of consent and the anatomy of 'refusal': Cases from indigenous North America and Australia. *Postcolonial Studies* 20(1): 18–33.

Sirriyeh A (2015) 'All you need is love and £18,600': Class and the new UK family migration rules. *Critical Social Policy* 35(2): 228–247.

Skeggs B (1997) *Formations of Class and Gender: Becoming Respectable*. London: Sage.
Skeggs B (2013) Values beyond value? Is anything beyond the logic of capital? *British Journal of Sociology*, 65(1): 1–20.
Slack J (2011) Human right to sponge off UK. *Daily Mail*, 17 June.
Smith C, O'Reilly P, Rumpel R et al. (2021) *How do I Survive Now?* London: Citizens Advice.
Spivak GC (1988) Can the subaltern speak? In: Nelson C and Grossberg L (eds) *Marxism and the Interpretation of Culture*. Urbana, IL: University of Illinois Press.
SSAHE (2020) *Migration, Racism and the Hostile Environment: Making the Case for the Social Sciences*. London: SSAHE.
Stoler AL (1995) *Race and the Education of Desire: Foucault's History of Sexuality and the Colonial Order of Things*. Durham, NC, and London: Duke University Press.
Sunak R (2023) PM speech on building a better future. 4 Jan. Available at: https://www.gov.uk/government/speeches/pm-speech-on-making-2023-the-first-year-of-a-new-and-better-future-4-january-2023 (accessed 8 June 2024).
Taha M and Salem S (2019) Social reproduction and empire in an Egyptian century. *Radical Philosophy* 2(4): 47–54.
Taylor S (2006) Critical policy analysis: Exploring contexts, texts and consequences. *Discourse: Studies in the Cultural Politics of Education* 18(1): 23–35.
Tazzioli M (2018) The temporal borders of asylum: Temporality of control in the EU border regime. *Political Geography* 64: 13–22.
Tazzioli M (2020) *The Making of Migration: The Biopolitics of Mobility at Europe's Borders*. London: SAGE publications.
Threipland C (2015) *A Place to Call Home: A Report into the Standard of Accommodation Provided to Children in Need in London*. London: Hackney Community Law Centre and Hackney Migrant Centre.
Ticktin MI (2011) *Casualties of Care: Immigration and the Politics of Humanitarianism in France*. Berkeley, CA: University of California Press.
Tonkiss K and Bloom T (2015) Theorising noncitizenship: Concepts, debates and challenges. *Citizenship Studies* 19(8): 837–852.
Tronto JC (2011) A feminist democratic ethics of care and global care workers: Citizenship and responsibilitly. In: Mahon R and Robinson F (eds) *Feminist Ethics and Social Policy: Towards a New Global Political Economy of Care*. Vancouver: UBC Press, pp. 162–177.
Turner J (2015) The Family Migration Visa in the History of Marriage Restrictions: Postcolonial Relations and the UK Border. *British Journal of Politics and International Relations* 17(4): 623–643.
Twum-Danso Imoh A (2022) Framing reciprocal obligations within intergenerational relations in Ghana through the lens of the mutuality of duty and dependence. *Childhood* 39(3): 439–454.
Tyler I (2013) *Revolting Subjects: Social Abjection and Resistance in Neoliberal Britain*. London: Zed Books.
Tyler I (2021) *Stigma: The Machinery of Inequality*. London: Zed Books.
UK Visas and Immigration (2023) *Policy Equality Statement (PES)*. London: Crown copyright.
Valluvan S (2017) Defining and challenging new nationalism. *Progressive Review* 23(4): 232–241.

Valluvan S (2018) Racial entanglements and sociological confusions: Repudiating the rehabilitation of integration. *British Journal of Sociology* 69(2): 436–458.
Valluvan S (2019) *The Clamour of Nationalism: Race and Nation in Twenty-First-Century Britain*. Manchester: Manchester University Press.
Valluvan S and Kalra VS (2019) Racial nationalisms: Brexit, borders and Little Englander contradictions. *Ethnic and Racial Studies* 42(14): 2393–2412.
van Baar H (2017) Evictability and the biopolitical bordering of Europe. *Antipode* 49(1): 212–230.
Van Der Leun J (2006) Excluding illegal migrants in the Netherlands: Between national policies and local implementation. *West European Politics* 29(2): 310–326.
van Oorschot WJH (2000) Who should get what, and why? On deservingness criteria and the conditionality of solidarity among the public. *Policy and Politics: Studies of Local Government and its Services* 28(1): 33–48.
Vincent D (2020) Coronavirus: Undocumented workers an 'invisible public health risk'. BBC News, 24 June.
Virdee S (2019) Racialized capitalism: An account of its contested origins and consolidation. *Sociological Review* 67(1): 3–27.
Vogel L (2000) Domestic labor revisited. *Science & Society* 64(2): 151–170.
Wacquant L (2009) *Punishing the Poor: The Neoliberal Government of Social Insecurity*. Durham, NC: Duke University Press.
Wacquant L (2023) The trap of 'racial capitalism'. *European Journal of Sociology* 64(2): 153–162.
Wall J (2021) *Give Children the Vote: On Democratizing Democracy*. London: Bloomsbury Publishing.
Watt P (2018) 'This pain of moving, moving, moving': Evictions, displacement and logics of expulsion in London. *L'Année sociologique* 68(1): 67–100.
Whitley L (2017) The disappearance of race: A critique of the use of Agamben in border and migration scholarship. *borderlands* 16(1): 1–23.
Williams F (2014) Making connections across the transnational political economy of care. In: Anderson B and Shutes I (eds) *Migration and Care Labour: Theory, Policy and Politics*. Basingstoke: Macmillan, pp. 11–30.
Williams M (2021) *The Next Story*. London: Solitudes Past and Present, Queen Mary University of London.
Woodhead M (2015) Psychology and the cultural construction of children's needs. In: James A and Prout A (eds) *Constructing and Reconstructing Childhood: Contemporary Issues in the Sociological Study of Childhood*. 3rd ed. London: Routledge, pp. 54–73.
Woodhouse C (2011) Curbs on migration to target sham weddings. *Evening Standard*, 13 July.
Woolley A (2019) *Access Denied: The Cost of the 'No Recourse to Public Funds' Policy*. London: Unity Project.
Work and Pensions Committee (2022) *Children in Poverty: No Recourse to Public Funds*. London: House of Commons.
Yeo C (2023) Last traces of Nationality and Borders Act 2022 erased with abandonment of 'differentiated status' for refugees. Available at: https://freemovement.org.uk/last-traces-of-nationality-and-borders-act-2022–erased-with-abandonment-of-differentiated-status-for-refugees/ (accessed 5 December 2024).

Yuval-Davis N, Wemyss G and Cassidy K (2018) Everyday bordering, belonging and the reorientation of British immigration legislation. *Sociology* 52(2): 228–244.
Yuval-Davis N, Wemyss G and Cassidy K (2019) *Bordering*. Cambridge: Polity.

Index

Abiola (interlocuter) 19, 28, 74, 76, 102–105, 108–110, 112, 122–123, 124
abuse 64
abusive relationships 69, 70–71, 75
accommodation 8, 25, 26, 46, 63, 66, 98–101, 110, 112, 115, 119–120, 124–125, 127, 148
Adkins L 125, 126
adult–child power relations 85
Agamben, Giorgio 1, 46
　bare life 1, 46, 47, 48–52, 57, 59, 61, 68
aid 94–96, 152
　refusal 96–97
Akin (interlocuter) 28, 102–105, 108–110, 112
Aliens Act 1905 26, 139
aloneness 62–65, 76, 90
Anderson B 4, 70
Andersson R 139, 154
anti-discrimination legislation 148
anti-EU discourse 32
anxiety 104–105, 109
applications 3, 20, 29, 36, 38, 54, 115, 117–118, 148, 156
Article 8 rights 20, 27–29, 31–32, 35, 38–39
austerity 5, 37, 139, 155

belonging 4, 33–34, 72, 76, 78, 116, 135, 137, 140, 144, 154
benefit tourism 33, 133

benefits 2, 20, 25, 33, 45, 146, 154
Beveridge Report 5
Bhambra GK 3–4, 143
Bhattacharyya, G. 10, 14, 84, 90, 95, 136, 140, 157
biological existence, denial of right to 46–47
Black and Minority Ethnic (BME) status 136–137
Black Lives Matter protests 131
blackness 27
blame, culture of 105
border technologies, racialised 23, 27, 29, 34–35, 132–149
bordering 6, 8, 21, 72–73, 144–145
borders 1, 6–7
Brexit 27, 40, 139
bureaucracy navigation 87–89, 115–116, 148
bureaucratic time 118

capitalism 5, 9, 125, 138, 141–142, 157
　racial 56, 63, 90, 94, 141–142, 149, 154, 155
　rentier 119
capitalist value, circuits of 94
care, feminist ethics of 92
caring labour 92–94
change of conditions 3, 36, 45–46, 115
charities 41, 54, 89, 94–95, 96
Child Benefit 41
child rearing 12–15

childbirth, 12–15
childcare 3, 35, 45, 55, 64, 105, 127–128
childhood sexuality 109–111
child-in-need framework 12, 78–79, 89, 96, 112
Children Act 1989 12, 63, 97n1, 155
  Section 17 3, 25–26, 36, 78, 89, 100, 110, 118–119, 156
children and childhood 22, 23, 78–79, 101, 150
  adultified 79, 97
  aid 94–96
  aid refusal 96–97
  ambiguous policy position 78–79
  bureaucracy navigation 87–89
  caring labour 92–94
  central role 77
  characteristics 80
  child-in-need framework 12, 78–79, 89, 96, 112
  citizenship 28, 145
  containing their own needs 93–94, 106–107
  deservingness 28, 153
  dominant imaginaries of 104
  exceptionalism 14, 153
  free school meals 24, 25, 41, 50, 134, 146, 151
  gendered responsibility for 35
  hopes and dreams 50–51, 128–129
  interlocuters 19, 22, 79
  interviews 16–17
  language brokering 88
  life-making practices 79–83, 87
  literature 12
  as lives to live for 74–75
  milestones 13–14
  positioning 80
  racial discrimination 134
  reparative work 89–94
  reproductive labour 79, 82–83, 92–93, 97
  sacrifices for 55
  shielding 103–105
  shielding parents 105–106
  social constitution of 13
  social reproduction and 12–15, 18
  socio-political positioning 79
  understanding 105–106
  weathering 87
  welfare contexts 22
Christmas 107
citizenship 4, 17, 20, 24, 57, 72, 94, 134, 144–145
  children 28, 145
Citizenship Act 1981 144
coercive control 3
cohabitation 12, 101, 108, 110
colonial extraction 142–143
colonialism 56, 126
Commonwealth Immigrants Act (1968) 139
cost-benefit calculations 33–35
cost-shunting 26
counter-transference 65
Covid-19 pandemic 15, 40, 41, 54, 86, 89, 100, 107, 148
criminalisation 24, 31–32, 147

Davis, AY. 51, 55
De Genova N 7, 70, 136, 138
De Noronha L 17, 72–73, 131, 145, 149
debt and debt servicing 21, 28, 35–37, 38–40, 45, 59, 75, 90, 99, 116, 124–126, 142, 145, 156, 157
decolonialisation 6
degradation 1, 2, 157
dehumanisation 47, 96
depletion 9, 11–12, 15, 47, 48, 51, 52, 57, 90, 92, 127, 152, 153, 157
deportability 7, 34, 70, 126, 156
deportation 1, 7, 9, 23, 37, 38–39, 56, 148, 150, 151, 156
depression 76
Destiny (interlocuter) 20, 29, 35, 38, 86, 91, 95, 110, 115–116, 117–121, 122–123, 124–126, 127–128, 129, 145, 151

destitution 3, 47, 145, 150, 155, 156
  enforced 21, 28, 35–37, 47, 51, 52–59, 63, 77, 91, 95, 98–99, 156
  intimate economies 98–99
  risk of 45
  and ten-year route 39
  weathering 52–59
destitution economies 86–87
developmentalism 145
digital technology 87
dignity 22, 49, 99, 113, 152, 157
discretionary leave 28, 30, 32
domestic violence 3, 69, 70–71, 75
dreams 57–58, 76, 85–86, 90, 126–130

economic burdens 33
economic contributions 33
education, schools and schooling 17, 80, 83–84, 84, 86, 88, 146
El-Enany N 34, 144
emotion 61
emotional care 91–92
emotional fortification 56
emotional labour 79, 97
endurance 22, 55, 56, 76
enforced destitution 47, 51, 77, 91, 95, 156
  intimate economies 98–99
  level of 63
  weathering 52–59
enforced proximity 98–99, 101, 102–108, 121
  physical intimacy 108–113, 114
  secrets and silences 102–108, 113, 117
Equalities legislation 17, 131–149
Equality Act 2010 133
ethics 15–19
EU Settlement Scheme 40
European Convention on Human Rights (ECHR) 20, 31–32
  Article 8 rights 20, 25, 27, 28, 29, 31, 32, 35, 38–39

European Economic Area (EEA) citizens 40
everyday bordering 8, 73
everyday interactions 71–72
everyday labour 47, 49
everyday mistreatment 71–72
everyday racism 131–132
evictions 100–101, 103
evictability 101
exclusion 14, 23, 26, 32, 37, 39, 41, 46, 94, 128, 143, 145, 156
existential erasure 1, 12, 21, 22, 61, 65, 116, 121
exploitation 3, 11, 19, 21, 64, 65, 77, 85, 90, 135, 143, 156

family 9, 14, 22, 155
  bonds 48–49
  criminalisation 31–32
  as an island apart 96–97
  multi-status structures 28–29, 96, 145
  reparative work 90
  as a site of crisis 13
family life, right to 31–32
family migration routes 27–40
Fanon, F 68
financial crisis, 2008 5
financial self-sufficiency 25
five-year route 40, 144–145
food, lack of 45
food banks 95
fortification 68
fortitude 49–50, 57
free school meals 24, 25, 41, 50, 134, 146, 151

gatekeeping 6–7, 37, 45–46, 48, 73
gendered inequalities 35
gendered violence 69, 70–71, 75
Gilmore, RW 1, 8, 63, 132, 152, 153
global care chain 10
global colour line 6
good migrants 107–108, 144–145
government selection rhetoric 33–35
gratitude, performances of 107–108

great replacement theory 137
Guentner S 5, 8

half-life application 20
hardship 3, 12, 21, 40–41, 46–48, 49, 51–52, 52, 59, 63, 75, 77, 84, 90, 91, 98
Home Office 30, 32, 35–36, 38, 38–39, 40, 66, 73, 101, 146, 156
homelessness 1, 3, 22, 46, 70, 98, 99, 118
homeplace 49, 55–56, 63, 80, 97
hooks, b 49, 54, 97
hope 50, 57–58, 126–130, 153
hostels 53, 66, 76, 87, 107, 110, 119, 121, 127, 129
hostile environment 6, 22, 26, 27, 41, 57
housing 3, 6, 22, 80, 86, 99–101, 110, 119, 131, 156
Housing Act, 1985 110
housing conditions 43–45, 47, 105, 109, 152
housing-related support 2, 25, 84, 99
human rights, right to family life 31–32
humanitarianism 152
hyper-exploitation 21, 65, 77
hyper-responsibilisation 96, 113, 152

Ijeoma (interlocuter) 19, 66–67, 68, 74, 75, 76, 101, 106, 109, 110–112
Illegal Migration Act 2023 40, 150
illegality 32, 38, 67, 70, 71
Immigration Act 1971 25, 132
Immigration and Asylum Act 1999 2, 25, 26, 97n1
immigration control 2, 25, 26, 27, 35–37
immigration detention 7, 98, 138
immigration health surcharge 38
immigration policy 3, 6, 37, 42, 47, 151
immiseration 51, 56, 96, 116, 143
impoverishment 1, 9, 10, 21, 37, 63, 75, 77, 141, 153, 155

Indefinite Leave to Remain 38
indirect discrimination 131, 133, 134, 136, 149
infantilisation 145, 147
informal networks, reliance on 3, 54, 64
injustice, resistance to 52
intergenerational family project 90
intergenerational reciprocity 49–50
interior life 61
interlocuters 19–20, 22, 157
interviews 16
Isaac (interlocuter) 86, 91, 95, 110, 118–119, 126, 127–128, 129, 143–144, 151

Jessica (interlocuter) 53, 55–56, 71, 82, 87–88, 107
John (interlocuter) 90–91
Joshua (interlocuter) 48, 64, 75, 80

Kevin (interlocuter) 84–85, 90, 95–96, 99
Kundnani A 6, 138, 139, 141

labour, of everyday existence 49
labour migration, control over 33–34
labour power 7, 33–34, 70, 88, 141, 156, 157
  hierarchising 139
  reproduction of 9–10, 58, 59, 83–87
landlords 7, 56, 99
language brokering 88
laundry 53, 107
legal categories 20
legal migration status 4, 19, 20, 29, 31, 32, 37, 38–39, 57, 72, 74, 75, 144
life-making practices 22, 51, 52–59, 62, 155, 157
  children 79–83, 87
Limited Leave to Remain 25, 27–28, 29, 39, 45, 86, 115
living conditions 13, 43–45, 47, 99, 101, 112, 141
loans 38, 121, 124–126

local authorities 1, 3, 17, 25–26, 36–37, 41, 44, 45, 53, 54, 56, 63, 70, 73, 78, 80, 95, 112, 115, 119–120, 127, 147, 148, 150
long durée, the 22, 48, 116, 126
Luke (interlocuter) 44, 47, 48–51, 51, 54, 55, 64, 75, 79, 79–80, 81, 84, 89, 128

marketisation 5, 6, 9, 138
Martha (interlocuter) 19, 89, 99–101
Marx, K 11, 59
meaningful lives 2, 9, 23, 42, 52, 57, 58, 59, 79, 113, 152
means of life, denial of 2, 9, 23, 28, 37, 46, 52, 70, 128
methodology 15–19
Mezzadra S 6–7, 139
micro-borders 20
migrants, representations of 33, 41
migration regimes 3–4, 7–8, 24, 26, 28, 123
Miriam (interlocuter) 43–45, 47, 48, 48–51, 51, 54, 55, 57, 58, 64, 75, 79–80, 81, 84, 86, 87, 89, 91, 93, 95, 106–107, 128, 146
mobile phones 53–54, 87, 107
Mobo (interlocuter) 26, 82–83, 89, 91–92, 99, 146, 147, 148
moral judgements 8
morality 108–110
mother blaming 13
mother–child relationship 74
motherhood 13, 14, 15, 21, 74–75, 91, 127–128
multiculturalism 148
multi-status family structures 28–29, 96, 145

nation state, the 1, 8, 23, 37, 49, 67, 73, 79, 135, 140, 142–144, 154
nationalism 26, 72, 137, 149
nationality 6, 23, 132, 132–134, 146
Nationality, Immigration and Asylum Act 2002 26

Nationality Act, 1981 32
Nationality and Borders Act 2022 40, 150
nationality policy 6
nativism 8–9, 24, 29, 41, 140, 144, 155
necropolitics 117, 156, 157
necropower 8
negative pronouns, use of 63
Neilson B 6–7, 139
neoliberal racial state
 the national we 155
 NRPF as symptom of 142–144, 157
 NRPF as technology of 144–148, 157
neoliberalism 5, 6, 9, 33–35
Netflix 41
no recourse to public funds (NRPF) 1–2, 24–25, 150–151, *passim*
 antecedents 25, 26–27
 basic rule 25–27
 destitution trap 3
 disproportionate impact 133–134
 duration 2
 future developments 40–42
 gatekeeping role 6–7, 37
 hardship 46–48
 increasing public profile 40–42
 interlocuters 20
 as internal border 99
 justification 24
 legal challenges 41
 legitimate aims 154
 numbers subject to 2
 omnipresence 118
 racialised effects 22–23
 relative invisibility 40
 research 2–3
 spatial operation 99–101
 as symptom of neoliberal racial state 142–144, 157
 as technology of the neoliberal racial state 144–148, 157
 temporary suspension calls 41

toll 45
as welfare bordering 2–9, 26, 151–152, 153–154
no recourse to public funds (NRPF) policy extension 24, 27, 27–40, 40, 153
  changes 27–29
  criminalising migrant families 31–32
  enforced destitution 35–37
  government selection rhetoric 33–35
  justification 29–30
  legal challenge, 2014 36
  neoliberal rationalities 33–35
  and ten-year route 38–40
  welfare-migration regime 33–35
non-citizenship status 4, 8, 20
non-existence 7
non-personhood 67
NRPF Network 25–26
NRPF teams 3

organized abandonment 8, 63, 65, 121
Otherness 126, 140

partial inclusions 7, 8, 10
police and policing 6, 55, 71, 72, 101, 111, 114
Policy Equality Statement (PES), August 2023 (UKVI) 132–135, 138–139, 142, 145
policy silences 29
policy terrain 46
political community 4
positionality 17
Powell, Enoch 139
practices under duress 22, 98, 102, 108, 113, 116, 152
precarious migrancy 1, 12–15, 52, 56, 59, 97, 116
precaritisation 130, 153
pride 80, 89
privacy 99, 101, 108–113, 113
probationary periods 29
profiteering 5, 9, 156
provisional belonging 72

psychic life 18, 21, 61, 68, 142
psychic erasure 65–68, 74, 77
psychic value 68, 70
public funds 25, 146
public health risks 41
public opinion 48
punishment, language of 35

race and racism 131–132, 149
  biological logics 137–138
  conceptualisation 135–142
  cultural 137–138, 140
  definition 136
  differentiation 141
  everyday 131–132
  indirect discrimination 136–137
  and nationality 132
  NRPF as symptom 142–144
  NRPF as technology 144–148
  racial discrimination 132–135, 136–137
  state 22–23, 131–132, 132–135, 147, 149
  structural 131, 138–139, 147
  systemic 1, 22–23, 49, 51, 52
race-migration nexus 139
racial capitalism 56, 63, 90, 94, 141–142, 149, 154, 155
racial discrimination 132–135, 136–137
racial logics 22–23, 132
racialisation 131, 135–142, 144, 145, 149, 156
radical aloneness 62–65, 66, 68, 76, 90, 93, 97, 125, 129, 130
radical responsibilisation 21, 62–65, 77
recourse to public funds 35–36, 143
recurrent displacement 101
rent arears 45
rentier capitalism 119
reparative work 89–94, 97, 153
reproductive labour 10–12, 14–15, 157
  children 79, 82–83, 92–93, 97
  depletion 11–12
  and psychic value 70

reproductive labour (*cont.*)
  resourcing 53–56
  stratification of 56
  value 68
  waged 83, 85
resistance, counterstrategies of 74–77
reverse discrimination 137
right to rent 45
Rita (interlocuter) 19, 68, 68–74, 76, 83, 90–91, 101
romantic relationships 112–113
Rwanda, processing of asylum seekers in 32, 150, 151

sacrifices 50, 55, 123, 127–128, 133
Sam (interlocuter) 19, 80, 84, 85, 106, 122
Samantha (interlocuter) 19, 57, 63–64, 65–66, 68, 80, 84, 85, 106, 112, 122, 147
savings 118, 119, 121, 122
secrets 98–99, 102–108, 113, 117
selection rhetoric 33–35
selectivity, state framing 33
self, loss of 65–68
Serwah (interlocuter) 35, 43–45, 46, 47, 48, 48–51, 53–55, 55–56, 57, 58, 62, 64–65, 75, 80, 84, 89, 93, 94
sexual boundaries 109, 110, 111, 114
sexual development, children 109–110
sexual relationships 68
sexual trauma 111
sexual violence 98
Shanice (interlocuter) 19, 82, 86–87, 87, 88, 89–90, 95, 101, 107–108
shielding 103–105
silences 98–99, 102–108, 113, 117
Skeggs, Bev 58, 68, 85
slow violence 116
social expectations 87
social housing stock 2, 99, 110, 119
social justice 6, 18–19
social networks 54–55, 63, 80, 101
social problems, creation 29–30

social reproduction 9–15, 64, 95, 157
  and children 12–15, 18
  costs 10
  depletion 11–12
  and exploitation 11
  and labour 9–10
  refamilisation of 13
  in schools 84
  theory 11, 70
  weathering through 21, 152, 154
  and welfare 10–11
  welfare bordering and 11
  women 10
social services 10, 16, 17, 26, 66, 67, 70, 71, 73, 76, 85, 86, 89, 100–101, 103, 105, 107–108, 110, 112, 113, 143, 147
social support, entitlement to 3, 4, 7, 8, 10, 26, 28, 35, 39, 47, 106, 119, 134, 144, 146, 155
social workers 7, 8, 66, 67, 76, 100, 103, 105, 110, 118, 145, 147
Southall Black Sisters 70
space and spatial constraints 98
  enforced proximity 101, 102–113, 113, 121
  physical intimacy 108–113, 114
  secrets and silences 102–108, 113, 117
  and time and temporality 120
  welfare bordering 99–101
spatial control 99–101
state control 34
state racism 22–23, 131–132, 132–135, 147, 149
Statement of Intent: Family Migration (Home Office) 32
statutory neglect 51
stereotypes, negative 148
stigma 5, 13, 61–62, 105
stop the boats campaign 30, 150
stories 57–58, 80
strength 49–50, 65, 75, 122, 123
structural neglect 63
structural racism 131, 138–139, 147

stuckness 67
subjecthood, negation of 66
suffering 41, 47, 50, 51, 58, 69, 71, 75, 93, 96, 129, 147, 148
support, lack of 63–64
surplus bodies 2
systemic racism 1, 22–23, 49, 51, 52

Tanya (interlocuter) 19, 20, 64
Tazzioli M 61, 117
temporal bordering 117, 126
temporal injustices 116, 121, 129, 130
temporary accommodation 8, 119, 121
ten-year route to settlement 20, 29, 35, 38–40, 118, 122, 133, 148
time and temporality 22, 56, 130
  bureaucracy navigation 115–116
  bureaucratic 118
  contradictions 129–130
  controlled 120
  debt 124–126
  everyday 118
  literature 116
  and space 120
  uncertain 119–120
  waiting 119
  weathering 116, 117
  weathering as 126–130
  weathering in 121–126
  welfare bordering as 117–121
tolerated citizens 72, 144, 145
Topboy 41
Troubled Families policy 13
Tyler, Imogen 61–62, 154, 155

UK Visas and Immigration, *Policy Equality Statement (PES)*, August 2023 132–135, 138–139, 142, 145
UN Convention on the Rights of the Child 7
unbearability 107
undeserving, the 27, 41–42, 76, 96, 108, 152
undesirables 2, 7, 13, 33, 34, 35, 36, 39, 76

ungrievable lives 2
unthought known, the 104, 113
uselessness 69, 77

value 58, 142
  community of 70, 72, 76, 145
  psychic 70
  racialised postcolonial hierarchy of 68–74
  reclaiming 21, 74–77, 77
  reproductive labour 68
values 58, 138, 139, 145
violence
  domestic 3, 69, 70–71, 71
  escaping 73–74
  gendered 69, 70–71, 75
  sexual 98
  slow 116
voluntary return 37

waged work 53–54, 58, 83, 85, 141
weathering 11–12, 21, 22, 23, 52–59, 59–60, 61, 75, 77, 82, 87, 90, 116, 117, 152, 152–153, 154
  children and childhood 87
  destitution 52–59
  enforced destitution 52–59
  NRPF as 151–152, 153–154
  through social reproduction 21, 152, 154
  time and temporality 116, 117
  in time and temporality 121–126
  as time and temporality 126–130
  welfare bordering 60, 126–130
welfare, and social reproduction 10–11
welfare bordering 1–2, 23, 42, 97, 98, 142, 150–157
  infrastructures 8–9
  justification 24
  legitimate aims 154
  and life-making 51
  NRPF as 26
  as organised state abandonment 121–122
  restraint navigation 54

welfare bordering (*cont.*)
  social reproduction and 11
  space and spatial constraints 99–101
  through NRPF 2–9
  as time 117–121
  weathering 60, 126–130
welfare bordering technologies 57
welfare chauvinism 8
welfare contexts, children and
    childhood 22, 78
welfare provision, marketisation 9
welfare regimes 3–4, 6, 11, 26, 52

welfare state 2, 5–6, 142–144, 144
welfare support 11, 25, 26, 36–37, 41,
    45, 63, 124, 142
welfare system 5, 24, 41, 48, 67, 143
welfare-migration regime 33–35
whiteness 13, 27, 137, 147
withstanding 12, 21, 52, 56–59, 61, 79
work options 45
world-making labour 15
worn down 61

xenophobic narratives 48

EU authorised representative for GPSR:
Easy Access System Europe, Mustamäe tee 50,
10621 Tallinn, Estonia
gpsr.requests@easproject.com

www.ingramcontent.com/pod-product-compliance
Ingram Content Group UK Ltd.
Pitfield, Milton Keynes, MK11 3LW, UK
UKHW031129130425
457215UK00006B/139